Admin911:
Windows 2000
Terminal Services

About the Author

Larry Seltzer is a freelance writer and contract programmer who has worked in the personal computer industry since 1983. He has written commercial and in-house corporate software, and directed testing laboratories at *PC Week*, *Windows Sources,* and *PC Magazine*. He currently writes for numerous business and technical publications, including *Fortune Small Business, Inter@ctiveWeek, Internet World, PC Magazine*, and *Windows 2000 Magazine*.

About the Series Editor

Kathy Ivens has been a computer consultant since 1984 and has authored and contributed to more than 40 books on computer subjects. She is a contributing editor at *Windows 2000 Magazine* and writes an internationally syndicated column.

Admin911: Windows 2000 Terminal Services

LARRY **SELTZER**

KATHY **IVENS**

Osborne/**McGraw-Hill**

Berkeley   New York   St. Louis   San Francisco
Auckland   Bogotá   Hamburg   London   Madrid
Mexico City   Milan   Montreal   New Delhi   Panama City
Paris   São Paulo   Singapore   Sydney
Tokyo   Toronto

Osborne/**McGraw-Hill**
2600 Tenth Street
Berkeley, California 94710
U.S.A.

For information on translations or book distributors outside the U.S.A., or to arrange bulk purchase discounts for sales promotions, premiums, or fund-raisers, please contact Osborne/**McGraw-Hill** at the above address.

Admin911: Windows 2000 Terminal Services

1234567890 DOC DOC 01987654321

ISBN 0-07-212991-3

Publisher
   Brandon A. Nordin

Vice President & Associate Publisher
   Scott Rogers

Editorial Director
   Wendy Rinaldi

Project Editor
   Elizabeth Seymour

Acquisitions Coordinator
   Timothy Madrid

Technical Editor
   Marc Mangus

Copy Editor
   Lunaea Weatherstone

Proofreader
   Susie Elkind

Indexer
   James Minkin

Computer Designers
   Gary Corrigan
   Jean Butterfield

Illustrator
   Michael Mueller

Series Design
   Gary Corrigan

Cover Series Design
   Greg Scott

Cover Illustration
   Joe and Kathy Heiner

This book was composed with Corel VENTURA™ Publisher.

For Danna, my wife.

Contents
at a Glance

Contents

Acknowledgments

This is the first book I wrote all by myself, and so I want to thank Lois Hirshkowitz, who taught me how to write. I also owe an unpayable debt to the late Stuart Mindlin, who gave me a job writing database management systems, even though I was fresh out of college with nothing but a bunch of lies on my resume.

Several people at Microsoft provided expert assistance, helping to make this book much better than it would have been. I wish to thank Chris Branson for helping me make the right connections, Mark Aggar for helping to clear up the Q238965 issue and, most of all, Greg Lirette for answering numerous technical questions and making me feel like I could actually finish the book.

I would also like to thank the Microsoft Knowledge Base (http://search.support. microsoft.com/kb/), the first place anyone should check when investigating problems in Windows and other Microsoft products. It's definitely not perfect, but there's always something new and interesting in it.

Of course, many people worked on this book, turning my submissions into the professional publication you hold in your hands. I wish to thank Wendy Rinaldi, Elizabeth Seymour, Timothy Madrid, and Lunaea Weatherstone, all of Osborne/McGraw Hill.

Chapter 1

Why Terminal Services?

Windows 2000, the next generation of Microsoft Windows NT, represents a significant leap in power for Windows computing. Some of the greatest improvements have come in Windows 2000 Terminal Services, a system for allowing multiuser access to Windows programs. Intelligent use of Windows 2000 Terminal Services improves the manageability of your network, and lets you more easily support remote users, including anonymous users across the Internet. Terminal Services is an integrated feature in all versions of Windows 2000 Server.

Windows NT has always been a multiuser operating system in one sense—many users can connect to a Windows NT server and perform tasks on that server, but only through specific services exposed by the server. For example, a Windows NT server can share files with client systems, share access to other networks (such as the Internet), share access to a database, and so on. But with Windows 2000 Terminal Services, you can share whole applications. What's the difference? With Terminal Services, users run a program, user interface and all, on the server. All the computing occurs on the server. The user's computer sends keystrokes and mouse events to the server; the server sends back display changes. As a result, very little processing takes place on the client. The client computer does not even need to have the application installed, and the application may very well be one that the client computer is incapable of running. There are Terminal Services clients for DOS, Windows 3.1, and Windows CE-based handheld devices, and you can use them to run Windows 2000 applications from the server. Even the load on the network is light.

Many Windows NT networks install their applications on the server and allow users to start the applications from there, but this too is very different from Terminal Services. When clients run programs off a network share, the program still loads on the client and processing takes place on the client. Since the program files must transfer to the client in order for the program to load, there can be a considerable delay, depending on network traffic. Once again, with Terminal Services the program loads on the server itself, and the only transfers on the network between the client and server are of screen changes and keyboard and mouse events.

Terminal Services itself places very little extra load on a server. If only for remote administrative purposes, you probably should activate it on all servers in your network.

Terminal Services administration is integrated into the Windows 2000 Active Directory. You can use the full power of Active Directory's group policy management to assign rights to users running Terminal Services applications.

A Quick Overview of Terminal Services

Windows 2000 Terminal Services works by sharing the user interface. Clients send keystrokes and mouse events to the server and receive display changes back. Even on a fairly slow connection, such as a 28.8K modem, the performance of Terminal Services connections is good enough to display all but the most multimedia-intensive applications. The protocol exchanged between clients and servers is called *Remote Desktop Protocol* (*RDP*). RDP is based on the International Telecommunication Union's (ITU) T.120 protocol, an international open standard first used in multiple virtual channel conferencing products like Microsoft's NetMeeting. RDP is a sophisticated protocol, supporting multiple levels of encryption and Unicode, a standard for character definition in all languages. At the network transport level, Terminal Services requires a TCP/IP connection. See Table 1 for some of the most important features of RDP.

Feature	RDP4 (Windows NT 4.0 Terminal Server Edition)	RDP5 (Windows 2000 Terminal Services)	ICA (Citrix MetaFrame)
32-bit Windows client	X	X	X
16-bit Windows (Win 3.x) client	X	X	X
MS-DOS client			X
Windows CE client	X	X	X
UNIX, Macintosh, Java clients			X
Browser-based client		X (with separate, free Terminal Services Advanced Client)	X
TCP/IP	X	X	X
IPX, SPX, NetBEUI, direct serial			X
Connect over LAN	X	X	X
Connect over WAN	X	X	X
Connect over dial-up network connections	X	X	X
Direct dial-up connection without network			X
Support for system beeps	X	X	X
Support for stereo sound	X (with third-party software from NCD)		X

Table 1-1. New Features Added in RDP5

Feature	RDP4 (Windows NT 4.0 Terminal Server Edition)	RDP5 (Windows 2000 Terminal Services)	ICA (Citrix MetaFrame)
Printing to a local PC printer	X (must share printer over network)	X	X
Local drives accessible to server-based applications	X (must share drives over network)	X (must share drives over network or use utilities in Windows 2000 Server Resource Kit)	X
Cut/paste of text and graphics between client and server applications		X	X
Can connect directly to an application on the server, bypassing the desktop	X	X	X
Can advertise server applications directly to clients			X
Load balancing of multiple servers for a single application		X (requires Windows 2000 Advanced Server or Datacenter Server)	X (requires add-on software)
Remote control of clients	X (RDP4 clients can be controlled, but this function requires Windows 2000 Terminal Services on the network)	X	X
Encryption of communications	X	X	X (requires additional software)

Table 1-1. New Features Added in RDP5 *(continued)*

Some applications may not run on Terminal Services. This problem exists, for example, for those applications that handle multiuser environments by tracking an IP address for each user, because Terminal Services forces all users to share the IP address of the Terminal Server. See Chapter 4 for more detail on why some programs don't work well with Terminal Services and what, if anything, you can do to make them work.

For the same reason, Terminal Services is incompatible with Windows Clustering Services, which allows multiple servers with different IP addresses to function as one large, fault-tolerant server. In lieu of clustering, Network Load Balancing Services for Windows 2000 does allow some load distribution for busy Terminal servers.

Why and When to Deploy Terminal Services

Terminal Services makes many things possible and many other things easier. You may have many computers that run old operating systems such as DOS or Windows 3.1, and perhaps even Windows 95 is inadequate for some of the applications you want your users to run. Upgrading systems is complicated and expensive, and can require user retraining.

Analysts often refer to the "total cost of ownership" (TCO) of computers, and how hidden costs, such as all the damage users do to their systems and the support costs they create, make computers more expensive than they seem. Bringing all the computing onto the server, where administrators can control users' options and more easily deploy new software, lowers TCO relative to running conventional Windows clients.

As shown in Figure 1-1, with Terminal Services, the permutations and combinations of applications and client platforms you can support are almost unlimited.

Servicing Mixed Platforms

Even if you are planning to upgrade your client systems, Terminal Services makes it easier to do so by letting you deploy applications aggressively, even if all your client systems aren't yet capable of running them. This lets you upgrade systems more gradually.

With Terminal Services, users can run Windows 2000 applications on a Windows 2000 server as long as they can connect to the server over TCP/IP. If you are contemplating migrating your clients to Windows 2000 Professional, Terminal Services is an especially attractive interim step, because it lets you deploy Windows 2000 applications without having all your Windows 2000 clients up and running. Since all the work is on the server, you can focus all your performance concerns there and do all your backups centrally.

The same goes for remote users: you may have no control over what computer users have at home, but if it's a DOS or Windows system connected to the Internet, they can log on to the server and run all the network applications they run at the office. By using a virtual private network, you can add strong encryption to the connection, making sure that only authorized users can connect.

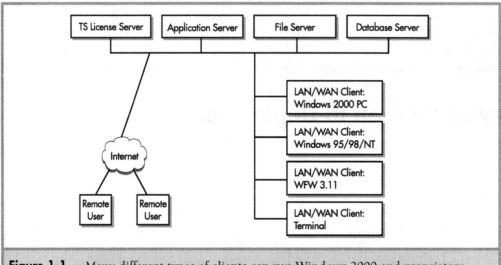

Figure 1-1. Many different types of clients can run Windows 2000 and proprietary applications under Terminal Services

NOTE: Of course, there are other ways to let users run applications on a server. There is Telnet, an interface most commonly used on UNIX and available for years on Windows NT. But Telnet is text mode only, and there are serious limits to the work you can do, at least easily, in text mode under Windows NT or Windows 2000.

You can also use the Web, deploying Web servers that let users access programs via a Web browser. However, the programs you want people to run probably aren't HTML-based (at least not yet). It's likely they're Visual Basic programs, Microsoft Access programs, or proprietary programs for your business—all Win32 native programs that don't run in a Web browser. Sure, with a lot of work and development expertise you might be able to make them accessible through a Web server, but Terminal Services makes this unnecessary. Terminal Services doesn't just present a dumb graphics terminal. Users can print to local printers, even though the application is running remotely. Users can also transfer clipboard data from the application running on Terminal Services to local applications. This makes it easier to work with Terminal Services applications as peers alongside other programs.

The more you rely on Terminal Services, the easier client management becomes. In a Windows 2000 network using Terminal Services, if a client develops any sort of problem you can simply replace it with another system off the shelf. Because the users' applications are installed on the server, all they need are links (potentially just one) to continue working. In the case of Windows-based Terminals, the situation is even simpler. Just replace the device and everything's fine.

Remote Administration

Many server products can be administered remotely using standard network protocols, but they are easier to administer if you're logged on at the actual server on which they run. Similarly, the remote administration interface may not be as full featured as the local version. By running an administration session under Terminal Services, you have almost all the power and convenience you would have if you were physically at the system. Since servers can be located in inconvenient locations like closets or even remote offices, Terminal Services can provide the environment that makes working on these systems possible.

You can administer file and print sharing over a Terminal Services connection. You can edit the registry of the server you're logged on to using that server's local copy of a registry editor. You can run any Microsoft Management Console (MMC)-based administration program on the server to remotely administer servers. Terminal Services provides a great way for an administrator working from a remote site or from home to administer entire domains, forests, or clusters.

Terminal Services also has a basic remote control facility that administrators can use to view or take control of client systems. This can be useful to demonstrate a technique or feature to a user, or to perform remote administration of the system.

Centralized Application Deployment

By deploying user applications on servers for access through Terminal Services, administrators can retain control over the use and configuration of the application.

Because Terminal Services integrates with Windows 2000's Active Directory, you can manage your users' access to applications and resources from applications more effectively and more automatically than in the past. If applications are installed locally on individual PCs, management of them can be tedious and dangerous, because user environments inevitably change from one system to another, even with a robust management system in place.

With Terminal Services, the applications are deployed centrally, so there is only one copy to manage. Upgrades and backups are much simpler. Each user is likely to have his or her own configuration settings in a personal folder (probably the Windows 2000 home directory). Changes users make don't affect other users.

Because most developers write applications for use in a single-user mode, these applications may need modifications to run properly in a multiuser system like Windows 2000 Terminal Services. Microsoft provides *application compatibility scripts* (in the %SystemRoot%\ Application Compatibility Scripts\Install folder) for modifying the application installation so that it runs properly. There aren't just Microsoft programs in there, but Corel Office, Lotus SmartSuite, and Peachtree Accounting as well. Other application vendors can help you make any necessary modifications. New and updated application compatibility scripts are available on a special Microsoft Web site.

Microsoft also certifies applications as Windows 2000-compatible, and all such applications are certified to work in multiuser environments like Terminal Services. See http://www.microsoft.com/windows2000/upgrade/compat/certified.asp for a list of such applications.

In-house and Other Proprietary Applications

Many companies have applications developed in-house using Visual Basic, Microsoft Access, and other systems, typically to access and input data to in-house databases.

Such programs are usually a piece of cake for Terminal Services, and potentially run much faster on it than on the client. Some older programs may engage in bad habits (discussed in further detail in Chapters 4 and 9) which would cause problems for Terminal Services, and if they are 16-bit programs they can be a performance drag on the system. 32-bit versions should work fine, however. Very little typically happens in the user interface of these programs, but they must exchange commands and data with file and database servers, which may communicate much more quickly with a server than with a client, depending on network topology and system configuration.

In other cases, companies may rely on vertically oriented applications for managing a particular business. For example, a publishing house might use a special program designed to manage authors by Social Security number, books by ISBN number, and so on. Terminal Services does just as well with these applications because it can make any Windows application available remotely.

Because Terminal Services works by running the applications on Windows 2000 Server and sharing the interface with the client, in-house developers can write applications utilizing the most modern and convenient facilities of Windows and the most current development tools, and not be concerned about outpacing the capabilities of client systems' hardware or operating systems.

Remote Access

There are many ways to enable remote users to access a network. You might need to do this for workers on the road, for workers who need to work from home, or to deal with freelance workers and consultants.

Depending on what you want to let users access, you might not need full-blown Terminal Services. If you only need to share e-mail, you can do so with conventional SMTP and POP3 mail. Some other systems, such as Lotus Notes, have their own remote access facilities. But Terminal Services is the most flexible. Once users are on the network, they can run all the same applications they run in-house. If you manage the network well, and especially if your network is based on a Windows 2000 domain, you don't have to treat your local and remote users differently. You need to allow users to connect into the network from outside, probably through the Internet. There are many ways to do this, the most common being through a virtual private network (VPN), which is a way to allow outside communication into your network using an encrypted channel. If all your communications are through Terminal Services, you can use its built-in encryption capabilities. In the United States and Canada, Terminal Services supports up to 128-bit encryption for all data on the wire. Even the logon information is encrypted.

This arrangement works better than other remote access methods in many ways. Consider e-mail: if your users access their remote mail via POP3, they will end up with two inboxes, one at home and one at work. With Terminal Services they are always using the same mail program and same inbox whether at home or on the road. Large amounts of mail or large attachments won't mean a long delay waiting for the mail to download, because the mail doesn't download. It stays on the server, and only the user interface gets transferred.

Application Types to Avoid

There are definitely applications for which Terminal Services is inappropriate or at least suboptimal.

Any heavily graphics-intensive application, particularly streaming video, will likely exceed the capacity of RDP to deliver adequate performance.

Applications requiring use of special hardware that you don't want to place in a mission-critical server are probably best used in a desktop system.

Finally, some applications, such as those used for software development, can require very large amounts of processor bandwidth and RAM. Running these effectively on Terminal Services would probably require more power than is practical to share, and they should be run on desktops in most cases.

Remote Administration versus Application Server Mode

Terminal Services has two basic modes of operation: Remote Administration and Application Server. When you install Terminal Services on a Windows 2000 server, you choose between these two modes.

Remote Administration mode is a special mode that allows administrators to perform certain tasks. You can perform all the normal administrative functions of Windows 2000 Server, such as file and print administration and user management, but you may not run non-administrative applications, such as Microsoft Office.

Remote Administration mode allows up to two users to connect to the server at a time. Only administrators can enable connections, so the server is safe from unauthorized use. The license for Remote Administration mode is built in to all copies of Windows 2000 Server, and no client license is necessary.

Application Server mode is the full version of Terminal Services, allowing any practical number of users, potentially hundreds, to run Windows applications on the server. The Remote Administration restrictions no longer apply, although administrators may perform administrative functions under Application Server mode as well. Use of Application Server mode requires a Client Access License (CAL).

Licensing

To access a Windows 2000 Server via Terminal Services running in Application Server mode, you must have a separate Client Access license for both Windows 2000 Server and Terminal Services. The Terminal Services Licensing program running on the Terminal Services Licensing Server on your network enforces the use of Terminal Services CALs. Terminal Services policies on these licenses are a little behind Terminal Services technology.

Windows NT and Windows 2000 administrators are familiar with CALs. You need a license for a client system to access a Windows NT or Windows 2000 server. You typically get some number of CALs with each copy of Windows 2000 and you can add more by purchasing additional licenses from Microsoft.

You can use your Windows 2000 CALs in two ways: per server or per seat. In per-server licensing, you must have one CAL for each system that might access the server at any one time. So even if you have 15 users, you can get away with only 5 CALs if at most 5 users will use the server simultaneously. Per-seat licensing provides a CAL for each client on the network. You choose one or the other based on how many clients and how many servers you have. Either scheme might make sense depending on how your users access your servers.

Sadly, Terminal Services only supports per-seat licensing. You must have one CAL for each client that may access the server. This can produce difficulties in some cases, but there are ways to work around the problems. Windows 2000 Professional clients come with a CAL for Terminal Services, so there is no licensing issue if your client computers are running Windows 2000 already.

If you're running Application Server mode on any of your servers, one of the servers on your network acts as the Terminal Services Licensing Server, running a special service to enforce the licensing of clients. In a Windows 2000 domain, the Licensing Server must run on a domain controller. In workgroups or Windows NT 4.0 domains, the Licensing Server can run on any Windows 2000 server.

After you activate the Licensing Server, you have to install licenses on it. Depending on how you usually communicate with Microsoft, you may be able to do this over the Internet or via phone or FAX. In any event, the requests are routed through the Microsoft Clearinghouse, a database at Microsoft that tracks all their active license servers and client license key packs. When you request license keys over the Internet, you are communicating directly with the database.

When clients running the Terminal Services client program attempt to access the server, they either present their CAL to the Licensing Server or are granted one from the available pool. If there are no licenses available, they can get a 90-day temporary license.

Problems can develop in this licensing scheme. For example, some early Windows Terminal devices fail to properly store their CAL information in non-volatile RAM, meaning they could lose their licenses in the event of a power failure. In such cases, you must call Microsoft and have them reissue the license. A similar process is necessary if you want to upgrade systems for a user or if a system is damaged. Troubleshooting license problems is covered in detail in Chapter 8.

There are two special types of licenses for Terminal Services for high-use scenarios. The Terminal Services Internet Connector license is designed for Web sites that use Terminal Services to expose an application to anonymous users on the Internet. For example, a software company could use this license to allow users to try a non-Web Windows application. Under the license, which supports up to 200 concurrent users, the users have to be anonymous and cannot be employees of the company. A Terminal Services Internet Connector license also requires a Windows 2000 Internet Connector license.

The Work At Home license is available only to Microsoft Select customers (typically very large corporations) and is designed only for employees. For each Windows 2000 Professional license or Terminal Services Client Access license the corporation buys, they can buy an additional Work At Home license to allow that user to work on the network at home.

Differences Compared to Windows NT 4.0 Terminal Server Edition

Many administrators are familiar with Windows NT 4.0 Terminal Server Edition (TSE). Windows 2000 Terminal Services is the next generation of this product, and it is much improved.

TSE is essentially a separate version of Windows NT 4.0 Server. The TSE functions are built into the kernel itself. As a result, when service packs and hotfixes come out for NT 4.0, Microsoft must make separate versions for TSE. This is in nobody's best interest.

In Windows 2000, Microsoft made Terminal Services a regular system service. You can install and uninstall it using the standard Add/Remove Programs applet in Control Panel.

Many of the other functions and features of Terminal Services are new in Windows 2000. Among these are:

+ Support for Network Load Balancing

+ Performance profile support specific to Terminal Services (you can prioritize performance for "Applications"—meaning Terminal Services applications—or "Background Services")

+ Performance improvements in the client software

+ Standard support for encryption on connections

+ Multilanguage support; any RDP client can talk to any RDP server

+ Administration tools are MMC snap-ins

+ New APIs for Terminal Services developers

History of Terminal Services

Multiuser computing is an old trick in this business—older, I'd wager, than most of the people reading this book. And yet it's a relatively new paradigm to many computer users, because of the history of the personal computing industry.

Before PCs, computers were expensive and difficult to administer. You couldn't get a computer for everyone, so you connected many users to one system and used a technique called time-sharing to allow everyone to perform tasks. The operating system on the computer, such as IBM's MVS or Digital Equipment Corporation's VMS, managed all users and juggled all the tasks those users were performing. The device used by individual users, a terminal, didn't do computing per se, but simply communicated the user's keystrokes to the computer and the output back to the cathode ray tube (CRT) or printer (the term for such a device is *dumb terminal*). Such systems are still in use today.

The revolution caused by the PC industry was that it provided a separate, inexpensive computer for each user. MS-DOS and other early operating systems were designed to manage a single user and to give that user complete control and the undivided attention of the system. Over the years, PC power has become cheaper and cheaper, and local area networks have developed to help businesses let users share data. The economic imperative for sharing computer power on PCs never materialized.

Actually, multiuser operating systems for PCs have always been around, but they never caught on in a big way. Around 1980, I remember working on a copy of MP/M, the multiuser version of CP/M, the dominant PC operating system before MS-DOS. Several companies attempted to build multiuser operating systems around MS-DOS. UNIX versions for PCs have also been available since the early 1980s. But PCs have always been cheap and simple enough to make it easy to justify purchasing them. Single-user systems were in the best interest of PC and software companies, because it permitted them to sell more units. PCs do waste a lot of computing power, but it's cheap power.

Now multiuser computing is back and in a big way. It's not the economics of the old world that makes it worthwhile; it's the management power of multiuser systems. System administrators know that installing and keeping track of all the software on client systems can make life miserable. Remote users are an even worse problem—how do you give users at remote sites, or users connecting across the Internet, access to applications on your servers? The answer can be Windows 2000 Terminal Services.

The same increases in computing power that have made PC power dirt-cheap have affected servers as well. As Windows NT matured over the years, it developed the capacity to handle many new types of tasks. Microsoft introduced Terminal Server Edition for Windows NT 4.0, but it was essentially a separate operating system with its own set of service packs, hotfixes, and problems. With Windows 2000, Terminal Services is built into Windows 2000 Server.

Some time after the first release of OS/2 in the late 1980s, a group split off from IBM to form a company to build a multiuser version of the operating system. Like Windows NT, OS/2 was a multiuser operating system in some ways, but did not allow multiple users to run interactive sessions at the same time. This company, called Citrix, created such a product, first to support text-mode sessions, then eventually GUI sessions as well.

When the market began to shift from OS/2 to Windows NT, so did Citrix, first creating WinFrame, which allowed multiuser interactive NT sessions. MetaFrame, their latest product, is built on Windows 2000 Terminal Services.

MetaFrame adds many useful features, especially for large, multiserver networks, over what Windows 2000 Terminal Services provides. Terminal Services is based, in part, on the MultiWin technology licensed from Citrix to Microsoft.

Finally, with Windows 2000 Terminal Services, just as on a mainframe in the 1960s, you can run a session from a dumb terminal where all the computing occurs on the server. Computer specialists like to say that there are very few new ideas in the software business, and surely that saying applies here.

Terminal Services Architecture

Although Windows NT, the precursor to Windows 2000, has always been a multiuser operating system from a network services perspective, it was never built to support simultaneous multiple interactive user logons. The way Microsoft (actually Citrix, on whose code the Terminal Services code is based) gets around the original design speaks well of the NT kernel design. The differences aren't radical at all, and they all build on design strengths in Windows 2000.

There are two obvious issues that need to be addressed in the underlying architecture of Windows 2000 to accommodate Terminal Services: multiple display sessions run, and multiple instances of applications run, even though those applications are not built to run in multiple instances on a single system.

Program Load Sequence

During Windows 2000 boot, the session manager (smss.exe) creates the console session, which gets the special session ID of 0. If you have installed Terminal Services, the termserv.exe process loads. Initially, it tells the session manager to create two idle sessions that sit and wait for connections from the network.

Each session under Terminal Services gets its own 2GB of virtual address space for user mode processes. Each gets a copy of the Client Server Runtime Subsystem (csrss.exe) that in turn loads a copy of winlogon.exe (the logon manager) to handle the client logon for the session. Figure 1-2 shows this in the context of an overall view of Terminal Services architecture.

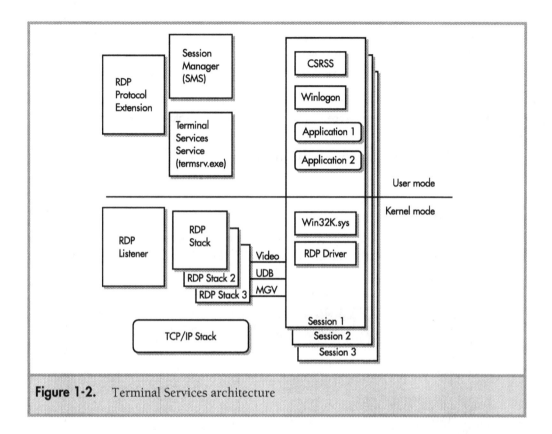

Figure 1-2.   Terminal Services architecture

In addition to those processes, a special version of win32k.sys (which implements the GDI and USER portions of the Win32 subsystem) is loaded into the session's address space. However, once it's in physical memory, that copy is mapped into the virtual space for each new session. The data areas of win32k.sys are mapped into physical memory for each session.

NOTE: That's 2GB of virtual address space, so it's only allocated to physical memory if needed.

As Figure 1-3 shows, by default Task Manager isolates the user processes in each session. When you load applications, they also load into this isolated space. If you check Show Processes From All Users, you can see everything running on the Windows 2000 server, and you'll see multiple instances of applications on the Processes tab. (At the least, explorer.exe and the applications listed in the previous paragraphs, in addition to all the user applications running in all the user sessions, will appear on the Processes tab.)

NOTE: You can type **query process** at the command line to display the same data.

Windows 2000 differentiates between objects and programs in the sessions by their session ID.

Display Changes

Normally, Windows 2000's GDI (the graphics display code) talks to display drivers that talk to the display hardware directly. Clearly, this wouldn't do in Terminal Services. Instead,

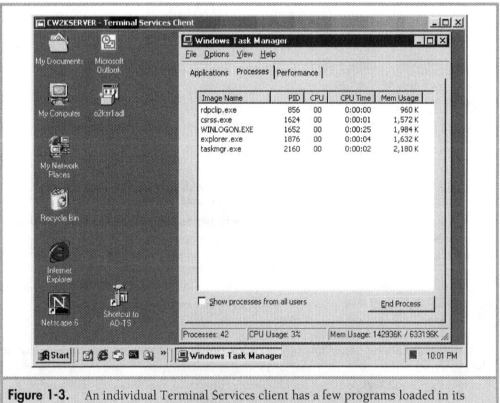

Figure 1-3. An individual Terminal Services client has a few programs loaded in its own session space by default

each session gets a copy of rdpdd.dll, the display driver for RDP. Instead of talking to the hardware, rdpdd.dll translates the display data into RDP data and sends it to the network. (The Terminal Services stack is actually protocol-independent, so if Citrix MetaFrame is installed, it talks to ICA instead of RDP.)

Kernel Name Spaces

In the Windows 2000 kernel, programs create objects to work with files, devices, other programs, and so on. In a normal Windows 2000 system, there is no chance that there will be naming conflicts between instances of these objects, but Terminal Services raises this possibility. Therefore, under Terminal Services, client sessions get individual namespaces for their own copies of the following types of objects: events, semaphores, mutexes, waitable timers, file-mapping objects, and job objects. These objects are not usually created directly by applications, but rather, indirectly by Win32 services, which are called through Windows APIs by the applications.

There is also a global name space for objects owned by the operating system and programs running at the console. Programs can create and reference objects in the global name space by prefixing the name with "Global\".

In the following example, a semaphore (MYSEM) is created in the global namespace. (The two backslashes in the name—"Global\\MYSEM"—are there because the example is in C, and it's a C convention that a literal "\" character must be written in the program doubled.)

```
hSem = CreateSemaphore(NULL, 0, 1, "Global\\MYSEM");
```

If the call had referred to MYSEM, the object would exist in the program's isolated name space, and other programs could create the same object without a conflict. This technique is used commonly with semaphores, providing a way for a program to determine whether it already exists. If you load a second copy of a program in a normal Windows session and it either brings you back to the first copy or displays an error message, it is likely using this or a similar technique to determine that the program is already running. But when you run a program in two different Terminal Services sessions and the objects are separate, the programs don't see each other, making it possible to run more than one copy.

Programs can also refer explicitly to the local name space by prefixing the name with "Local\" but since local is the default, there isn't much of a reason to do so.

Also, because the global objects are accessible to applications, the applications and operating system can communicate using these synchronization objects (semaphores, mutexes, and so on) through the use of "Global\".

Connection Time Processes

The RDP software running on the client system initiates a connection to the Terminal server through TCP port 3389. On the Terminal server, the RDP listener thread detects this session request and creates a new instance of the RDP stack to handle it. The stack takes over connections on that session and negotiates with the client over details such as the encryption level, display resolution, and so on. Prior to the logon, the client and server also negotiate licensing details.

Once all these messy details are handled, the server RDP stack instance is mapped into the session space for the new Terminal Services session, using either a new session space or a waiting idle one. If a new one is needed, the session manager creates it in the manner described above. Then it's logon time.

The username, password, and domain name information is received on the server by the session's instance of winlogon.exe. This program performs the necessary authentication to ensure that the user has the permission to log on to the location where they are attempting to log on. Then the username and domain name are passed to the Terminal Services service (which maintains a list of associations between usernames and session IDs) to see if an existing disconnected session is available for this user.

How Applications Run

When the session manager exits, the session inherits the user attributes of the csrss.exe process that created it, which are those of the user who logged on. All programs that run in the session also inherit, and are subject to, the user rights of the user who logged on.

Windows 2000 uses copy-on-write page protection extensively for efficient use of memory. What this means is that when programs are loaded for one user when they already exist for another, the memory for the first copy is mapped into the second instance rather than consuming new physical memory. I've already explained that this is done with win32k.sys, and it is also done with applications. Data areas for programs are user-specific and therefore need new memory for each session.

When 16-bit programs run, just as in regular Windows 2000, they run in the context of ntvdm.exe and possibly wowexec.exe.

Chapter 2

Terminal Services Deployment

Planning for a successful Terminal Services deployment depends in large part on having a good idea of how you are going to use the product. That plan for use has an impact on the proper hardware for the job, the proper network hardware and software configuration, and the proper licensing scheme. A successful deployment plan involves people with an understanding of the business purposes for the deployment, as well as the technical capabilities of the hardware.

You must also be conscious of your domain configuration. If your network is a "native" Windows 2000 domain using Active Directory, you have some additional features available, although Terminal Services will also run on a Windows NT 4.0 domain or even a workgroup.

A Terminal Services server can require anywhere from a minimal to high-end capacity of the network and the server itself, depending on the applications that users run and how many users there are per server. Review the requirements for your applications and what you consider to be acceptable performance.

In some cases, Terminal Services will turn out to be an inappropriate solution. Your specific needs for a Terminal Services installation is something only you can calculate, but I'll give you some guidelines to follow to create a feasible plan.

Finally, licensing in Windows 2000 Terminal Services is different than for conventional Windows 2000 Server access, and can be complex. You must consider licensing issues before deployment, because they can have a big impact on your costs.

Remote Administration

If you plan to use Terminal Services as a remote server administration tool, your planning needs may be relatively simple. Terminal Services places a minimal load on a server if it is enabled in Remote Administration mode and only authorized administrators can log on. Furthermore, the two-user Remote Administration license is included with all versions of Windows 2000 Server. Finally, according to Microsoft, Remote Administration mode installs only minimal additional software on the server, and has no impact on BackOffice or other server programs running on the server. Therefore you can enable Remote Administration mode on all Windows 2000 servers. If you are not comfortable with allowing all administrators access through Terminal Services to their servers, you need to decide what makes you comfortable.

Because the programs you run as a Terminal Services client must run on the Terminal server, Remote Administration mode is only useful for administering Windows 2000 networks. For example, if you have Windows NT 4.0 servers in your network, you won't be able to run a remote desktop or application. You will only be able to administer them remotely through standard NT management tools such as User Manager and Server Manager.

The type of client is unimportant for Remote Administration mode; administrators can work on the server from any Terminal Services client, including non-Windows clients (assuming you install the appropriate add-on software from Citrix). In fact, there's no particular advantage to using Windows 2000 as a Terminal Services Remote Administration client, apart from the generic reason that Windows 2000 is a good client. See Chapter 5 for more details about running Remote Administration mode.

Application Server

If you plan to allow regular users to run conventional applications on Terminal Services, planning is much more complicated than for Remote Administration mode. The good news is that your application management will become much simpler than when you had to distribute actual binaries of the applications to each desktop.

You have to configure your users to have a home directory and you should use groups to administer them. The applications have to be configured to save their user-specific data in user-specific areas. For example, a program should record its registry settings in the key HKEY_CURRENT_USER (which is copied for each user) and not HKEY_LOCAL_MACHINE (for which there is one copy for the entire server). Good applications do this, but there are some applications that can cause problems. See Chapter 4 for more on application problems.

Small Applications

Many applications are small in terms of code and do not transfer a great deal of data either way on the network. Data entry programs are the classic example. In the context of Terminal Services, such programs also have the advantage of relatively quiescent user interfaces.

Because of these characteristics, you can run many more instances of these applications, and support many more users, on a given Terminal Services server than you could run on programs with richer, more active user interfaces, such as Microsoft PowerPoint.

Even larger applications can have these characteristics depending on how they are used. In the long term, what matters are the *working set size*, meaning the amount of physical RAM the program occupies, and the amount of change in the user interface during normal usage.

Large Applications

Many users deal not only with programs that consume potentially large amounts of RAM, such as Microsoft Access or Lotus Notes, they also use large data sets with the programs or subsets of the applications that produce complex screens.

Consider the project management user who designs and manages a large project. Such programs consume large amounts of memory, potentially transfer large amounts of data between the Terminal server and database server, and have complex screens in the form of grids and Gantt charts. Finally, they are taxing on the CPU as well, at least for certain periods. All of these factors make such applications more taxing on the Terminal server. You can still use them, but the more they are used on a server, the greater the performance impact on all users.

Of course, there are applications which are small in terms of their own size, and therefore in the amount of memory they consume on the server, but which send large amounts of data across the network. For example, Microsoft Paint is only a few hundred K, but can be used to display complex graphics which could slow Terminal Services performance for the user.

Application Selection

In general, Win32 applications will run normally on Terminal Services, but there are exceptions. It is important to investigate this issue for your important applications by checking with the application vendors for their statements of compatibility. You may have to talk to them about the implications for support and your application license for running under Terminal Services. (Microsoft maintains a list of third-party applications at http://www.microsoft.com/ntserver/ terminalserver/exec/vendors/showcase/ showcasesearch.asp that have been tested successfully under Terminal Services.)

Whatever the vendor says about the application, you should test yourself. Of course, for the applications you have developed in-house, this is the only route to take. There is no substitute for building a test network with a test server. Fortunately, you probably won't have to worry about Terminal Services Client Access Licenses (CALs) for the test network, since Terminal Services will issue temporary licenses for 90 days after installation. The 90-day grace period was made for evaluations like this.

Other programs are inappropriate for Terminal Services because the architecture cannot support adequate performance. Streaming video is the classic example of this. Any program that requires fast graphics response, such as many video games, is also unlikely to perform adequately under Terminal Services. The RDP protocol also doesn't support sound (other than simple system sounds like beeps), and display is limited to 256 colors.

NOTE: Citrix has a product called VideoFrame for sending streaming video to a thin-client device running the ICA protocol.

Some applications just won't work with Terminal Services. Consider a program that uses a barcode scanner or special card reader. To work under Terminal Services, the devices would have to be wired to the server. This is probably not the way you want to run them, so these applications should run locally. On the other hand, if the barcode scanner works through the keyboard port, it should work under Terminal Services. Because RDP can send keystrokes and mouse events, devices that look like keyboards and mice should work, but those that connect via the serial or parallel ports or USB or special cards probably won't.

See Chapters 4 and 9 for more technical details on how applications run under Terminal Services as opposed to the normal Windows environment.

Application Installation

If you plan to use Application Server mode, any applications you share on that server must be installed on the server after Terminal Services is installed. Terminal Services has a special Install mode for applications that you must enter before installing applications. While in this mode, Terminal Services watches changes to the registry and other system events to separate them out properly for a multiuser environment.

If you use the Add/Remove Programs Control Panel applet to install the program, Windows 2000 enters and exits the mode automatically with the applet. You can also enter and leave the mode with the **CHANGE USER [/EXECUTE | /INSTALL]** command line program.

If you have servers to which you want to add Terminal Services, you will have to reinstall existing applications on them if you want those applications to be available via Terminal Services.

Planning Your Terminal Services Network

The characteristics for a network running Terminal Services are not necessarily the same as those running other access methods. When planning for a Terminal Services deployment, you need to consider some issues in advance.

Don't Make Domain Controllers Application Servers

It's a good idea to use only member servers for application serving. Domain controllers must be available for many tasks and responsibilities in a Windows 2000 network. Running applications on them increases their performance burden considerably, potentially at the expense of overall network performance.

User Permissions: Windows 2000 Applications versus NT 4.0

During the installation of a Windows 2000 server in Application Server mode, you have to decide whether to set Permissions Compatible With Windows 2000 Users as opposed to Permissions Compatible With Terminal Server 4.0 Users (see Figure 2-1).

This choice affects the permissions users have when running under Terminal Services. If you choose Windows 2000 User permissions, users run with the permissions of the Windows 2000 Users group, which restricts their access to certain critical resources, like some system areas in the file system and registry. If you choose the 4.0 permissions, users have rights as NT 4.0 users, with access to these areas.

When you plan your Terminal Services testing and deployment, this is a critical issue to consider. In general, it is better to allow lesser permissions (the Windows 2000 permissions) for your users, but this may not be possible, depending on the needs of your applications. Only you will know from your own testing whether you need to open up the 4.0

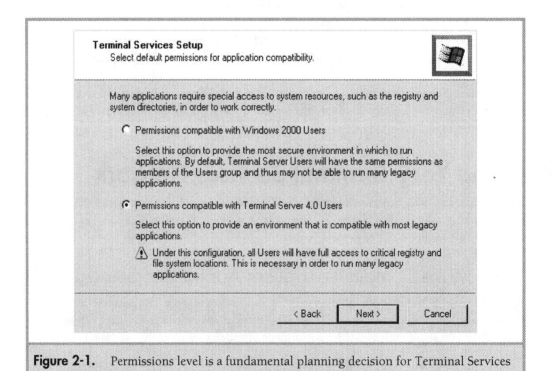

Figure 2-1. Permissions level is a fundamental planning decision for Terminal Services

permissions. Fortunately, you can easily change this setting later on in the Terminal Services Configuration program. See Chapter 6 for more detail on how to deal with this problem when it arises.

This decision is necessary because most applications on the market were not written specifically to work with Windows 2000's user permissions, but with the more liberal permissions in Windows NT 4.0. The fact that Windows NT 4.0 permissions is the default selection indicates that Microsoft is aware of this

Use NTFS

It would be possible, but supremely unwise, for you to use the FAT file system for any server, including a Terminal server. FAT is included in Windows 2000 only for compatibility with applications which you never want to run on a server. It has no facilities for security. The NTFS file system has built-in support for security, including limiting access to specific files and subdirectories to specific users and groups. Without NTFS, all users have access to everything in the Terminal Server's file system.

Domain Structure

The advantages for Terminal Services of various domain structures are pretty much the same as for other network applications.

You can choose to have no domain structure at all. This has an element of simplicity to it, but if you have multiple servers, users have to have separate accounts on each Windows 2000 Terminal Server from which they run programs. In the long term, this becomes unmanageable with more than a few users.

If you have a Windows NT 4.0 domain structure, you can choose to keep it and run your Terminal servers as member servers. But you will lose out on the benefits that come from Active Directory. NT 4.0 doesn't handle very large numbers of users as well as Active Directory. Moving to Windows 2000 Terminal Services can be an important first step in migrating your whole network to Windows 2000, as it moves your applications and network infrastructure in that direction.

If you use Active Directory and a full Windows 2000 domain, you are running Terminal Services in its own element. This brings advantages in terms of both performance and manageability.

If you run Active Directory, Microsoft recommends that you place all your Terminal Servers in the same organizational unit (OU). This allows you to create and employ policies specifically for those servers more conveniently than applying them to individual servers.

Home Directories

Home directories for your users are essential in any Terminal Services installation. Instead of storing configuration information in the %SystemRoot% directory (where it would conflict for each user), Terminal Services relies on each user having a private space for this information. Home directories, usually under the Documents and Settings folder in Windows 2000, are the answer.

You have to plan for the space that these home directories will consume—and it may be a lot of space. In addition to settings, each user will have My Documents and My Pictures folders in the same location, so if users have large amounts of data it will be on the file server, not their local hard disks.

If you have more than a few users, you should probably plan to keep users' home directories on a server other than the Terminal server. On a fast, switched network the performance will be acceptable, and backup and restore will be much simpler.

Roaming Profiles

In a large and complex network, users will likely be connecting to multiple Terminal servers. Just as in a non-Terminal Services environment where the user logs in from multiple systems, the users want their environment and preferences, such as their Start menu and desktop settings, to follow them around to all the systems from which they log on. For this purpose, Active Directory supports roaming user profiles.

Roaming user profiles allow users to retain their settings as they move from client to client or, in the case of Terminal Services, from server to server. You need to store profiles in network locations separate from the user's home directories. These profiles can get large, depending on what the user does with them, and with a sufficiently large number of users they can consume a large amount of space. You need to provide a network share that users can access with read/write privileges.

If you use roaming profiles, it is important that the Terminal servers to which users will connect have identical operating system and application configurations. For example, the %SystemRoot% directory and application installation directories need to be the same on the systems, because the profile will expect them to be the same. It is possible to have multiple profiles in multiple OUs and to administer them separately, but this is probably more work than you want to do.

CAUTION: If you are combining roaming profiles and home directories in Terminal Services, you need to take extra steps to separate the profile and home directories to avoid performance problems at logon time. See Chapter 5 for more on this.

Encryption

In some cases you may want to use encryption for the connection between the Terminal Services client and server. With remote access clients you definitely want to consider this, especially since it's easy and brings almost no cost. In other cases, you may plan to have network users connect to servers across insecure links, such as the Internet, between branch offices.

Encryption Levels

You can use any of three levels of encryption for the traffic between Terminal servers and clients—low, medium, and high. Username and password information is also encrypted according to the ITU T.120 protocol, which is the basic communication protocol on which RDP is based.

Under RDP 5 (Windows 2000), low encryption uses the RC4 encryption algorithm with a 56-bit key, but only traffic from the client to the server is encrypted. If a client uses RDP 4, a 40-bit key is used. The data sent from the server to the client is difficult to intercept even if unencrypted.

Medium encryption uses the same key sizes and algorithm as low encryption, but encrypts traffic in both directions. If you're not concerned with the traffic from the server to the client, you could lighten the processing load on the server somewhat by using low encryption, but you're probably better off looking elsewhere for performance savings.

High encryption encrypts traffic in both directions using the same RC4 algorithm, but with a 128-bit key. This key is only available in the North American version of Terminal Services. In the export version, it is essentially the same as medium encryption.

Hardware Authentication

Windows 2000 supports interactive logon with smart cards that have X.509 version 3 certificates with private keys, but Terminal Services does not support these devices, or any other hardware-based authentication.

Firewalls

All communication between Terminal Services clients and servers using the RDP protocol requires TCP/IP and uses TCP port 3389. It is possible to change the port number, but doing so is not likely to be practical, since would have to make the change on all client systems. Check to make sure that port 3389 is not blocked at your firewall, assuming you want to allow Terminal Services access from the outside.

Packet-level firewalls are comparatively easy to configure to allow Terminal Services access, as you need only open up port 3389. If the firewall works at the application level, it will need to have a specific filter for RDP; some do, some don't. Check with the firewall vendor.

Some firewalls and other facilities use the IP address of the client to determine security characteristics and physical location. This won't cut it with Terminal Services since all clients have the same IP address (the server's).

In network terms, it's not unlike what a proxy server does. All the clients behind the proxy server have the same IP address from the point of view of external services, like a Web server. In fact, since users could be working with multiple Terminal servers, each with their own IP address, you can't even assume that a single user has a single IP address.

Remote Access

There are many ways to provide remote access to networks, but Terminal Services may be the most flexible method of all. As long as the client has TCP/IP connectivity to the Terminal Server, they can use any computing function available to a Windows 2000 system on the server's network. Rather than restricting access to applications specifically configured for remote access, such as special mail clients, Terminal Services users can use regular applications.

As with any remote connection, the performance of the remote client is gated by the slowest connection between it and the server, and potentially by slow connections between the server and other systems. For example, even if the client is connecting by a relatively fast connection method, such as DSL or a cable modem, if the server is connected to the Internet by an overloaded connection of any speed, the results may be dissatisfying. Consider the communications infrastructure between the server and clients and how many clients may be connected at any one time. See "Performance Requirements for Terminal Services" later in this chapter for typical bandwidth requirements for Terminal Services clients.

You can also connect two separate computer networks through a dedicated line or the Internet and use the connection to allow users on one network to run applications on a Terminal Server on the other network. Such connections are likely to be used for other purposes, so you must consider the additional bandwidth requirements of Terminal Services usage and the capacity of your connection.

Terminal Services Advanced Client Web Package

With the recent release of the Terminal Services Advanced Client Web Package, you can now use a Web server as a gateway to Terminal Services. The new client is an ActiveX control that lets you design Web pages with an embedded Terminal Services session. The main advantage of this is the ease with which users can find the right links to their applications and servers.

Upgrading from Windows NT 4.0 Terminal Server Edition

Windows 2000 Server provides a smooth upgrade from Windows NT 4.0 Terminal Server Edition (TSE). The TSE server must be running Service Pack 4 or later.

If you are running Citrix MetaFrame on your TSE server, you must first remove it using the appropriate entry in Add/Remove Programs. Windows 2000 requires MetaFrame 1.8a or later and TSE requires earlier versions. It is important that you remove MetaFrame before the upgrade, because you won't be able to do so afterward.

It's also important to note that TSE uses a different default directory for %SystemRoot%: Windows NT 4.0 and Windows 2000 use \WINNT, but TSE uses \WTSRV. If you upgrade Windows 2000 over a TSE installation, the system will retain the \WTSRV directory as the %SystemRoot% directory. The same goes for TSE's use of the \WTSRV\PROFILES directory to store profiles and user data and Windows 2000's use of \Documents and Settings. Almost all software should work properly in this environment, but there are certainly programs, or at least batch files, that make bad assumptions about the \WINNT directory.

As with any NT 4.0 to Windows 2000 upgrade, you need to make sure that all the hardware in the system is compatible with Windows 2000. Check the Hardware Compatibility List at http://www.microsoft.com/hcl/default.asp. See Chapter 3 for details on performing the actual upgrade.

Just as with most other operating system upgrades, you should think seriously about doing new, clean installations of Windows 2000 and migrating your applications over rather than upgrading existing TSE installations. As with everything else in the Terminal Services setup process, be sure to test this on a test network before subjecting your users to it.

CODE BLUE

If you upgrade a Windows NT Server to Windows 2000 and select Terminal Services, the Winlogon DontDisplayLastUserName value, which controls whether the name of the previous user to log on is displayed in the logon dialog, may not be preserved. The upgrade forces the value to 0.

You can reestablish this feature either with a group policy or edit the registry directly. To edit the policy, load MMC and add the Group Policy snap-in. Open Local Computer Policy, then click Computer Configuration | Windows Settings | Security Settings | Local Policies | Security Options. In the right pane, double-click "Do not display last user name in logon screen" and select Enable.

To change the registry directly, go to HKEY_LOCAL_MACHINE\Software\ Microsoft\Windows\CurrentVersion\Policies\System\DontDisplayLastUsername. Change the value to 1. This value controls the behavior for local logons. Also go to HKEY_LOCAL_MACHINE\Software\Microsoft\WindowsNT\CurrentVersion\Winlogon DontDisplayLastUsername. Also change the value to 1. This value controls behavior for Terminal Services users.

NOTE: Activating this feature can interfere with the automatic logon feature in Client Connection Manager (see Chapter 3).

License Planning

Terminal Services licensing can be complicated, in fact, deceivingly so. Planning a Terminal Services installation requires that you evaluate the implications for your software licenses, and not just your Terminal Services licenses.

Consider all the applications you want users to run under Terminal Services. You may need to acquire new licenses for doing this. For example, suppose you want to use Terminal Services to allow employees to have access to the network from home, and be able to run the same Microsoft Office applications that they use at work. You may or may not need new Windows 2000 Server Client Access Licenses (CALs) for the remote clients, because per-server licensing would allow you to assume that any user working from home would not be at the office, or vice versa, and therefore would never consume more than one CAL. You will need new Terminal Services CALs because it has no per-server licensing. You will need new Office CALs, because Office requires a separate license for every client system on which a user uses it, including Terminal Services clients.

You also face the issue of planning your Terminal Services Licensing Servers. Every Terminal Services network that has a server running in Application Server mode requires at least one Licensing Server, a server on which licenses are stored and managed. On a Windows 2000 domain, the Licensing Server must be on a domain controller. On a

Windows NT 4.0 domain, or Workgroup, the licensing server may be on any Windows 2000 member server. But if you are considering a migration from an NT 4.0 to Windows 2000 network, try your best to place the licensing server on a Windows 2000 server that may be promoted to be a domain controller in the future. It's possible to move licenses from one server to another, but it's cumbersome.

See Chapter 8 for a detailed treatment of Terminal Services licensing.

Performance Requirements for Terminal Services

A significant rollout of Terminal Services can have large effects on performance, both at the network level and at individual servers.

Hardware Requirements

The load on a Terminal server can range from light to immense. You need to plan the hardware for your server to accommodate memory, CPU, registry, and file system needs of the maximum number of clients you expect to run on it.

See the "Capacity Planning" section below for test results and information on how to perform your own tests.

Memory

The base minimum you should plan for Windows 2000 Server is 128MB. In addition to this, you need to plan for additional memory per user, the specific amount depending on the size of the applications they will be running. A good rule of thumb is to allocate 13MB for the user's desktop. When more than one user runs the same application on a server, the code for the application itself is shared between the users, so only data areas in memory need to be considered in addition to one copy of the application code.

Ironically, 16-bit applications require about 25 percent more memory than 32-bit applications because of the overhead of the Win16 support subsystem that needs to be loaded.

16-bit applications also impose other performance burdens on the system, and you might think about isolating them on a specific server or servers so they don't interfere with the performance of Win32 applications.

The amount of memory consumed by Win32 applications depends on the application. Some simple applications could take less than 1MB each, but Microsoft Word 2000 consumes (on my system) between 10MB and 15MB. You can investigate application sizes by running them and then bringing up Task Manager and looking at the application's entry on the Processes tab (see Figure 2-2). Bear in mind that this amount of memory will vary with different functions in the applications.

Disk

In addition to the amount of space consumed by data files, you need to consider page and dump files for each user. Paging files are the files used by the Windows 2000 Memory Manager to swap areas of memory out to disk to make room for other uses. Windows 2000's Virtual Memory Manager does not operate strictly on a least-recently-used basis; even in a system where physical RAM is not depleted, Windows 2000 performs some paging of relatively unused parts of memory to have sufficient free memory available when needed.

Individual users under Terminal Services don't have their own paging files. Windows 2000 can support multiple paging files, although in most cases there will be one. For performance reasons, it's a good idea to place the paging file on a physical drive separate from the operating system itself.

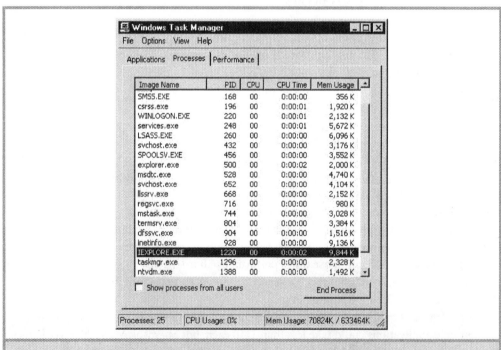

Figure 2-2. Task Manager can show you the amount of memory consumed by an application

Dump files are created when the system crashes, and they contain the contents of memory at the time of the crash. In a system with large amounts of RAM, you have to be concerned that the file system has sufficient free disk space for the dump file, which is placed on the system partition. Unless you're a programmer with great debugging skills, dump files aren't usually helpful, though, so you might also want to consider disabling them. You can do this by going to the Control Panel's System applet, selecting the Advanced tab, and clicking the Startup And Recovery button. Here, in the Write Debugging Information section, you can change the selection from the default Complete Memory Dump to "(none)" (see Figure 2-3).

Of course, dump files are sometimes useful, especially if you are working with Microsoft support, which may ask for one as part of debugging your problems. There are three types of dump files you can set the system to create. Complete Memory Dump is all of the system memory, so you need to have enough free disk space on your boot volume for the amount of physical RAM plus 1MB. A Kernel Memory Dump stores only the contents of the kernel

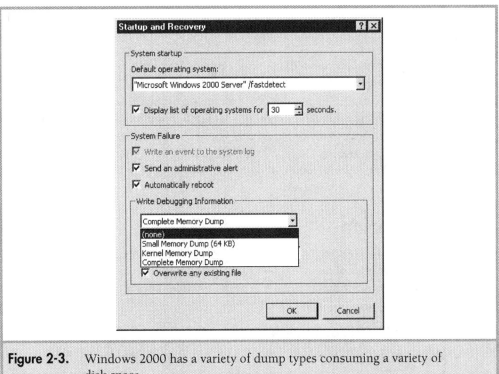

Figure 2-3.   Windows 2000 has a variety of dump types consuming a variety of disk space

memory. According to Microsoft, this could be anywhere between 50MB and 800MB, depending on how much RAM is in your computer. You can see how much memory is being used by the kernel on the Performance tab of Task Manager. Finally, a Small Memory Dump, which stores a minimum of information, requires only 2MB of disk space, but the system will create new files at each error rather than overwriting the old ones.

CPU

To the extent that your server is CPU-bound, meaning that there is more demand for CPU resources than are available, adding more CPUs or using faster CPUs will increase your performance. Under Terminal Services, adding CPUs tends to give you better performance improvements than with many other applications. This is because Windows 2000 can more easily allocate the tasks of different users to different CPUs than, for example, the work of one user with an especially intensive task.

If you have many users running a relatively small number of applications and the system is CPU-bound, you will get better performance improvements out of adding CPUs than adding memory, because Terminal Services needs to load only one copy of the code in an application for all users who use that application.

Registry

Registry size in Windows 2000 is set dynamically at install time and is based on the page file size. If you have large numbers of users logging in to a Terminal Server, depending on the way their applications use the registry, the default size of the registry could prove insufficient. You may want to expand the maximum registry size to accommodate growth.

You can do this by going to the Control Panel's System applet, selecting the Advanced tab, and clicking the Performance Options button, then the Change button. In the Virtual Memory dialog box that appears, you can change both the paging file sizes and the maximum registry size (see Figure 2-4).

Capacity Planning

One of the Windows 2000 Resource Kit tools is the Terminal Server Capacity Planning tool. This tool is actually a series of programs you can use to create and run automated tests to measure the capacity of your hardware in a Terminal Services environment. These tools are covered in detail in Appendix A.

The Microsoft/NEC/Groupe Bull Tests

While we should all test our environments under Terminal Services to see if they run correctly, we can't all do performance testing on large networks. But we can get some idea

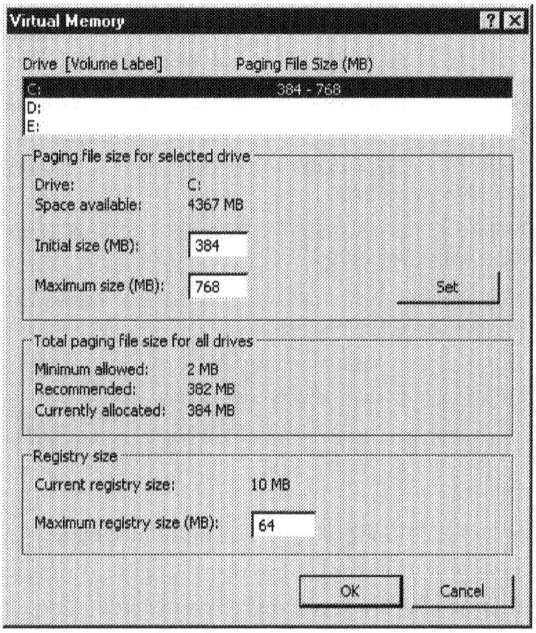

Figure 2-4.   Consider the size of your paging files and registry when planning a
Terminal server

of the performance characteristics of Terminal Services from tests run by Microsoft in
conjunction with NEC and Groupe Bull. The full test descriptions and results are available
at http://www.microsoft.com/WINDOWS2000/library/technologies/terminal/tscaling.asp.
The information and tables in this section are adapted from that paper.

   For these tests, Microsoft used a version of the automated testing tools described in
Appendix A, and also wrote test scripts for three test scenarios. The programs were designed
to simulate the workloads of three types of workers identified by the Gartner Group:
Knowledge Worker, Structured Task Worker, and Data Entry Worker. The applications
range from simple data entry to large and complex operations. The automation facilities, like
most test automations, lead to work patterns which are not exactly real world, but they do
provide a good estimation of how the server performs under various loads. Table 2-1 shows
the configurations of the test servers and the maximum number of different types of workers
the server could handle.

Server Configuration	Server Model	Structured Task Workers	Knowledge Workers	Data Entry Workers
4-way Pentium II – 400 MHz 1.0MB L2 Cache, 4096MB RAM	Express5800 140Ha	70 Users	120 Users	210 Users[1]
2-way Pentium III – 450 MHz 0.5MB L2 Cache, 1024MB RAM	Express5800 MC2400	40 Users	70 Users	210 Users[1]
1-way Pentium III – 450 MHz 0.5MB L2 Cache, 1024MB RAM	Express5800 MC2400	20 Users	40 Users	Tests incomplete

[1] These tests reached their limits not due to a limit on performance, but because Windows 2000 exhausted a fixed resource known as the "paged pool." It might be possible to go further in such a test using the /3GB switch in BOOT.INI.

Table 2-1. Results of Microsoft and NEC/Bull's Tests

The capacities expressed in Table 2-1 show the point at which a separate script, known in testing jargon as a "canary" script, took 10 percent longer to complete than it would on a single user load. In other words, the servers were considered at capacity when they had a meaningful impact on the performance of a control program running on the same server.

The tests involved 64 client workstations, in some configurations running more than one session to the server at a time. Apart from the Terminal server, there was a Test Manager system that controlled the test process; a domain controller; a Web server (which was used in some of the Knowledge Worker and Structured Task Worker tests); a Microsoft Exchange mail server; and a Microsoft SQL database server.

In Table 2-2, we deduce from the performance results in the previous table the memory needs per user. Given a fixed amount of memory for the system and the number of users, you should be able to get a rough estimate of your memory needs.

	Structured Task Workers	Knowledge Workers	Data Entry Workers
Memory Per User (MB)	9.0	7.5	3.4
System Memory (MB)	128		
Total Memory	System + ((# of users) * (memory per user))		

Table 2-2. Memory Requirements Guidelines

Microsoft's definitions of the types of workers simulated in the tests are important, as you may be able to analogize some of your own users to them:

Knowledge Worker   Works in an ad hoc fashion and needs flexibility in applications. Examples include project management, desktop publishing, data mining, and financial analysis.

Structured Task Worker   Performs the same tasks repeatedly, and the work is defined by a set process rather than ad hoc needs. Examples include claims processing, accounts payable, and accounts receivable.

Data Entry Worker   Inputs data into a database.

Network Load Balancing

Terminal Services is incompatible with Windows Clustering, but you can improve server performance in some cases by using Network Load Balancing. This is a service provided in Windows 2000 Advanced Server and Datacenter Server that turns a group of servers into a single server with a single IP address. This is usually best suited to such applications as a database or Web server where a large number of users need access to a relatively small and simple application.

By configuring a group of servers identically and storing the user and profile data external to all the Terminal servers in the load-balanced group, users can connect to any of the servers and have an identical experience. See Chapter 7 for detailed information about Network Load Balancing for Windows 2000 Terminal Services.

NOTE: You can also use round-robin DNS to provide load balancing in a similar fashion.

Network Design

In addition to performance considerations for any particular client or server, you must plan for the network bandwidth that Terminal Services will consume. To do this, you must map out which client will be using which servers and over what connections they will be communicating. Of course, there will be other traffic on these connections at the same time.

License Server Planning

License Servers have small traffic requirements, which is why it's okay to put them on domain controllers. In a relatively small and simple network, you can just put your License Servers on the domain controller and be done with it. In a larger network with discrete segments and multiple domains, you may want to consider how the Terminal Services server discovers and communicates with the License Server.

When you enable a Terminal server, it starts polling the network for License Servers. In an Active Directory environment, the Terminal server searches the directory for License Servers; in a workgroup or Windows NT 4.0 domain, the Terminal server broadcasts to all servers in the subnet looking for a License Server. Once a Terminal server finds a License Server it checks for it every hour (or two, depending on the configuration). The network traffic from these checks is trivial.

There are many ways to activate a license server: through a direct connection to the Internet from the activation program, through a Web page, via fax, and over the telephone to Microsoft. The first method is the fastest and easiest, and requires that the License Server be connected to the Internet. You only need to do this once per License Server, so don't inconvenience yourself or compromise your server's security to activate your server over the Internet.

Chapter 3

Setting Up Terminal Services

Installing the Server

Installing Terminal Services is relatively simple (although installing the Terminal Services License Server can be tricky). You can install and configure Terminal Services either during the installation of Windows 2000 Server or at any time afterward.

Adding Terminal Services During Server OS Installation

During the GUI portion of Windows 2000 setup, after you enter the computer name and administrator password, you begin the Windows 2000 Components setup process. This window has a scrolling list of Windows components, and near the bottom of the list, unchecked by default, are Terminal Services and Terminal Services Licensing. The latter option installs a Windows 2000 License Server. Choose Terminal Services, or both, and click Next.

After setting the server date and time (and possibly other screens, depending on the options you may have chosen), the Terminal Services Setup screen appears, whether or not you have chosen to install a License Server. You have two choices for installing Terminal Services:

- **Remote administration mode**   This is the default selection. If you select this option, Windows 2000 Setup continues with no further steps regarding Terminal Services at this point.

- **Application server mode**   Selecting this option requires you to configure the permissions for users who log on to the Terminal Server.

Application server mode configuration offers two choices for setting Terminal Services client user permissions:

- Permissions compatible with Windows 2000 users
- Permissions compatible with Terminal Server 4.0 users

Windows 2000 user settings are far more restrictive than NT 4.0 settings.

NOTE: You can change the user permission settings later, using the Terminal Services Configuration program.

The networking portions of the Windows 2000 setup continue after you make this selection. If you are also installing the Terminal Services License Server, you need to

configure that separately. See Chapter 8 for details on the License Server and other
licensing issues.

Adding Terminal Services After OS Server Installation

To install Terminal Services on your Windows 2000 Server after the initial installation of
the operating system, open the Add/Remove Programs applet in Control Panel. Click on the
Add/Remove Windows Components button on the left side of the dialog box to open the
Windows Components Wizard. Scroll down until you reach the lines for Terminal Services
and Terminal Services Licensing (see Figure 3-1). Select Terminal Services and, if you want
this server to be a License Server also, select Terminal Services Licensing.

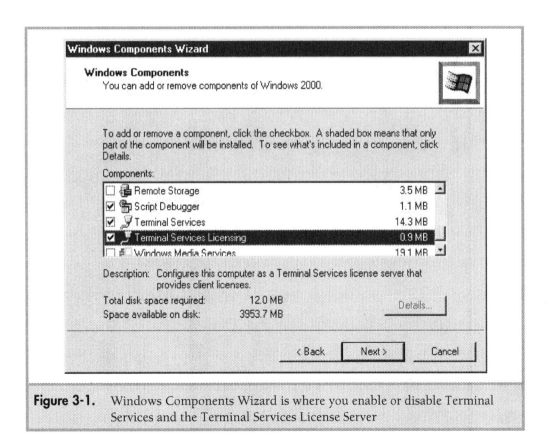

Figure 3-1. Windows Components Wizard is where you enable or disable Terminal
Services and the Terminal Services License Server

CAUTION: In a Windows 2000 domain, the License Server must be on a domain controller. On a Windows NT 4.0 domain or workgroup, the License Server may run on any member server.

In the Windows Components Wizard window (see Figure 3-2), select the Terminal Services mode you want to install.

 NOTE: All Windows 2000 Servers come with a two-user license for Remote Administration mode, but you must have Windows 2000 Server CALs and Terminal Services CALs for Application Server mode clients.

If you select Remote Administration (the default) and click Next, Windows 2000 Setup installs the components.

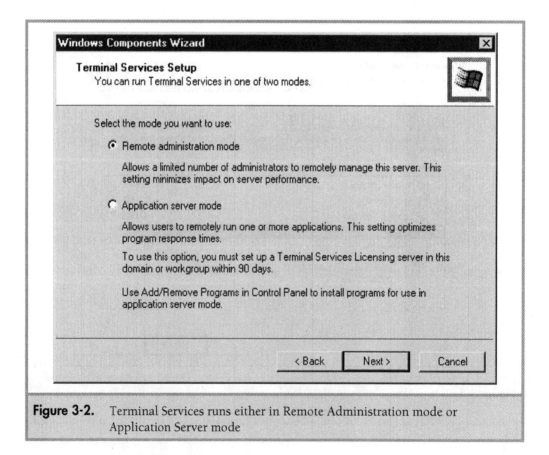

Figure 3-2. Terminal Services runs either in Remote Administration mode or Application Server mode

If you select Application Server Mode, the next window asks you to select the permissions level for users who log on to the Terminal server (see Figure 3-3).

This setting affects the permissions that users and applications have when they log on the server using Terminal Services. Windows 2000 user settings are far more restrictive than Windows NT 4.0 settings.

If you choose Windows 2000 user permissions, the wizard displays a list of applications that may not work correctly because of the permissions issue. Don't be surprised to see the Windows 2000 Support and Administration Tools in this list. These tools are meant to be used by Administrator users, so don't be too worried.

If you are also installing a License Server, you must specify the location of the License Server database, and you may also be asked to specify the scope of the server (see Figure 3-4). In other words, does the License Server support the entire enterprise or just the local domain/workgroup? If you choose Your Domain Or Workgroup, Terminal Services will look no further when attempting to connect to the License Server. If you choose Your Entire Enterprise (this is called the Enterprise Licensing Configuration), Terminal Services will

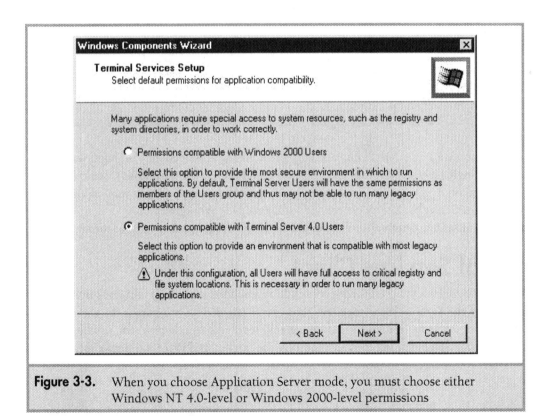

Figure 3-3. When you choose Application Server mode, you must choose either Windows NT 4.0-level or Windows 2000-level permissions

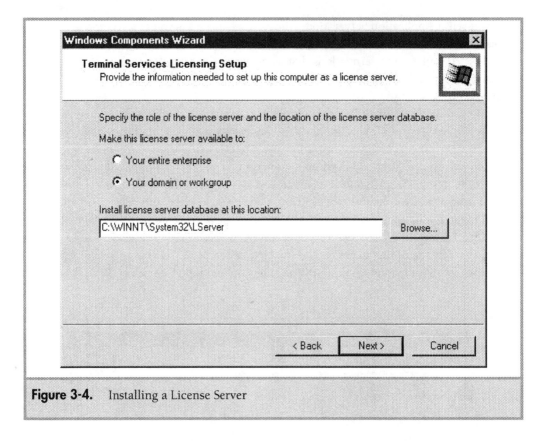

Figure 3-4. Installing a License Server

look beyond your domain. If you have multiple domains at a location, you might want to use a single License Server for them, so you could choose the Enterprise Licensing Configuration. If you have multiple sites, each with a domain, you might want to enforce one License Server per site by choosing Your Domain Or Workgroup.

After installing Terminal Services or the License Server, you must reboot the server.

Terminal Services Client

In order to connect to a Terminal server and run applications from it, a client system must have the Terminal Services client software installed. This program is the client for the Remote Desktop Protocol (RDP). In general, it's a very simple program, sending the mouse clicks and keyboard events to the Terminal server, and there is a simple local user interface for managing connections to Terminal Services servers.

Supported Client Platforms

Microsoft provides Terminal Services client software on the CD of all versions of Windows 2000 Server. In June 2000, Microsoft released the Terminal Services Advanced Client (TSAC) which adds two new versions of the Terminal Services client, one as a Microsoft Management Console (MMC) snap-in and the other as an ActiveX control to allow users to connect to Terminal Services through a Web page. It also adds a Windows Installer version of the conventional client, which makes distribution of the client easier in Windows 2000 networks. This version of the conventional client included with the TSAC also includes an ActiveX client control and new command-line parameters.

This new client is available for download from Microsoft's Web site at http://www.microsoft.com/ windows2000/downloads/recommended/tsac/tsac.asp. At that site, you have three separate download options for the three different types of clients. The new clients are also included as part of Service Pack 1 for Windows 2000, both in the download and on the CD in the \Valueadd\TSAC directory.

The original Terminal Services client supports the following platforms:

+ Windows 3.11
+ Windows 9x
+ Windows NT
+ Windows 2000

NOTE: Windows Millennium Edition (Windows Me) comes with the Terminal Services client software (and Citrix MetaFrame client software) on its own CD. Windows CE provides its own client as part of the Windows CE system software. If you add Citrix MetaFrame, you can connect to numerous other platforms, including DOS, UNIX, Macintosh, and Java clients.

Another platform advantage for MetaFrame is that it supports numerous network protocols, including IPX/SPX, NetBEUI, and direct asynchronous connections to the server.

Terminal Services, unaugmented by MetaFrame, only supports TCP/IP connections. You can connect over dialup to the server, but only by creating a TCP/IP connection through Remote Access Services (RAS).

The new client versions and Windows Installer file in TSAC do not support Windows 3.11, so if you want to run Windows 3.11 clients you must use the old client. There's really no loss to Windows 3.11 users, because all the advances in the new client work is only on Win32 platforms anyway.

Installing the Standard Terminal Services Client

The Terminal Services client program installs like most other Windows programs, and the process is very simple. You have a number of options for the method of installation. For large or physically distributed networks, you may want to push the installations to clients using Active Directory (I'll explain how to do this later in this section).

Standard Client Installation

The Terminal Services clients are included in a normal Windows 2000 Server installation. Go to the %SystemRoot%\System32\Clients\TSClient subdirectory, where you find three subdirectories: net, win16, and win32.

The win16 and win32 subdirectories have floppy disk images of the client software for win16 (for Windows for Workgroups 3.11) and Win32 (for Windows 9x, Windows NT, and Windows 2000). If you need to use "sneakernet" to distribute the client, you can copy the individual disk subdirectories to disks. The net subdirectory contains its own win16 and win32 subdirectories with all the necessary files in them, and is meant to be used across the network.

To install the client software on a workstation, connect to it over the network from the workstation machine, and run setup.exe to open the installation program. Then follow these steps:

1. Click Continue on the banner screen.

2. Enter the default name and organization.

3. Read the license agreement very carefully; check with your lawyer and then click "I agree."

4. Confirm the target installation directory. Click on the big graphic icon of a window.

5. Specify whether all users on this system or just the current user will use these settings for Terminal Services. Click Yes for all.

When the client program is installed, a confirmation dialog box announces that fact. Click OK.

Sneakernet versus Shared Install Files   Sometimes the most convenient way to install the client is to bring or send the floppies to users, but this is an unlikely event these days. Terminal Services users are, by definition, networked in some way, so there's probably a better way to install the client over the network. Uncompressed, the client takes up about 1.4MB, just a hair too big for a single floppy.

The simplest way to install over a network is to make the client install files available on the network and give users a shortcut to the setup.exe program. Alternatively, you can use a logon script to have users execute setup.exe with parameters to do what Microsoft calls an unattended install.

Performing Unattended Installs   You can perform silent installs of the client software by using the appropriate switches:

- ✦ **SETUP /Q**   Installs the client silently with default selections for options such as the target directory. At the end of the installation, the exit dialog box displays.

- ✦ **SETUP /Q1**   Installs the client silently with default selections for options such as the target directory. The exit dialog box does not display at the end of the installation.

- ✦ **SETUP /QT**   Installs the client silently with default selections for options such as the target directory and hides all user interface for the installation, including the copy gauge and the exit dialog box at the end.

Creating Client Installation Floppies   If you need to make floppies, you can copy the files from the relevant directories to the disks, but Terminal Services provides a handy program for this purpose. Open the Terminal Services Client Creator program in Administrative Tools. There you can select the 16-bit or 32-bit client and whether you want to format the disks (see the following illustration).

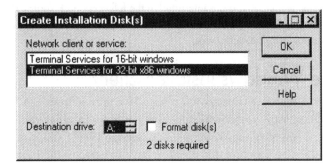

Using the Windows Installer Version in the TSAC
You might want to consider using the Windows Installer package that comes with the Terminal Services Advanced Client. Windows Installer is a technology new to Windows 2000 that automates installation of applications. It's available as an add-on to Windows 9x and Windows NT 4.0, and is built into Windows Millennium Edition.

Windows Installer uses a new file format with a .msi extension. When you have such a file you can right-click on it in Windows Explorer and select Install from the shortcut menu. The program installs with no user interaction.

If you have large numbers of earlier clients that don't have Windows Installer support, you have two options: you can install Windows Installer support on them or you can use the old client. In the long term, you are better off with your clients supporting Windows Installer, especially if you are building a Windows 2000 network. You'll also find that many third-party programs now use the Windows Installer format, so you may have to end up installing it anyway.

NOTE: You can find the Windows Installer program at http://www.microsoft.com/msdownload/platformsdk/instmsi.htm

If you are running Active Directory to manage your network, you can create a policy that says that specific users or computers (that you specify) should install the client automatically. See "Distribute the Terminal Services Client Through Active Directory" later in this chapter.

NOTE: Windows 2000 comes with a third-party tool, Veritas WinINSTALL LE, which you will find in the \VALUEADD\3RDPARTY\MGMT\WINSTLE directory of the install CD. This tool allows you to take non-Windows Installer installation files and repackage them for use by the Windows Installer service. If you are interested in the full version of Veritas WinINSTALL, which has additional capabilities for software distribution to desktops across an enterprise, see http://www.veritas.com/products/wile/.

Installing the Windows Installer Client

Back at the download Web site (http://www.microsoft.com/windows2000/downloads/recommended/tsac/tsac.asp), you downloaded the Windows Installer version of the TSAC as Tsmsisetup.exe. If you have the Windows 2000 Service Pack 1 CD, you can find it in the \Valueadd\TSAC directory. Execute this file. You have to agree to the license, and then select a directory in which to install the client. When you proceed, the Terminal Services client is not actually installed on the computer, but rather placed in a directory from which it may be installed.

The default location in which the program installs the Windows Installer client is \Program Files\Terminal Services Client MSI\, but this may not be the best location for you. You will likely want to place this file in a network share from which clients can access it.

Which location is best depends on your own network setup. The file is named Terminal Services Client.MSI, and it is not the only file in the directory. The other files and subdirectories are necessary as well.

Installing the Windows Installer Client on One Computer

Using the system on which you want to install the client, navigate to the share where the Windows Installer file is located and either double-click on it or right-click and select Install. In the wizard that launches, you have to decide whether the client should be available only to the currently logged-in client or to all users on the system (see the following illustration).

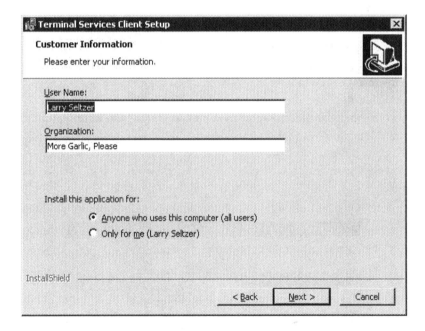

There is also a Complete setup and a Custom setup, but all Custom allows you to do is determine whether the client is installed immediately or upon first use.

The installation program creates a Terminal Services Client program group in either the user's profile or the All Users profile, depending on your decision in the dialog box.

To install the Windows Installer client on multiple computers on a Windows 2000 network, see "Distribute the Terminal Services Client Through Active Directory" later in this chapter.

Installing the Microsoft Management Console-Based Client

The MMC snap-in version of the Terminal Services client is named Tsmmcsetup.exe and you either download it from http://www.microsoft.com/windows2000/downloads/recommended/tsac/tsac.asp or find it in the \Valueadd\TSAC directory on the Windows 2000 Service Pack 1 CD.

Execute this file. You have to agree to the license, and then select a directory in which to install the client. The default location for the snap-in is \Program Files\Terminal Services MMC Snap-in.

Installing the Web-Based Client

The Web-based client, also known as the ActiveX Client Control, installs on a Web server running Internet Information Server 4.0 or later. Sample pages are included with the client which requires support for Active Server Pages (enabled by default in IIS).

The installation file is named Tswebsetup and may either be downloaded from http://www.microsoft.com/windows2000/downloads/recommended/tsac/tsac.asp or found in the \Valueadd\TSAC directory on the Windows 2000 Service Pack 1 CD.

When you run the program and agree to the usual license, you'll see that the default install directory is in your Web server directory.

The dialog box indicates that this is the location for the sample Web pages, which it is, (see the following illustration) but it is also the location for the .cab file that contains the ActiveX control.

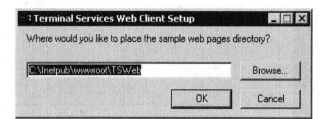

Distribute the Terminal Services Client Through Active Directory

To distribute the client software via AD, create a group policy in the Active Directory for the Windows 2000 domain in which you're installing the package. You can specify this

Create Organizational Units to Apply Policies to Groups or Computers

Unfortunately, you can only apply group policies to domains or organizational units (OUs). If you haven't already organized your network around OUs, you can create one specifically for the purpose of distributing the Terminal Services client.

If you want to distribute the Terminal Services client to specific users, whether or not that group of users corresponds to groups you have created for your network, it's easiest to create a group in the OU specifically for this distribution, and include the relevant users and groups in that new group.

If you want to distribute the Terminal Services client to specific computers, the tasks get a little more complicated. You can't make groups of computers or shortcuts to them (take note, Microsoft), so you need to organize your computers into OUs to which you apply the group policy. In fact, it's generally a good idea to organize your computers into OUs. (For more information about all of this, read *Admin911: Windows 2000 Group Policies*, by Roger Jennings, published by Osborne/McGraw-Hill, 2000.)

policy for users, groups, or computers of your choice if you know how to organize your AD for that purpose.

1. Start the Active Directory Users and Computers MMC (Start | Programs | Administrative Tools | Active Directory Users and Computers).

2. Right-click the organization unit or domain to which you want to apply the policy for auto-installation of the Terminal Services client and choose Properties.

3. Click the Group Policy tab, then click New to create a new policy.

4. Name the policy, using a name such as Install TS Client (see the following illustration).

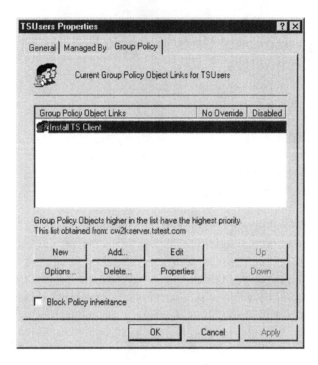

5. Click Edit to open the Group Policy Manager (see the following illustration).

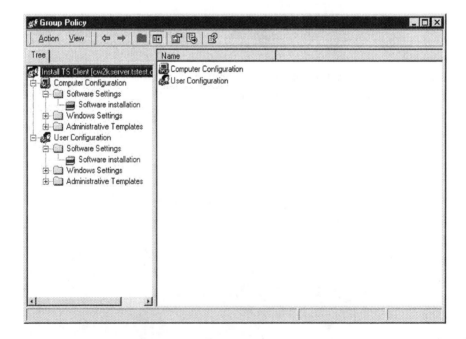

6. To create a policy to install Terminal Services for certain users, expand the User Configuration section in the left pane. If you are setting this policy for computers, expand the Computer Configuration section. Use Computer Configuration if you want it to apply to all users on that computer. Use User Configuration if you want to apply the policy to those users, regardless of what computer they were on. Exactly which of these you should use depends on your goals and users' habits.

7. Click the plus sign to the left of the Software Settings policy object in the appropriate section.

8. Right-click the Software Installation object and select New | Package from the shortcut menu.

9. In the File Open dialog box, browse the network to the share where the Terminal Services client files, including the Windows Installer package, are located (remember the default was \Program Files\Terminal Services Client MSI). Select the Installer file (Terminal Services Client.MSI) and click Open (see the following illustration).

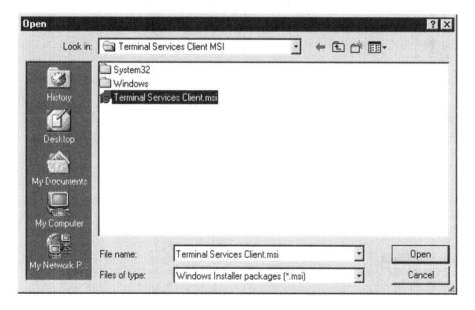

10. In the Deploy Software dialog box, choose whichever option you want, but Assigned is probably the appropriate one (see the following illustration).

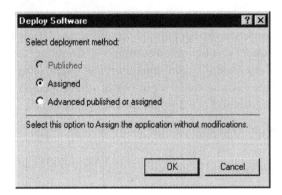

11. The new policy object is created and appears in the right pane of the window when Software Installation is selected (see the following illustration).

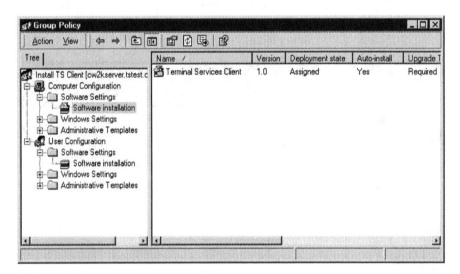

TAKE COMMAND

It takes a while for a policy to replicate through the network, so you can force instant replication with the secedit command. Open a command prompt and enter the following:

Secedit /refreshpolicy machine_policy (for computer policies)

Secedit /refreshpolicy user_policy (for user policies)

Uninstalling Terminal Services

If you find it necessary to uninstall Terminal Services, either at the client or the server, the process is remarkably easy.

Uninstalling the Client

The Terminal Services client always creates an entry in the Add/Remove Programs applet in Control Panel. Sometimes you also see an Uninstall entry in the submenu of the Terminal Services Client menu item on the Programs menu. In either case, running the program brings you to the same setup screen you saw when you installed the client.

To uninstall the client, click Remove All and confirm that you want to do so. You must reboot to complete the process, even if you are running Windows 2000 Professional.

TIP: You can also reinstall the client at this point, either to replace files you've deleted, or because you messed up your settings and want a fresh installation to go back to the default settings.

Uninstalling the Server

Uninstalling Terminal Services is also simple. To do so, go to Control Panel on the server and select Add/Remove Programs, and click the Add/Remove Windows Components button on the left of the dialog box. You see the same Windows Components Wizard you saw when you installed Terminal Services. Deselect Terminal Services and, if necessary, Terminal Services Licensing, and click Next to continue.

The Windows Components Wizard removes Terminal Services from the system (or at least it stops the component from running and removes its program entries from the Start menu). You must reboot the server to have the configuration changes take effect.

Working with the Standard Client Software

After you install the client software, a Terminal Services Client entry appears in the Programs group of client machines. The listing contains three entries:

- ✦ Terminal Services Client
- ✦ Client Connection Manager
- ✦ Uninstall

CODE BLUE

Immediately after installation of the client and server, users should be able to connect to the server and begin working, with one problem: if the server is a domain controller and the user is just a normal user, the client receives an error message that says the local policy forbids an interactive logon.

This occurs because Terminal Services requires users to have Log On Locally permissions for the server. Normal users have this right on a member server, but not on a domain controller. The following types of users have Log On Locally rights by default on a domain controller:

- ◆ Account operators
- ◆ Administrators
- ◆ Backup operators
- ◆ Print operators
- ◆ Server operators
- ◆ Service-based users such as TsInternetUser

There are two ways to troubleshoot this problem:

- ◆ Assign Log On Locally rights to the appropriate users and groups
- ◆ Don't let regular users run applications on a domain controller

In most cases, this latter policy is the right one. Domain controllers have many duties in a Windows 2000 network, and must be ready to perform authentications and other services to other systems on the network. Running Terminal Services in Remote Administration mode on a domain controller adds a trivial extra load to the server and so is worth the administrative convenience it brings. However, running applications in Application Server mode could make the domain controller unresponsive when you need it.

If you feel it won't interfere with the DC's work load, and you want to assign rights for users to run applications in this mode, here's how:

On the domain controller, choose Start | Administrative Tools | Domain Controller Security Policy. In the left pane, expand Security Settings, then Local Policies, and then select User Rights Assignment.

Double-click Log On Locally in the right pane to open the Security Policy Setting dialog box. The list contains the users and groups that have this right. You can add the users and groups you want to allow access by clicking the Add button.

Terminal Services Client Program

The Terminal Services Client program is basically a File Open-type dialog box for choosing Terminal Servers. You can either enter a server name or browse the domain or workgroup for a server. You can specify a screen resolution, whether to enable compression and local bitmap caching, and then you can connect (see the following illustration).

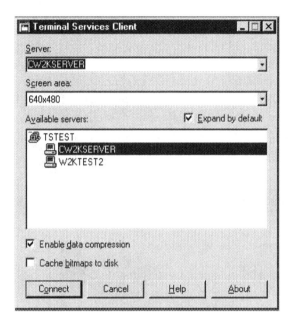

Even though the server browsing area won't let you out of your domain, you can enter names of servers outside the domain by typing them into the Server field, assuming you have proper credentials for the server. For instance, you can type the domain name or IP address of a server across the Internet.

Client Connection Manager

The Client Connection Manager is a more sophisticated way to connect. It allows you to predefine connections to Terminal servers and to build into them all the available user settings for a connection. For example, you can predefine a connection to a server that includes all the logon information and the display resolution.

You can even define connections that load a program on the server. In that case, when the user quits the program, the connection also drops, making the remote application seem just like a local one to a user. You can create shortcuts to these connections and place them anywhere in the menu system.

Creating a Connection

To create a new connection, either select File | New Connection, press CTRL-N, or click the first icon on the left of the toolbar of the Client Connection window.

The Client Connection Manager Wizard opens so you can create the connection by stepping through the wizard windows (clicking Next to move along).

Name the connection (you can change the name later, as you would change any Windows filename) and specify the server to connect to by name or IP address.

In the Automatic Logon window, you can specify the logon info for the server in advance. If no password is entered, the user will have to log on to the server manually. If you supply the username and/or domain, those items will be preloaded into the logon dialog box (see the following illustration).

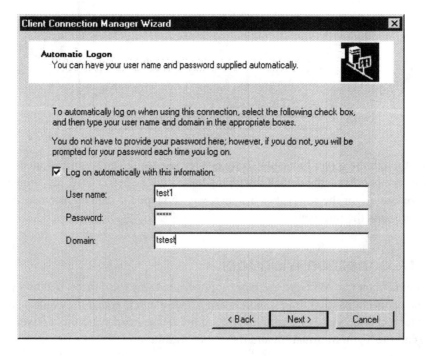

CODE BLUE

The Winlogon DontDisplayLastUserName feature interferes with the Automatic Logon feature of Client Connection Manager. In spite of supplying a valid username and password, you will be prompted for both when you connect if the DontDisplayLastUserName feature is enabled.

To disable the feature, edit the registry on the Terminal server and go to the value HKEY_LOCAL_MACHINE\Software\Microsoft\WindowsNT\CurrentVersion\Winlogon DontDisplayLastUsername. Change it from a 1 to 0. Alternatively, you can disable the group policy at Local Computer Policy\Computer Configuration\Windows Settings\ Security Settings\Local Policies\Security Options\ Do not display last user name in logon screen.

CODE BLUE

If you log on to Terminal Services using a User Principal Name (UPN) and have the server set up to display the name of the last user who logged on, the Winlogon service only displays the username and not the full UPN. A UPN is in the form: *username@domainname*. For example, if you log on successfully as lseltzer@mydomain (notice that the Log On To box grays out as soon as you type the @), the next time you log on, the User Name box says "lseltzer".

Even though the display of the last username is controlled by registry settings on the server (see Code Blue above), the actual value displayed is stored on the client in the registry key: HKEY_CURRENT_USER\Software\Microsoft\Terminal Server Client\Default\Username, and contains the username in Unicode form.

There's a kind of workaround for this: on the Terminal server, in registry key HKEY_LOCAL_MACHINE\Software\Microsoft\WindowsNT\CurrentVersion\Winlogon, create a new value of type REG_SZ called TSForceUPN and give it a value of 1. Once this value exists, if it is 1, *all* logons are resolved with UPNs. In other words, even if a user logs on with only a username, the next logon displays a UPN (*username@domainname*). The user can backspace over the @domainname, but who's going to do that?

Specify the resolution of the session, limited, of course, by the resolution of the client system on which it will run. You can also define a session to run full-screen on the client. By default, the session runs in a window.

If necessary, enable data compression and local bitmap caching, both of which are only useful over slow connections, like a dial-up.

Defining Sessions for Specific Programs

The next screen is one of the really cool things in Terminal Services. You can define a connection so it loads a specific program rather than a desktop session of Windows. Unfortunately, Microsoft ignored the obvious need for a Browse button for the field in which you specify the filename of the application to load (see Figure 3-5).

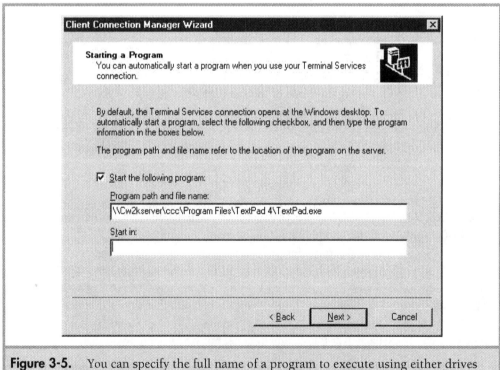

Figure 3-5. You can specify the full name of a program to execute using either drives local to the Terminal server or UNCs for any server

CODE BLUE

You need to be careful about the Start In directory specification in this window, which designates the current directory for the program after it loads. If you simply copy the settings from a Windows Explorer icon of the program on the server, there's a good chance that the program will fail to load for a normal user under Terminal Services because the user will not have rights to that directory.

The default for the Start In directory is the user's home directory (%HOMEPATH%). Since you really, really ought to create and enforce home directories for Terminal Services users, this is a good default and you may as well leave the field blank unless you know a better directory to specify for a particular application. You can use environment variable names (like %HOMEPATH%) in specifying the directory.

After the Starting A Program dialog box, you have the option of changing the icon on the connection you are creating. There's a choice of three very boring icons or you can browse other Windows exe files for other icons. In addition to the connection icon in the Client Connection Manager itself, the wizard puts a shortcut to the connection in a Program folder on the Start menu. By default, the Terminal Services Client folder is used, but you can choose another location. Click Next and the process ends.

TAKE COMMAND

Use the **mstsc** command to run the Terminal Services client from the command line. The syntax is:

```
mstsc.exe [session name] [-v:server name] [-f] [-w:width -h:height] [/?]
```

where:

/? display syntax

session name specifies the name of a session in the Client Connection Manager for that system

-v:*server name* specifies the name of the Terminal server to which you want to connect

-f starts the session in full-screen mode

-w:*width* -h:*height* specifies dimensions of the session in pixels (for example, -w:640 -h:480)

Import/Export Connections

Connections can be imported and exported in Client Connection Manager, which you might want to do to distribute connections to different users.

To export connections, select one or more connections and choose File | Export or choose File | Export All to export all the connections. If you have a password in the connection for the Automatic Logon feature, the Export function asks you to confirm that you want to include it in the export file. The file is in standard Windows ini format, with a series of sections and variables in the form *variable=data*. The password is not stored in plain text, but in a hexadecimal representation of something which is not a plain text password. Even though the password has been obscured somewhat, treat it as if it's out in the open.

If you choose Export All, you find an entry for the [Default] connection in the export file. This connection represents the current settings of the Terminal Services Client program. Beware—if you import a file with the [Default] connection in it, that connection is imported into the Terminal Services Client.

Sample Client Connection Manager Import/Export File

What follows is the contents of a sample cns file that runs Excel on a Terminal server.

```
[Excel On Main Server]
WinPosStr=0,1,0,0,640,480
Expand=1
Smooth Scrolling=0
Shadow Bitmap Enabled=1
Dedicated Terminal=0
Server Port=3389
Enable Mouse=1
Disable CTRL+ALT+DEL=1
DoubleClick Detect=0
Full Screen Hotkey=3
Icon Index=0
Desktop Size ID=1
Screen Mode ID=1
Compression=1
BitmapCachePersistEnable=0
Desktop=2
Auto Connect=1
Icon File=
Progman Group=Terminal Services Client
MRU0=192.168.0.1
AutoLogon 50=1
UserName 50=6C73656C747A657200
MaximizeShell 50=1
Password 50=EE116426169F3FAF637D1835510B328D5B6C35C22AE968C1FFFF4C4B0ADB912E00
```

```
Salt 50=96CAEB1802DAB4CC57C94E32FE9C4A9C314410D900
Domain 50=6C6172727973656C747A657200
Alternate Shell
50=443A5C50726F6772616D2046696C65735C4D6963726F736F6674204F66666963655C4F66666963655C4578636
56C2E65786500
Shell Working Directory 50=00
AutoLogon=0
UserName=00
MaximizeShell=1
Password=A2E2D4F2E53086058B1CB2353858663688FF9AAA6BA84B5F666A8C4F6231B96C00
Domain=00
Alternate
Shell=443A5C50726F6772616D2046696C65735C4D6963726F736F6674204F66666963655C4F66666963655C4578
63656C2E65786500
Shell Working Directory=00
[Word On Main Server\Hotkey]
CtrlEsc=36
AltEsc=45
AltTab=33
AltShiftTab=34
AltSpace=46
CtrlAltDelete=35
[Private Reserved Section]
Excel On Main Server=
[Excel On Main Server\Hotkey]
CtrlEsc=36
AltEsc=45
AltTab=33
AltShiftTab=34
AltSpace=46
CtrlAltDelete=35
```

CODE BLUE

When you create a connection in the Client Connection Manager, you have the opportunity to enter a username, password, and domain for the connection in the Automatic Logon screen. The explicit instructions on the Automatic Logon screen say that if you enter all the information, including the password, the connection will automatically log you on to the server.

Well, not quite. Set it up correctly and you'll find that the logon dialog box still appears for the connection, although the username and domain you specified is in the dialog box.

The problem is that the Connection Properties on the server are configured for a default setting for all connections of Always Prompt For Password, and you need to change that setting. To do so, on the server choose Start | Administrative Tools | Terminal Services Configuration. Select Connections on the left, then double-click the appropriate connection object on the right (almost certainly the RDP-TCP connection). In the Properties dialog box that opens, select the Logon Settings tab and then uncheck the Always Prompt For Password box at the bottom.

BUG ALERT The Client Connection Manager has a bug in the Automatic Logon screen: it can only save up to 14 characters of a password. If your password is longer, you will either have to enter it manually or see an error message like this:

```
The system could not log you on. Make sure your User name and domain are
correct, then type your password again. Letters in passwords must be typed
using the correct case. Make sure that Caps Lock is not accidentally on.
```

There's no good workaround for this bug in the shipping Windows 2000 Client Connection Manager. Your choices are to enter the password every time or select a shorter password.

CODE BLUE

Here are some troubleshooting suggestions for some of the commonly encountered problems users see and call the helpdesk about.

A user sees an error message that says, "You do not have access to this session."

This message indicates that the user doesn't have sufficient privileges for the RDP-TCP connection. To fix the problem, open the Terminal Services Configuration program on the server and select Connections. Right-click the RDP-TCP connection on the right and choose Properties. Select the Permissions tab and assign rights to the relevant user or group.

A user sees the message "Your interactive logon privilege has been disabled. Please contact your system administrator."

The user attempting to log on does not have the Allow Logon To Terminal Server permission enabled on the Terminal Services Profile tab of his account in the Active Directory Users and Computers program. You can remedy this by opening Active Directory Users and Computers, and double-clicking the affected user or group object. Select the Terminal Services Profile tab, and check the Allow Logon To Terminal Server checkbox.

A user sees the message "The terminal server has exceeded the maximum number of allowed connections. The system cannot log you on (1B8E). Please try again or consult your system administrator."

This indicates that the server is possibly running in Remote Administration mode, and that the maximum number of two connections is already active when the client attempts to connect.

A user sees the message "Terminal Services sessions disabled. Remote logons are currently disabled."

This message indicates that an administrator has issued the command **change logon /disable** from the command line. To remedy the situation, the administrator must run the **change logon /enable** command at the command line.

A user sees the message "Because of a network error, the session will be disconnected. Please try to reconnect."

The administrator has set a limit on the number of connections, and the maximum number was reached at the time the user attempted to connect. To check and/or increase the limit, open the Terminal Services Configuration program on the server. Click Connections, right-click the connection on the right (RDP-TCP in a normal install), and choose Properties. Select the Network Adapter tab. At the bottom of the page is an option for Maximum Connections, which you can increase, or switch to Unlimited Connections.

A user sees the message "The client could not connect to the Terminal server. The server may be too busy. Please try connecting later."

This message indicates that the administrator has disabled one or more of the connections to the server. Open the Terminal Services Configuration program on the server, click Connections, and look for connections in the right pane with a red X superimposed on the object. If there are none, right-click the connections available object (RDP-TCP in a normal install). If All Tasks | Enable Connection is an available option, the connection is currently disabled (which had to have been accomplished deliberately). You have the option of enabling it, but you should check with the person who disabled it to make sure it's okay to change the option.

 BUG ALERT If you make changes to the input locale under a Terminal Services session, they are reflected in the local settings for the user on the Terminal server. Input locale is set in the Control Panel Regional Options applet, on the Input Locales tab.

BUG ALERT If you create a connection with Connection Manager and then copy the connection and paste it to the desktop, an access violation may occur in explorer.exe.

Microsoft reports this problem in Knowledge Base article Q262137, but I have not been able to replicate it on either the standard client or Terminal Services Advanced Client, under either release-level Windows 2000 or Service Pack 1. This probably means the problem requires circumstances that are not specified in the article.

Microsoft states that the bug is caused by a problem in conman.exe (the Client Connection Manager program). They say they have a hotfix for it, but that the fix is not fully tested. The bug does not appear in the list of bugs fixed in Service Pack 1.

BUG ALERT If you use a password-protected screen saver on a client system while running a Terminal Services session, and the session is minimized at the time the screen saver kicks in, the Terminal Services session may display a blank screen after you enter the password to exit the screen saver. The administrator may need to reset the session using Terminal Services Manager (see Chapter 5).

Microsoft recommends as a workaround that you not minimize Terminal Services sessions if you are using a password-protected screen saver ("Doctor, it hurts when I do this!" "Don't do that!").

Working with the MMC Snap-In Client

The main point of the Terminal Services MMC snap-in client is for administrators to be able to connect to multiple servers and easily switch between them. It does a good job of this, but it definitely feels like a prerelease product.

You invoke the Terminal Services MMC snap-in client from Start | Programs | Administrative Tools | Terminal Services Connections.

The snap-in begins life in a rather bare state. The first thing you need to do is create a connection (see Figure 3-6). Right-click on Terminal Services Connections and select Add New Connection.

First, you must specify the name of the server to which you will connect (use the Browse button). The Connection Name is what will appear in the left pane of the snap-in, so you'll need to name it in a way that allows you to distinguish between your servers. You can optionally specify a username, password, and domain to log on to. Remember, in order to log you on automatically, the server must also be configured to omit the requirement of an interactive password entry.

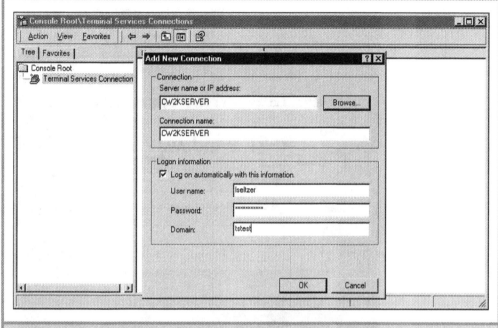

Figure 3-6.   As in the standard Terminal Services client, you can predefine connections
to specific servers and automatically log on

Once you have one or more connections, you can right-click on them in the left pane
and select Connect to establish the connection listed in the right pane. See Figure 3-7 for
the results.

You can right-click and connect to other Terminal servers at the same time. When you
click back on the connection name for a server to which you are already connected, it brings
you back with the connection intact.

BUG ALERT The initial version of the MMC snap-in client cannot adjust the resolution of the
Terminal Services session once established. So, for example, if you were to open a connection
with the MMC not maximized and then maximize it, the Terminal Services session would remain
at its original resolution with a blank border around it.

For this reason, it is best to maximize the MMC before establishing any Terminal Services
connections.

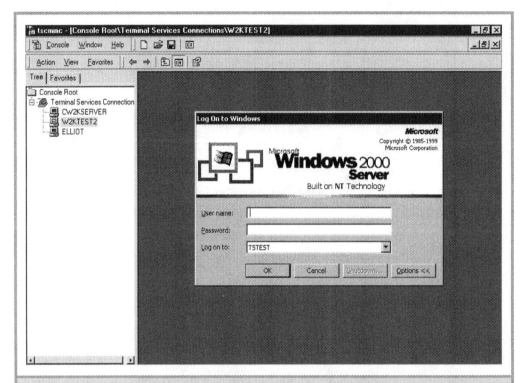

Figure 3-7. Terminal Services MMC snap-in client lets you establish connections to multiple Terminal servers and switch between them

BUG ALERT Another bug can cause the MMC to crash. If, while a session is open, you resize the panes of the MMC by dragging the band between them, the MMC will crash. Microsoft acknowledges this bug, says the problem lies in the Microsoft Management Console, and that it may appear with other snap-ins as well. Microsoft says that this is fixed in Service Pack 1 of Windows 2000, but my testing indicates otherwise. After installing SP1 and then the snap-in, I resized the panes, and the program exited ungracefully. (Don't bother, I've already reported it to Microsoft.)

Because the MMC diminishes your Terminal Services screen space to begin with, you may want to adjust this band before establishing connections, but while still leaving enough left pane visible so you know what you're clicking on.

When this happens, you may find yourself with sessions open on the server. These will eventually time out, but you can go to the server and open Terminal Services Manager from the Administrative Tools group. Select the user or session labeled "disconnected," right-click on it, and select Reset.

Unlike the procedures available with the Client Connection Manager, you cannot specify the resolution of the session nor an application to run in the MMC snap-in. If you include your password in a connection definition, it is encrypted and stored in the .msc file (the snap-in).

Working with the ActiveX Client

After you install the ActiveX client there's nothing else to do on the server, unless you want to create your own Web pages. Microsoft provides two sample Web pages utilizing the Terminal Services ActiveX client, and you can use the code in them to produce your own if you want.

The default installation for the sample files is in the TSWeb subdirectory of the wwwroot directory, which itself is the root of the Web server. Using the example in Figure 3-8, the URL is http://w2ktest2/tsweb/default.htm. w2ktest2 is the name of the server (you can also use an IP address). The /tsweb directory and default.htm are from one of the sample files. Because it is the default document in the directory, you can also launch it as http://w2ktest2/tsweb/.

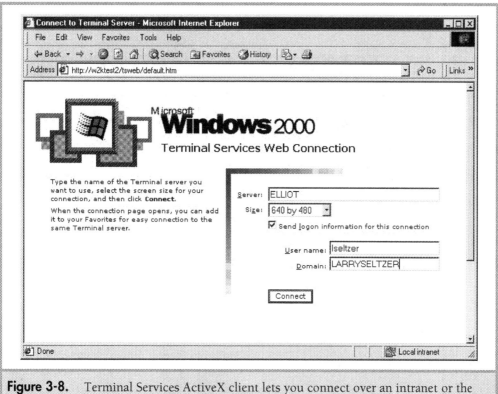

Figure 3-8. Terminal Services ActiveX client lets you connect over an intranet or the Internet and run Terminal Services sessions on your server

The default.htm document is just about functionally equivalent to the Terminal Services Client program. You can specify a server name (warning: there is no browse capability), you can select a resolution from a list of them in a combo-box, or you can specify that the session run full-screen. You can optionally specify the username and domain to which the session should connect, although Microsoft thought it too great a security risk to allow users to preset a password this way.

Of course, since this client is an ActiveX control, it will only work in Internet Explorer. If you have a need to use Netscape Navigator, Citrix has product called NFuse that allows you to access MetaFrame servers using a Netscape plug-in.

Bear in mind, in case you rely on a firewall for security, that the ActiveX control runs on your Web server. If you were relying on a firewall to protect your Web server, you may be surprised to learn how much a user of Terminal Services can do. Because Terminal Services users communicate over RDP, firewalls won't be able to detect if the user is, for example, compromising critical system files on the server. Only proper administration techniques (see Chapters 5 and 6) can do that.

Press the Connect button and you get the standard Windows logon screen, possibly preloaded with the specified username. Complete the logon and you're in (see Figure 3-9).

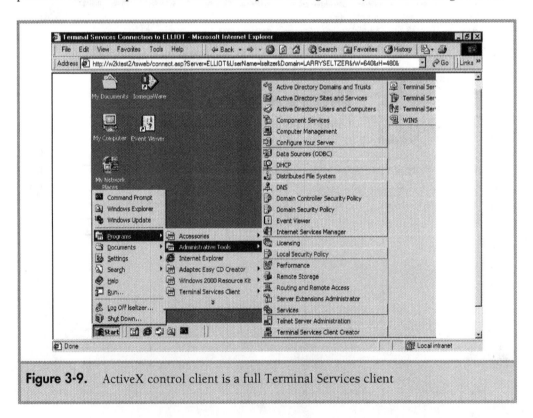

Figure 3-9. ActiveX control client is a full Terminal Services client

The second sample page, manyservers.htm, is not designed to be useful as much as flashy. It has four Terminal Services sessions in a 2x2 table (see the following illustration). There is also a field for you to type in a server name and Connect and Disconnect buttons. When you connect to the server, separate sessions open up in all four cells.

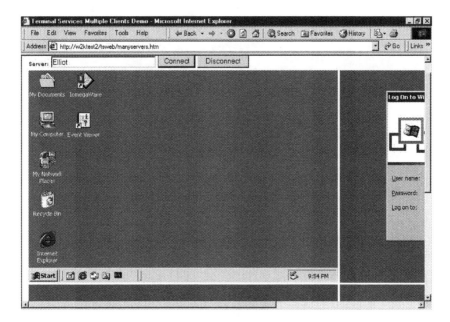

Chapter 4

Troubleshooting Application Issues

Configuring Shared Applications

You can't just install an application under Windows Terminal Services and expect it to run. To work successfully with applications under Terminal Services, you must not only break yourself of some well-ingrained habits, you must also develop a high level of mistrust and doubt.

If you installed any applications on your server before enabling Terminal Services, tough luck, buddy. You have to uninstall them and then reinstall them the right way.

Overcoming Common Problems

Programmers who write Windows applications don't normally think about their programs running in a Terminal Services environment or any multiuser environment. Most people think of Windows systems as single-user systems, so they make assumptions about the computer's configuration that do not always work well in a multiuser environment. In this section, we discuss some of the reasons a Windows program may not work properly in a multiuser environment. You can apply some measures to help applications behave in a multiuser environment, and this chapter will help you apply them. Alas, some behaviors are irreparable.

You can avoid much of this grief by trying to use applications that have been certified by Microsoft to run under Windows 2000. One requirement for such certification is that the application work correctly in a Terminal Services environment.

Data Storage Mistakes

Back in the old days of the early 1990s, when every Windows computer had but one user and dinosaurs roamed the earth, programs stored their configuration information in .ini files. Those configuration files were stored in a fixed location, such as %SystemRoot% or the program directory.

Such techniques don't work in Terminal Services. If only one file exists, every user who sets a configuration option is creating a global setting for all users. This, of course, assumes a user has Write permission for the files in such a directory (which isn't likely).

This is why you must create home directories for users (discussed later in this chapter), so that well-designed applications can have a place to store user-specific files.

User Configuration Data Storage Errors

Programs that store user configuration data in privileged areas present enormous problems to administrators of Terminal Services. Windows 2000 is a secure operating system, and normal users don't have Write permission for all areas in the file system. In fact, users don't even have Read permission for all areas. If a program installs configuration data to the %SystemRoot% directory, normal users will not be able to make modifications. Incidentally, even Microsoft makes this mistake (see "Microsoft Office in Terminal Services" later in this chapter).

Menu Items Errors

Software installation programs that create menu items in the current profile create serious problems for Terminal Services. Menu items must be written to the All Users profile and its menu folders to ensure that the program's listings are available to all users.

Writing User-Specific Information to HKEY_LOCAL_MACHINE

The registry has two main areas to which programs may write configuration data, HKEY_LOCAL_MACHINE and HKEY_CURRENT_USER. The former stores information relevant to all users on the system, and the latter is for information relevant only to the current user. Some programs, sloppily assuming that systems have only one user, write user information to the keys and subkeys in HKEY_LOCAL_MACHINE. When users make changes for themselves, it results in changes for all others as well.

Writing Global Information to HKEY_CURRENT_USER

This problem is the complement to the previous one. Some programs, once again mistakenly assuming there is only one user on the system, write all their information to HKEY_CURRENT_USER. Other users attempting to use the program may experience problems because the program will not find configuration information it expects. This means that only the user who installed the program will be able to use it. (This may be intentional on the application vendor's part, as they may consider their license for the program to be for one user.)

Failure to Support Multiuser Access to Certain Files

Some programs may require access to a certain file in their program directory and open that file for exclusive access. This means that when a second user attempts to access the file, that attempt will fail, probably displaying a message indicating a "sharing violation."

Creating Settings at First Runtime

Some programs create new registry settings and establish settings in configuration files when the program is first run, instead of during installation. Because Terminal Services specifically monitors installations to look for such settings, the system misses them if they're created at runtime. As a result, settings aren't propagated to all users. This may or may not cause a problem, depending on the application. For a workaround for such applications, see the section "Using the Add/Remove Programs Feature" in this chapter.

Using Home Directories

It's generally a good idea in a Windows NT or Windows 2000 network to assign home directories to users. In Terminal Services, it's absolutely mandatory. As some of the software problems above indicate, Terminal Services has problems with applications that assume that there is one user on the system, and with applications that do not properly differentiate between configuration information that is global to the system and that which is specific to individual users.

By default, Windows 2000 users have home directories that are named for their logon names, in subdirectories in the Documents and Settings directory. You can set up separate home directories for users when they are logged on under Terminal Services. It's as simple as setting up a directory, preferably on a separate file server, where these home directories may be stored, and then specifying the appropriate UNC for the user in the entry in Active Directory Users and Computers.

See Chapter 5 for more detail on home directories and user profiles.

Remote Administration Mode and Applications

Because only administrators can run sessions in Remote Administration mode, you don't need to make any special provisions for setting up applications in this mode. That's the good news.

The bad news is that some applications won't work in Remote Administration mode. There are two main causes for this. In some cases, applications create user interface components which, because of the absence of portions of Terminal Services that load only with Application Server mode, appear on the server console rather than the terminal. The second problem arises when applications don't make use of per-session name spaces (see "Terminal Services Architecture" in Chapter 1).

Using the Add/Remove Programs Feature

Terminal Services has two new modes of operation to Windows 2000: Install mode and Execute mode. When you install a program, you must first put Terminal Services into Install mode, and then return to Execute mode in order for users to run the program. The simplest way to accomplish this is to use the Add/Remove Programs applet in Control Panel.

To install a program, run the Add/Remove Programs applet and click the large Add New Programs button on the left side of the window (see Figure 4-1).

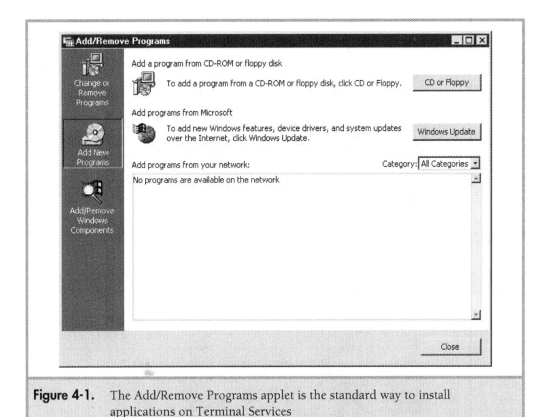

Figure 4-1.   The Add/Remove Programs applet is the standard way to install applications on Terminal Services

Click the CD or Floppy button, and if your software installation disk is in either location, the system displays a dialog suggesting that program. If no installation programs are available on the CD or floppy disk, the system brings up a dialog box with no suggestions, so you can specify the location of the installation program. In either event, enter a program name or browse to the program's location to begin the installation (see Figure 4-2).

After the installation routines are complete, click Next. The fact that the next dialog box has appeared does not mean the installation is complete. Be sure to finish any portions of the installation program, including quitting the application itself, before clicking Finish (see Figure 4-3).

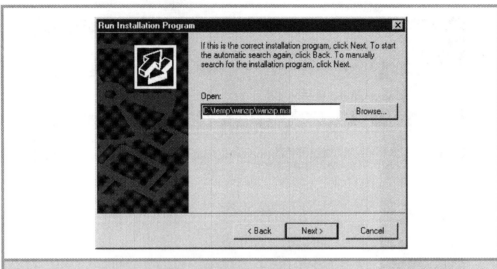

Figure 4-2. Specify the name and location of the install program

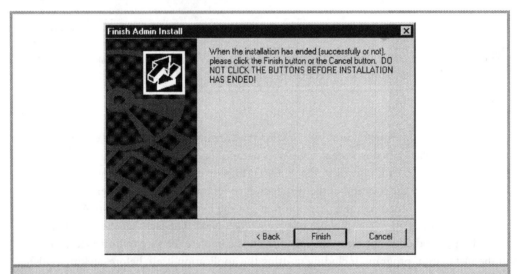

Figure 4-3. Clicking Finish in the dialog box is equivalent to switching the system back into Execute mode, so be sure all installation routines are completed

CODE BLUE

Some poorly written applications make configuration settings the first time the program runs in addition to the settings written during installation. If you follow the standard procedure above, these additional settings will not be monitored by Terminal Services Install mode.

Instead, run the application once before you click Finish in the Add/Remove Programs applet. This will ensure that the settings are written while Terminal Services is still operating in Install mode.

If you have already left the Install mode before running the application, you can uninstall it and start again. Alternatively, you can re-enter Install mode with the **change user /install** command (see the next section, "Using the Command Line"). You can create another Administrator account, log on with that account at the server console, run **change user /install**, run the application, and then re-enter Execute mode with **change user /execute**.

Often, installation programs require a reboot of the system to complete the installation process. Fortunately, the Add/Remove Programs applet is intelligent enough to put the system back into Install mode after the system reboots. The setup finishes and the system returns to Execute mode.

However, you must remember that this is a server. If you need to install an application that requires a reboot, you must make sure that all users are logged off beforehand.

Additionally, if you install an application that requires rebooting from a Terminal Services session, your session will (of course) be disconnected during the reboot. When the server has restarted, you need to reconnect and log on to test the installation.

Using the Command Line

You can put the system into Install mode manually using the command **change user /install**. After you install the application, use the command line to put the system back into Execute mode with the command **change user /execute**.

The main reason to prefer the Add/Remove Programs applet to the command-line method is that Add/Remove Programs automatically changes the system into Install mode and back to Execute mode. This reduces the chance that you will forget to perform the last step.

However, if you perform automated installations, perhaps using batch files, the **change user** command is the way to go. You can also use the **change user** command to perform any operation in Install mode after program installation has completed.

TAKE COMMAND

The **change user** command switches the system between install and execute modes. When you need to install an application for use in Terminal Services, you need to first switch the Terminal server to install mode, which you may do either with this command or with the Add/Remove Programs applet in Control Panel. If you switch manually, using the change user command, it is critical to remember to switch back!

The syntax for **change user** is:

```
change user [/execute | /install | /query]
```

where:

/execute puts the system into execute mode the default and normal mode.
/install puts the system into install mode, so that Terminal Services monitors changes in the system and makes the changes effective for all users.
/query displays the current mode for the system.

CODE BLUE

Many applications won't successfully install from a remote Terminal Services session. You have to install them from the server console. When you attempt to install a program under a Terminal Services remote session, you may see this message:

```
Setup cannot start or configure program name
```

SQL Server 7.0 is an example of programs that present this difficulty. When you encounter this error, you must install the program at the server console.

CODE BLUE

Because Windows 2000 erroneously allows a program running from the RunOnce keys in the registry to switch a normal user into Install mode, users may lose some settings and gain others in a sporadic manner.

Allowing a RunOnce program to change modes was intentional, but the intent was for administrators to run these programs. If a normal user logs in and makes registry changes while the server is in Install mode, these changes may be propagated to other users' registries.

Microsoft has a hot-fixed version of Kernel32.dll that addresses this problem. At this point, the fix has not been completely tested, so you have to call up Microsoft tech support and specifically request it.

You can also avoid this situation by assuring, as you should for many other reasons, that no other users are logged on to a server when you install software. You should also make sure, if a program creates RunOnce or RunOnceEx settings, that you log in after the install and any reboot to complete the installation as Administrator.

Using Windows Installer

Many newer programs, including Microsoft Office 2000, use the Windows Installer service. Windows Installer is a technology new to Windows 2000, and it automates application installation. It's available as an add-on to Windows 9x and Windows NT 4.0. It is built into Windows Millennium Edition.

Behind the Scenes

When you enter Install mode, Terminal Services monitors the application installation looking for changes in the system, which may need modification to work correctly in multiuser mode.

For example, during Install mode, if an installation program writes data to HKEY_CURRENT_USER, Terminal Services mirrors it to a special area in HKEY_LOCAL_MACHINE\Software\Microsoft\Windows NT\CurrentVersion\ TerminalServer\Install. When a user needs these settings, Terminal Services copies them to the appropriate keys in HKEY_CURRENT_USER.

One major problem with Windows Installer service under Terminal Services is that Windows Installer allows programs to install parts of themselves and then allow other parts of the programs to be installed when a user needs them. This saves on disk space that the program occupies.

But imagine what happens under Terminal Services: the administrator installs the program, and then a user attempts to run it. Some new feature is needed, but the user does not have sufficient rights to perform the installation of the files for that feature.

Partly as a solution to this problem, the Windows Installer supports *transform files,* which use a .mst extension, and which apply live changes to an installation as needed. In general, you need to get .mst files from the vendor.

You have more than one way to apply a transform file to an installation. In the case of Microsoft Office 2000, add the **transforms=***path**transform_file*.**msi** parameter to the command line of the setup.exe program (discussed later in this chapter in "Microsoft Office in Terminal Services"). You can also run the Windows Installer from the command line specifying both the program installation package and the transform file:

msiexec /I *path**application_package*.**msi transforms=***path**transform_file*.**msi allusers=1**

NOTE: The **allusers** parameter isn't always necessary for the Windows installer, but is applicable for Terminal Services installations.

Creating Installer Packages for Legacy Programs

It's possible to create Windows Installer packages (.msi files) for programs with conventional setup routines. This is a multistep process you must follow carefully, but it can make program distribution easier. For example, you can use Active Directory to push installations to systems on the network using Windows Installer.

To perform the steps discussed in this section, you need a server on which the Windows Installer package resides for clients to access. You also need a client system on which to perform some tasks, including the important task of testing the installation.

Windows 2000 comes with a third-party tool, Veritas WinINSTALL LE. This tool allows you to take non-Windows Installer installation files and repackage them for use by the Windows Installer service. If you are interested in the full version of Veritas WinINSTALL, which has additional capabilities for software distribution to desktops across an enterprise, see http://www.veritas.com/products/wile/.

You should create a test client on which to create the Windows Installer package, because the process involves installing the client. You don't want to do this on your server.

Installing Veritas WinINSTALL LE

If you haven't already done so, install Veritas WinINSTALL LE, which is included with Windows 2000 in the \Valueadd\3rdparty\Mgmt\Winstle directory of the Windows 2000 CD. You can do this on the test client or on some other system, as long as you can access the WinINSTALL program directory from that client across the network.

To perform the actual installation, right-click swiadmle.msi in the Winstle directory and select Install. Veritas WinINSTALL LE installs into the %SystemDrive%\ProgramFiles\ VERITAS Software\Winstall directory. The test client needs to be able to access this folder.

Creating the Installation Package

You need the original install programs in addition to the .msi file, so copy the installation files to a network share that you can access. This is also the directory into which you should place the Windows Installer file you are creating.

On the test client, start the process with either of these actions:

- ❖ In the Programs menu, choose VERITAS Software | VERITAS Discover.
- ❖ Browse My Network Places (or Network Neighborhood) to reach the \ProgramFiles\VERITAS Software\Winstall directory on the appropriate server.

Then follow the wizard using the following instructions:

1. Open Discoz.exe (WinINSTALL Discover), read the text on the first screen of the wizard, and click Next.

2. In the next screen of the wizard, specify the name of the application in the first field.

3. Click the ellipsis (...) next to the second field to browse the network and find the folder that is the target for the Windows Installer package clients will use.

4. In the filename field, enter an appropriate name with a .MSI extension. (See Figure 4-4 for an example). Click Next to continue.

5. Select the target drive for the Discover program's temporary files (choose a drive with sufficient free space).

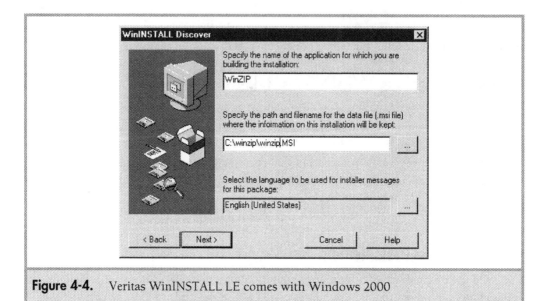

Figure 4-4.   Veritas WinINSTALL LE comes with Windows 2000

6. Tell the Discover program which drives to scan for changes. Generally, this means the drive on which the program will be installed, but specifically it means all drives that may be affected by the installation. You can be prudent and add more drives than may be necessary, but this makes the scanning process longer. Click Next.

7. Define the file scan exclusion list (usually the default listing works fine). Click Next.

Discover displays a message telling you that the "Before" snapshot is complete, meaning that it has captured the state of the computer prior to installing the program (see the following illustration).

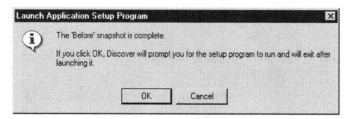

Click OK to open a dialog box where you can browse for the installation program. Start the install program (setup.exe or whatever is appropriate for the application) and then click

OK. The Terminal Services client installation begins. The next step of the process is just the normal installation process for the program. Follow it through to completion, and if the application starts immediately after installation, close it.

Now that you have finished the installation, you must create an "After" snapshot. WinINSTALL LE compares the two snapshots, and the differences between them create the Windows Installer package.

Start the Discovery program (discoz.exe) again. On the test client, either run the program or browse through My Network Places or Network Neighborhood to the %ProgramFiles%\VERITAS Software\Winstall directory on the server. Click Next to begin creating the "After" snapshot.

As the screen in Figure 4-5 indicates, if you want to abandon the package creation and start over, you can do so at this point.

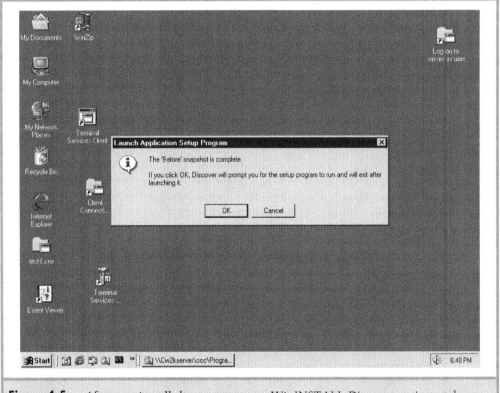

Figure 4-5.   After you install the program, run WinINSTALL Discover again to take an "After" snapshot

WinINSTALL LE Discover searches the file system and registry for changes made by the installation (see the following illustration).

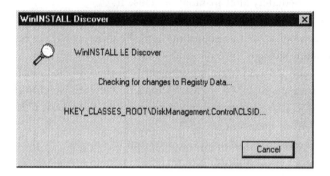

At the end, you should see the "Conversion Successful" dialog box, which may contain some errors or warnings. Some warnings don't represent important problems. For example, you may see a warning that the installation ran from a network drive to which some clients may not have access. Bear this in mind and click OK to continue.

You should also see a confirmation dialog telling you that the "After" snapshot is complete and specifying the location of the Windows Installer package.

CODE BLUE

If you insert an Autoplay-enabled CD in your Terminal server's drive, you will probably see a warning dialog instead of the Autoplay window (see the following illustration). (If the install program on the CD has a name other than setup.exe or install.exe, you won't see this warning.)

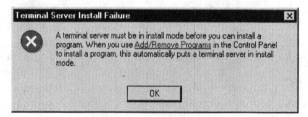

Because you don't want to run the normal installation routine for an application on a Terminal server, you probably don't want the Autoplay feature of Windows (also known as Auto-Insert Notification or AIN) enabled. In fact, you should disable Autoplay on all your servers that run Terminal Services. See the next section for instructions.

Disabling Autoplay on Terminal Services Servers

Your Terminal Services servers shouldn't have Autoplay enabled, and you have two ways to accomplish this: use Group Policy or edit the registry.

Using Group Policy

To use Group Policy effectively, you need to have your Terminal servers grouped into organizational units (OUs) in Active Directory. At that point, you can apply this group policy object (GPO) to the OU, and then possibly disable it for subunits of the OU if you need to.

Follow these steps to apply the policy:

1. In Active Directory Users and Computers, right-click the appropriate OU or domain and select Properties.

2. On the Group Policy tab, click New and then enter the name of the policy object (for example, **disable autoplay**).

3. Click the Edit button to bring up the Group Policy Editor.

4. Expand Computer Configuration, then expand Administrative Templates and select System.

5. In the right pane, double-click the Disable Autoplay policy object (see Figure 4-6).

6. Select Enabled (make sure you've selected CD as the policy target).

7. Click OK, close the GPE, close the Properties dialog box, and close the MMC.

TIP: Remember that it could be some time before the policy replicates throughout the domain.

This policy also exists in the User Configuration section of the GPO, but if it makes sense to disable Autoplay on a Terminal server it makes sense to do so globally.

Using the Registry

If you want to edit the registry, there are at least three ways to disable Autoplay for a drive (there are probably a half dozen more known to a few individuals inside Microsoft). Note that the registry consistently refers to this feature as "AutoRun."

The first two values are of type REG_DWORD and are located in the HKEY_CURRENT_USER\ Software\Microsoft\Windows\CurrentVersion\Policies\Explorer key.

NoDriveAutoRun has a value that is a bit mask with bits corresponding to the drive letters in the system, from drive A on up, starting with the least significant bit. For example,

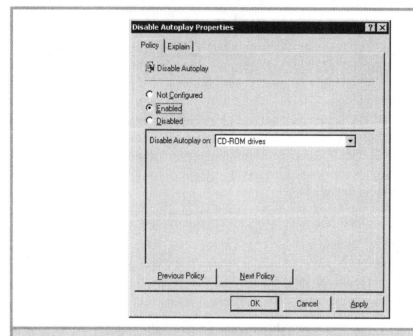

Figure 4-6. Active Directory lets you disable Autoplay on your servers as a group if you set them up in an organizational unit

if the CD-ROM drive uses drive letter D, set this value to 8 (the dialog box in Regedit asks for decimal or hexadecimal, but 8 is the same in both).

NoDriveTypeAutoRun also has a bit mask value, and lets you specify the types of drives on which you want Autoplay disabled. The default value is 0x95 (hex). By changing the value to 0xB5 (which turns on the 0x20 bit), you disable Autoplay on CD-ROM drives in the computer.

Table 4-1 contains a list of other drive types and their bit numbers, but in general the Group Policy and drive-specific registry methods are more precise. Note that for many of the drive types, such as RAM disk, Autoplay is irrelevant.

NOTE: For I-can't-imagine-what reason, Microsoft did not include a standard user interface for disabling Autoplay on a computer. Windows 9x has always included such a feature, and I suspect that Windows 2000's developers were aware of it. Go figure.

Bit Number	Description
0x04	Removable disks (such as floppies, but not CD-ROMs)
0x08	Non-removable disks (such as hard disks)
0x10	Network drive
0x20	CD-ROM
0x40	RAM disk

Table 4-1.   Drive Types Addressed by the Bit Mask in the NoDriveTypeAutoRun Value

The third value disables Autoplay globally for the computer. Go to HKEY_LOCAL_MACHINE\System\CurrentControlSet\Services\Cdrom and check the AutoRun value. 1 means Autoplay is enabled, 0 means it's disabled.

CODE BLUE

Some CD-R and CD-RW drives work better with Autoplay enabled. Some of the methods above allow you to differentiate between drives in your system, so that, for example, if you have a regular CD and a CD-R, you can disable one and not the other.

If you are using Adaptec's DirectCD for Windows, you must leave Autoplay on or the software will not function properly. With some other configurations, Autoplay will interfere with writing to the CD-R or CD-RW.

Application Compatibility Scripts

Terminal Services comes with a system of batch files called application compatibility scripts. You run these scripts, which are customized to specific applications, after installing the application on the Terminal server. The script makes changes in the application so that it will work correctly under Terminal Services. The scripts are located in the %SystemRoot%\ Application Compatibility Scripts directory.

The main part of this process is to change the application so that it saves files for individual users in their home directories rather than one specific location. The process accomplishes this through the use of a setting called RootDrive.

To use Terminal Services effectively, it is essential that you designate a single drive letter that will map to the home directory for all users. The convention for home directories is Z, so in these examples I will use that letter.

The first time you run an application compatibility script, it notices that you have not set a RootDrive, so it opens Notepad with a specific batch file in it. This batch file (RootDrv2.cmd, shown in Figure 4-7) contains instructions showing you exactly which character to edit and why you are doing this.

After you edit the batch file, the script you are running launches it, thereby setting the variable. Another script permanently sets this letter as RootDrive in the registry at HKEY_LOCAL_MACHINE\Software\Microsoft\Windows NT\CurrentVersion\ Terminal Server\RootDrive.

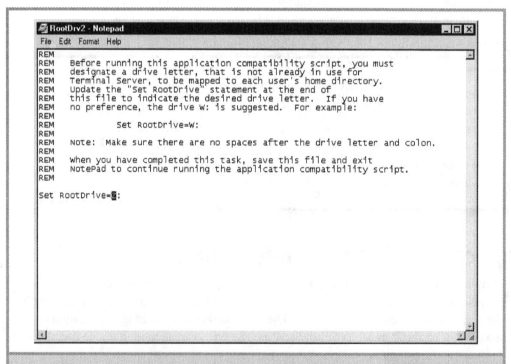

Figure 4-7.   Before running application compatibility scripts, you must designate a drive letter for applications to use when storing user-specific information

Scripts Available from Microsoft

Table 4-2 lists applications that have compatibility scripts available. Most of these are in the standard location, %SystemRoot%\Application Compatibility Scripts.

 NOTE: Microsoft posts updates to this list of scripts at http://corporate.windowsupdate. Microsoft.com. Click Product Updates, then click Continue. In the Operating Systems area, click the Windows 2000 checkbox. In the Component Types area, click the Terminal Services checkbox, then click Continue. Click Continue one more time to see a list of available updates to Terminal Services, including application compatibility scripts.

Application	Filename
Corel Office 7	Coffice7.cmd
Corel Office 8	Coffice8.cmd
DiskKeeper 2.0	Diskpr20.cmd
Eudora Pro 4.0	Eudora4.cmd
Lotus Smart Suite 9	Ssuite9.cmd
Lotus Smart Suite 97	Ssuite97.cmd
Microsoft Access 2.0	Office43.cmd
Microsoft Access 7.0	Office95.cmd
Microsoft Access 97	Office97.cmd
Microsoft Excel 5.0	Office43.cmd
Microsoft Excel 7.0	Office95.cmd
Microsoft Excel 97	Office97.cmd
Microsoft Excel 97 (standalone installation)	Msexcl97.cmd
Microsoft Exchange 5.0 and higher	Winmsg.cmd
Microsoft ODBC	ODBC.cmd
Microsoft Office 4.3	Office43.cmd
Microsoft Office 95	Office95.cmd

Table 4-2.   Compatibility Scripts Available from Microsoft

Application	Filename
Microsoft Office 97	Office97.cmd
Microsoft Office 2000	Requires Transform file
Microsoft Outlook 97	Outlk98.cmd
Microsoft Outlook 98	Outlk98.cmd
Microsoft Outlook Express	Outlk98.cmd
Microsoft PowerPoint 4.0	Office43.cmd
Microsoft PowerPoint 7.0	Office95.cmd
Microsoft PowerPoint 97	Office97.cmd
Microsoft Project 95	Msproj95.cmd
Microsoft Project 98	Msproj98.cmd
Microsoft Schedule+ 7.0	Office95.cmd
Microsoft SNA Client 4.0	Sna40cli.cmd
Microsoft SNA Server 3.0	Mssna30.cmd
Microsoft SNA Server 4.0	Sna40srv.cmd
Microsoft Visual Studio 6.0	MSVS6.cmd
Microsoft Word 6.0	Office43.cmd
Microsoft Word 7.0	Office95.cmd
Microsoft Word 97	Office97.cmd
Microsoft Word 97 (standalone installation)	Msword97.cmd
Netscape Communicator 4.0x	Netcom40.cmd
Netscape Communicator 4.5x	Netcom40.cmd
Netscape Communicator 4.6x	Netcom40.cmd
Netscape Navigator 3.x	Netnav30.cmd
Peachtree Complete Accounting 6.0	PchTree6.cmd
PowerBuilder 6.0	PwrBldr6.cmd
Visio 5.0	Visio5.cmd

Table 4-2. Compatibility Scripts Available from Microsoft *(continued)*

Much of Microsoft's documentation on this subject is not entirely reliable. However, Microsoft has an excellent document named "Terminal Services Application Compatibility Notes," available at http://www.microsoft.com/windows2000/library/operations/terminal/tsapcompat.asp. The document discusses each of the application compatibility scripts included with Windows 2000. The document also covers each of the applications, the problems they have under Terminal Services, and the limitations that will remain even after the script is run.

Microsoft online resources indicate that there are additional scripts at the http://corporate.windowsupdate.Microsoft.com site, but I found none there. Some of the scripts that are supposed to be at the update site are in fact in the standard Windows 2000 installation. By the time you read this, there may be many scripts available.

Microsoft also indicates that there is a Lotus Notes script named Lnote4u.cmd, but I couldn't find it. On the other hand, there are scripts in the standard Windows 2000 Terminal Services installation (for DiskKeeper, for example), which are not discussed in the document.

It's also worth noting that Microsoft's list of applications is filled with old versions of applications and missing some current ones.

Microsoft's "Terminal Services Application Compatibility Notes" also discusses applications for which there is no script, presenting workarounds for problems, or presenting a diagnosis of terminal incompatibility.

Here are some of the more interesting notes from the document:

❖ Microsoft Clipboard Viewer will not work in a multiuser environment.

❖ Microsoft FoxPro 2.6a, while running under Terminal Services, may allow multiple users access to the same files simultaneously, causing data corruption.

❖ Many applications, such as Lotus SmartSuite 97, cannot be effectively upgraded under Terminal Services. Instead you have to uninstall the program and then install the new version.

Help from ISV Web Sites

If you plan to install an application for which you don't have an explicit fix for Terminal Services, save yourself some time in advance and go to the vendor's Web site. If they have a knowledge base or some similar repository of support information, search it for "Terminal Server" or "Terminal Services," possibly even for "Citrix," as many of the same issues will apply.

For example, Corel Office 2000 (equivalent to version 9) is not mentioned by Microsoft and there is no compatibility script. I went to Corel.com, found the knowledge base, searched for "Terminal Server" and found a document entitled "Installation of WordPerfect Office 2000 on Windows Terminal Server" at http://kb.corel.com/kbdocs/WP90WIN/ WP90WIN/WP90WIN_202326.htm. Take a look at this document. You'd never figure this out on your own.

While you're visiting ISV sites, look for other problems related to Terminal Services. In fact, check these sites before you buy applications you want to run on Terminal Services.

Post-Installation Failures

Sometimes a program will install just fine but fail when you attempt to run it, especially in a non-privileged user context. For example, a poorly written program might be hard-coded to write to the %SystemRoot% directory, which would fail for any normal user.

One way to test for the specific problem is to create a temporary user account on the server with the same privileges as a user experiencing problems with the application (you can copy that user in the Active Directory Users and Computers program). Log on as that user and test the application. Then log on again as Administrator, run Event Viewer and see what files, registry entries, and other system resources were accessed and when the errors occurred.

Uninstalling Applications

Uninstalling programs properly is the same as installing them properly: use the Add/Remove Programs applet.

An application's uninstall routine will not necessarily remove it properly if it has been modified by an application compatibility script to run under Terminal Services. In fact, even the Add/Remove Programs applet will at times leave files around—in the user home directories, for example.

This is not really a Terminal Services problem, but rather a Windows 2000 problem. No uninstall routine has the ability to seek out all user profiles on the system and root out all the program references; perhaps they should, but they don't.

Microsoft Office in Terminal Services

Microsoft Office is a special case in many ways. Not only is it the most significant application for users in many companies, it also requires special steps to install properly on Windows 2000 Terminal Services.

To install Office 2000 successfully for Terminal Services, you need a transform file of the type described above in the section "Using Windows Installer." Microsoft includes this file as part of the Office 2000 Resource Kit, a book/CD that's worth having around for any administrator who deals with Office.

If you install the Office 2000 Resource Kit, the file, named Termsrvr.mst, is in the \Program Files\ORKTools\ToolBox\Tools\Terminal Server Tools directory. Or, you can find it on the \ORK\PFiles\ORKTools\Toolbox\Tools\TermSrvr\ folder of the Resource Kit CD.

Installing Office 2000

You must install Office 2000 from the Terminal Services console, starting with these steps:

1. Insert Office 2000 CD 1 in the CD drive of the Terminal Services computer.

2. In Control Panel, select Add/Remove Programs.

3. Click the Add New Programs button.

4. Click the CD or Floppy button.

5. Click Next.

At this point you should see a dialog box with the name of the program to run (see the following illustration).

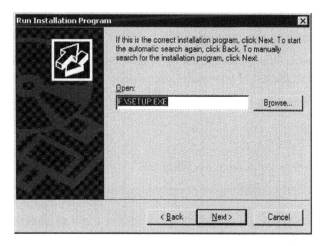

If the program name is not the Office install program (setup.exe in the root of the CD drive), either type in the correct entry or use the Browse button to find it.

Before pressing Enter, append the following parameter to the end of the program name in the dialog: **TRANSFORMS=<*path*>\TermSrvr.mst** (see the following illustration).

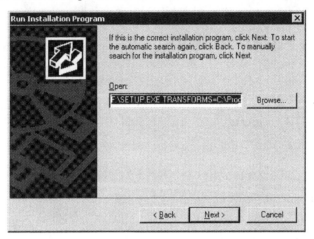

Press Enter or click Next to begin installation of Office 2000, and perform the following tasks:

1. Type the CD key number and organization, but leave the username and initials blank.

2. Accept the license agreement and click Next.

3. At the Microsoft Office 2000: Ready To Install dialog box, select Customize.

4. Specify the path for the Office installation and click Next.

5. At the Microsoft Office 2000: Selecting Features dialog box, click the disk with a down-arrow to the left of Microsoft Office and select Run All From My Computer.

6. Expand the feature tree and select Not Available for any features you don't want to install.

7. Click Install Now.

8. When the installation is complete, click OK.

9. Click Finish in the Add/Remove Programs applet.

After the installation, run Outlook 2000 as an administrator to allow it to complete its installation.

Features to Omit from Your Office Installation

The following features don't work well under Terminal Services, and Microsoft says that the supported state for them in Terminal Services is Not Available:

✦ All individual Office Assistant characters

NOTE: You can choose Run From My Computer for the Office Assistant itself, but you must install the Motionless Office Assistant, which is available on the Office 2000 Resource Kit.

✦ Microsoft Small Business Tools

✦ Scanner and Camera Add-In

✦ System Information

CODE BLUE

If you do work in Office programs before leaving Install mode (either by clicking Finish at the end of the Add/Remove Programs applet or running **change user /execute**), any tasks you perform are applied to all users when you switch to Execute mode.

For example, if you start using Outlook before switching out of Install mode, other users might see your personal folders. Be careful to switch out of Install mode at the correct time.

Installing Disk 2 of Office 2000

To install disk 2 of Office, which includes Microsoft Publisher, you must follow a process similar to that described above:

1. Insert Office 2000 CD 2 in the CD drive of the Terminal Services computer.

2. In Control Panel, select Add/Remove Programs.

3. Click the Add New Programs button.

4. Click the CD or Floppy button.

5. Click Next.

At this point you should see a dialog box prompting you with the name of the program to run. If the program is not the Office install program (setup.exe in the root of the CD drive), either type in the correct entry or use the Browse button to find it.

Before pressing Enter, append the following to the end of the program name in the dialog box: **NOUSERNAME=True** (see the following illustration).

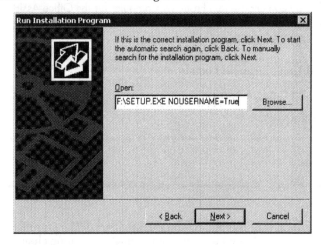

Now press Enter or click Next. The Publisher installation process begins, and you must take the following steps:

1. Type in the CD key number and organization, but leave the username and initials blank.

2. Accept the license agreement and click Next.

3. At the Microsoft Office 2000: Ready To Install dialog box, select Customize.

4. Specify the path to install Office and click Next.

5. At the Microsoft Office 2000: Selecting Features dialog box, click the disk with a down-arrow to the left of Microsoft Office and select Run All From My Computer.

6. Expand the feature tree and select Not Available for any features you don't want to install (refer back to the sidebar on features that don't work well under Terminal Services).

7. Click Install Now.

8. When the installation is complete, click OK.

9. Click Finish in the Add/Remove Programs applet.

10. After the installation, log on as the same user so that Office can finish the installation.

Office 2000 SR-1/1A

Some of the problems described later in this chapter refer you to Office 2000 Service Release 1/1a for solutions. This section explains how you install the update on a Terminal Services system.

CAUTION: Be sure to run the SR-1/1a update only once on a Windows 2000 server, as running it multiple times can cause problems with Internet Explorer.

First, you must obtain the SR-1/1a update either on CD from Microsoft or download it. If you have the CD, you can skip the first three steps here. You may be asked for the Office 2000 CDs during this update, so have them ready.

1. Point your Web browser to http://www.microsoft.com/office/ork/ 2000/appndx/toolbox.htm#o2sr1au.

2. Click on O2ksr1adl.exe and in the File Download dialog box, select Save This Program To Disk. Save it somewhere accessible from the Terminal server. The program is quite large (52MB).

3. When the download is complete, execute the program from a Terminal Services server. Specify the location for extracting the software (the program creates the directory you name if it does not already exist; see the following illustration).

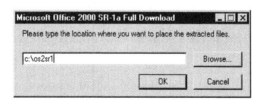

At this point, make sure that no users are logged on to this server who are running Office applications.

Then, when the extraction is complete, open the Add/Remove Programs applet and take these steps:

1. Click Add New Programs.

2. Click the CD or Floppy button.

3. In the Run Installation Program dialog box, click Browse and find setup.exe for the Service Release (wherever you extracted it, or the root directory of the CD if you have a CD).

4. Click Next.

5. Accept the licensing agreement and click Next.

6. Click the Update Office button (see the following illustration).

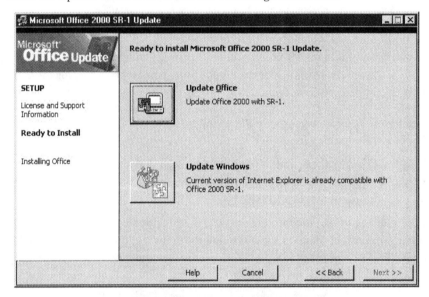

7. Click Next at the next screen to continue the installation (you may be asked for the Office 2000 CD).

At the end of the Service Release installation, you must reboot. After rebooting, log on again as the same user who installed the update to complete the installation.

Problems in Office 2000 on Terminal Services

I've run into, or heard about, a number of problems installing and running Office 2000 on Terminal Services. This section presents information about bugs and problems, along with solutions (if available).

NOTE: The largest assortment of problems and bugs are attached to Outlook. These issues are covered later in this chapter in the section "Outlook Problems in Terminal Services."

Error Message During Setup

You may see the following message when you run the Office Setup program:

```
The Windows Installer service could not be accessed. Contact your
support personnel to verify that the Windows Installer service is
properly registered.
```

The message means you're attempting to run the Office Setup program as a user who does not have sufficient permissions. You must be logged on as a user with administrator rights to perform this operation.

EraseCD2.exe Bug in Terminal Services

Microsoft has a utility named EraseCD2.exe, which removes the Office 2000 CD-2 files from an installation. Microsoft specifically warns that this utility does not work on Windows 2000 Terminal Services. Do not run it.

Problems with HTML Files

If, in a Terminal Services client session, you save a file in Microsoft Word 2000 or Microsoft Excel 2000 as HTML, the file may become damaged. According to Microsoft, this is caused by a conflict between the file permissions that Microsoft FrontPage 2000 and Microsoft Internet Explorer use when processing a file with a cached entry.

Microsoft released a "critical update" to Windows 2000 for this problem that you can find at http://windowsupdate.microsoft.com. It is also fixed in Service Pack 1 of Windows 2000.

Microsoft also suggests a workaround for the problem, should you not want to apply the fix. After you save the file, open it in Internet Explorer to see if it is correct or blank. If it's blank, save the file again and refresh the browser. Repeat this until the problem is corrected. Honest, that's the workaround.

Grammar Check Problems in Non-English Versions

If you are using a language in Microsoft Word 2000 other than English and run a grammar check, you may see the following message:

```
Word cannot start the grammar checker.
```

Office 2000 Service Release 1/1a fixes this problem. Alternatively, you can use Regedt32 to edit the security permissions at HKEY_LOCAL_MACHINE\Software\Novell\Grammatik\ 6.1\Microsoft. Make sure that the following subkeys are not locked down:

- ✦ Query Value
- ✦ Set Value
- ✦ Create Subkey
- ✦ Enumerate Subkeys
- ✦ Notify
- ✦ Delete
- ✦ Read Control

Users need to have Allow permissions for these areas of the registry.

Script Editor Bug in Access 2000

The Microsoft Script Editor will not run in Microsoft Access 2000 under Terminal Services. When you attempt to load it, it just doesn't load. No error message, no muss, no fuss, no program. Microsoft has acknowledged the bug. As of this writing, there is no fix.

Problems Displaying PowerPoint Slide Show

If you want to display a slide show in PowerPoint 2000 under Terminal Services, there are performance issues you should consider when designing the show. Use the following guidelines for slides shows in Terminal Services:

- ✦ **No audio**   Audio effects won't play on a Terminal Services client, so you may as well not include them.
- ✦ **No video**   Video will almost certainly perform badly, if at all, under Terminal Services, so avoid it like the plague.

- ❖ **Avoid animations, including animated GIFs**   Some animations work acceptably, some don't. Spiral and Swivel are the biggest problems. Animated GIFs don't work well under Terminal Services, so try not to use them.

- ❖ **Slide transitions may not perform well**   Most slide transitions will be slower than on a regular workstation. Fade Through Black transition does not work at all. According to Microsoft, the following transitions show the least amount of degradation:

  - ❖ Cover Down
  - ❖ Cover Left
  - ❖ Cover Right
  - ❖ Cover Up
  - ❖ Cover Left Down
  - ❖ Cover Left Up
  - ❖ Cover Right Down
  - ❖ Cover Right Up
  - ❖ Cut
  - ❖ Cut Through Black
  - ❖ Uncover Down
  - ❖ Uncover Left
  - ❖ Uncover Right
  - ❖ Uncover Up
  - ❖ Uncover Left Down
  - ❖ Uncover Left Up
  - ❖ Uncover Right Down
  - ❖ Uncover Right Up
  - ❖ Wipe Down
  - ❖ Wipe Left
  - ❖ Wipe Right
  - ❖ Wipe Up

- ❖ **Color scheme**   Remember that Terminal Services is limited to 256 colors, so use of graphics and photos that require richer colors will provide disappointing results.

Outlook Problems in Terminal Services

Microsoft Outlook 2000 has such a laundry list of issues on its own that it needs its own section. First, as stated earlier in this chapter, be sure to run Outlook 2000 while logged on as an administrator after installing the program. This step is needed to complete the installation process.

IMO Mode Not Supported

The Outlook Internet Mail Only (IMO) option is not supported under Terminal Services. This does not mean you cannot use Outlook 2000 for Internet mail or that it requires Exchange Server. But you must configure Outlook for the Corporate or Workgroup (CW) setup option.

CAUTION: The Microsoft Office 2000 Resource Kit states that you can use the IMO option, but it is mistaken.

Choose Help | About Microsoft Outlook to see which type of Outlook installation is running. To change the option, choose Tools | Options and click the Mail Services tab. Choose Reconfigure Mail Support and change the installation type to CW.

Outlook Custom Forms Need Special Permissions

If you have configured your system to restrict Write permission for portions of the registry for the group Users, those Users will have problems with custom forms in Outlook 2000.

You need to allow Write permission for HKEY_CLASSES_ROOT\CLSID for any users who use Outlook custom forms.

Team Folders Don't Work

Outlook Team Folders and Terminal Services don't mix. Microsoft does not support running Team Folders on Terminal Services.

Problems with Outlook Runtime Demand Installation Option

If you are using Windows 2000 Advanced Server with Terminal Services in Remote Administration mode, and install Outlook 2000 without a transform file, the runtime demand installation feature won't work. Omitting the transform file means the Windows Installer does not detect Terminal Services. Therefore, the first time you run Outlook it will not allow runtime demand installation.

Even though you might expect on-demand installation to work in Remote Administration mode, Office checks at runtime to see if it's running in Terminal Services, and prevents the on-demand install from working.

There are two solutions to this. One is to mark everything you might need as Run From My Computer at install time. The other is to get Office 2000 Service Release 1/1a, which addresses this problem.

Non-English Spell Checker Fails

The spell checker fails when run in a language other than English in Outlook 2000 under Terminal Services. To work around this problem, log on as Administrator at the Terminal server and perform the following steps:

1. Open Control Panel and start the Add/Remove Programs applet.

2. Click the Microsoft Office entry, then click the Change button.

3. Click Add or Remove Features.

4. Expand the Office Tools entry in the list of features.

5. Select the icon next to the Proofing Tools (*language*) entry (where *language* is the language you want to use), and choose Run All From My Computer.

6. Click Update Now.

Bug in NetMeeting

Outlook's online meeting facility, which uses Microsoft NetMeeting, has serious problems under Terminal Services. If you attempt to join such a meeting, you may see the following message:

```
Microsoft NetMeeting
You have called your own computer. Please make sure that the address or
name you have specified is correct.
```

What has happened is that another user on the same Terminal server has already joined the meeting, and NetMeeting cannot distinguish between two users on the same server. Microsoft has acknowledged the problem, but no fix is available at this time.

Problems After Switching to IMO Mode

If you switch Outlook under Terminal Services from the Corporate or Workgroup (CW) mode to the Internet Mail Only (IMO) mode, Outlook stops responding when another user logs on through Terminal Services.

The problem is that if one user makes this change, it is made for all users on that server. Outlook can't handle some users running CW and others IMO.

Problems Creating Blank New Word Documents in Outlook

The Outlook option to create a new blank Microsoft Word document may not be available under Terminal Services. If you have this problem, you'll have to create your Word documents in Word.

Ecco Pro Imports Fail

If you attempt to import Ecco Pro data into Outlook, you will receive a message stating that Ecco Pro must be running for the import to continue and that the program cannot start. This is because Ecco Pro cannot run under Terminal Services. Perform the import on a non-Terminal Services system.

Schedule+ Option Is Automatically Global

If one Outlook user on a Terminal Services server selects to use Schedule+ as his or her primary calendar, the same setting will be used for all users. This is probably not a welcome change.

Troubleshooting Office 97 on Terminal Services

Microsoft Office 97, like most other complex applications, works under Terminal Services, but you need to run an application compatibility script (included in Windows 2000 Server) to fix some problems. In addition, there are some limitations in the program's use.

Installing Office 97 Under Terminal Services

Use the Add/Remove Programs applet to run the Office 97 CD-based setup. After the reboot following the installation, log back on as an administrator and go to the %SystemRoot%\ Application Compatibility Scripts\Install directory and run Office97.cmd. Set the home directory in Notepad to the appropriate drive for your users and save the file.

The script makes several changes in the default install of Office 97 to make it work under Terminal Services, including the following:

- It removes the FindFast feature (some would call this an improvement even without Terminal Services).
- It moves certain files to the home directory.
- It changes permissions on certain files.

After the scripts complete, clients can run Office 97 applications, but there are many documented problems, which are addressed in the next section.

Problems with Office 97 on Terminal Services

You and your users may encounter all sorts of problems running Office 97 under Terminal Services. This section presents information about many known problems, and many of them don't really have solutions. However, if you're aware of the problems you can counsel users or avoid configuration options linked to the problems.

The following Office 97 features can cause problems in Terminal Services:

- **Custom dictionaries**   The only private user custom dictionary allowed is custom.dic in the Office97 subdirectory of the user's home directory. All users share all other custom dictionaries.
- **Menu animation**   Avoid using the Office 97 menu animation feature, as it can have an inordinate performance cost on the server.
- **Toolbox**   Only administrators can use or create additional controls in the toolbox. More specifically, only users with Write permission for the %SystemRoot%\System32 folder are able to perform this task.
- **Clippy**   The stupid paper clip is still enabled by default.
- **Data map dictionary**   This dictionary (Geodict.dct) is shared by all users. If one user deletes a map, other users no longer have access to that map.
- **PP Presentation Conference**   Only one user can use the PowerPoint Presentation Conference command on the Tools menu at a time. Because it is not possible for several people on a server to conference among themselves, the feature loses a good deal of its value.
- **Auto Signature**   The Outlook 97 Auto Signature is not user specific. You can create a unique profile by defining each user in the Mail And Fax utility in the Control Panel.

✦ **Access tools and wizards**   Many Microsoft Access 97 tools and wizards do not support concurrent use, including the Combo Box Wizard, List Box Wizard, Lookup Wizard, Option Group Wizard, Database Documenter Wizard, Table Analyzer Wizard, Table Wizard, Field Builder, and Switchboard Manager. Only one user can use them at a time. Preferences for the wizards are shared by all users. To allow non-administrator users to run the Access wizards (or Access add-ins in Excel), find the following lines in the Office97.cmd application compatibility script and remove **Rem** from beginning of the following lines:

> Rem If Exist "%O97INST%\Office\WZLIB80.MDE" cacls
> "%O97INST%\Office\WZLIB80.MDE" /E /P "Authenticated Users":C >NUL: 2>&1

> Rem If Exist "%O97INST%\Office\WZMAIN80.MDE" cacls
> "%O97INST%\Office\WZMAIN80.MDE" /E /P "Authenticated Users":C >NUL: 2>&1

> Rem If Exist "%O97INST%\Office\WZTOOL80.MDE" cacls
> "%O97INST%\Office\WZTOOL80.MDE" /E /P "Authenticated Users":C >NUL: 2>&1

✦ **Access Database Documenter Wizard**   This wizard does not run on NTFS properly. To access its database, you must modify access to the %SystemRoot%\System32\System.mdw file. To use the wizard, users must have Write permission for the file.

✦ **Access workgroups**   If you use Wrkgadm.exe to create a new Access workgroup, you need to give Read permission for the workgroup information file to the Everyone and Administrator groups (the default workgroup information file is %SystemRoot%\System32\System.mdw). In addition, only administrators can create workgroup information files. If you want to add users to a workgroup information file, you must first change permissions to Write.

✦ **Access 97 spelling options**   Access spelling options are shared among all users. Only administrators can change them.

Troubleshooting Other Applications

The list of applications that have limitations or require modifications to run properly under Terminal Services is large. In this section, I will list some of the problems in applications, and some of the actions you can take to work around them.

✦ **Lotus Notes**   Lotus Notes Client version 5.0.3 and later versions are considered supported, but not certified, when running under Terminal Services. Use your own judgment (depending on your level of risk-taking) about whether you want to run this application under Terminal Services.

◆ **Outlook 98 configuration** If you use the Mail applet in Control Panel to configure Outlook 98, you may see the following message:

```
You may need more memory or system resources. Close some windows and
try again.
```

This is not a memory problem. To work around this problem you must first change Terminal Services to Install mode. At the command line, type **change user /install** and press Enter. Retry the operation.

◆ **Microsoft Narrator bug** If you're using Microsoft Narrator (a program that speaks keystrokes as they are typed, designed for those with impaired vision) under Terminal Services, the program will read your username, domain name, and password out loud. Since Terminal Services sends back bitmap images to the client computer and no field information, Narrator does not know that these fields are passwords and other sensitive information. Normally, Narrator would say "password." Microsoft suggests you provide Narrator users with headphones.

◆ **Fax service** If a normal user sends a fax job using the Microsoft fax service, he may see a dialog box indicating that the job completed successfully. However, checking Print Manager reveals the job is not there. The problem is that, by default, the normal Users group does not have sufficient access to the fax service. To fix the situation, open an MMC (choose Start | Run, and type **mmc** in the Run box). Add the Fax Service Management snap-in. Right-click the service name in the MMC and select Properties. Select the group (probably Users) to which you want to grant rights, and click the Manage Fax Service checkbox (see illustration).

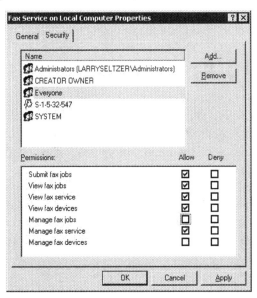

◆ **NetMeeting**   If you attempt to connect to another user with Microsoft NetMeeting, you may see one of the following messages:

```
The call could not be established because all protocols are disabled or
not functioning properly.
NetMeeting could not start. Please restart your computer and try again.
```

NetMeeting does not work properly under Terminal Services. It cannot distinguish between two users running on the same server because it requires that all users have unique IP addresses, and all Terminal Services users on the same server have the same IP address.

◆ **Timex Data Link**   If you have a Timex Data Link watch and you attempt to synchronize it to a Terminal Services session using either the CRT Mode 5 – DOS Framed or CRT Mode 3 – DOS Fast Framed settings, the program will fail to initialize and give you the following message:

```
The video device failed to initialize for fullscreen mode. Choose 'Close'
to terminate the application.
```

You can choose the Close or Ignore buttons at this point. Ignore does not permit you to continue and Close closes the DOS window and returns you to the Calibration Wizard. Unfortunately, Terminal Services cannot handle DOS full-screen mode. Your best bet is CRT Mode 4 – Windows Framed. You'll also need a network connection faster than a dial-up line to make this operation reliable.

◆ **Ecco Pro**   This program will not run in a Windows Terminal Services environment. If you're an Ecco Pro user, you're probably used to disappointments like this, since NetManage discontinued the product some years ago, although there are still users out there. Abandon all hope, ye Ecco Pro users who enter Terminal Services!

DOS and Win16 Apps

The first rule about legacy applications, especially Win16 and DOS applications, is that if they don't run on conventional Windows 2000 installations, they won't run on Terminal Services. There are many reasons why older legacy programs would fail in such circumstances, such as bypassing the file system calls to write directly to disk. Programs like this don't work on Windows 2000 and they won't work under Terminal Services.

If a 16-bit DOS or Windows application runs under Terminal Services, it probably won't run as smoothly as an analogous Win32 program. According to Microsoft, running 16-bit programs can reduce the user capacity of a processor by 40 percent and increase the memory requirements of the system per user by 50 percent. Such programs also tend to be less stable than Win32 programs and, while it's rare that they would bring down a Windows 2000 server, it's possible that a badly written legacy application will affect the stability of other Terminal Services users on the same server.

In general you should try to avoid all but Win32 programs in a Terminal Services environment, but many installations need to run legacy programs and you can do so by taking care to follow considerations needed for Terminal Services.

A common technique is to isolate all DOS and Win16 programs on a single Terminal server or set of Terminal servers, so they don't interfere with the performance of the Win32 programs. You may actually need to use more memory in these servers, depending on the number of users using them.

In a multiserver environment such as this, another common technique to make things easier for users is to let them run the legacy applications through a Terminal Services client on the main Terminal server. In other words, if the users normally log on to one server and get their desktop there, some of the icons on that desktop should be connections made in Client Connection Manager (see Chapter 3) directly to the legacy applications on the other Terminal server.

Inappropriate Terminal Services Applications

Some programs are not poorly written per se, but are inappropriate for Terminal Services nonetheless. This includes both server and client applications.

Graphics

The largest category of inappropriate programs are graphics-intensive applications. Consider Doom and other such games, which require fast graphics response and, sometimes, intensive CPU effort. The need to transfer the graphics through the RDP protocol to the client makes it unlikely that these programs would perform adequately.

The other significant problem for games such as this is that the RDP5 protocol can only handle 256-color displays. This can be a significant problem for games.

Many other graphics-intensive programs, such as Adobe Photoshop, deal with huge amounts of memory and graphics that will likely tax any Terminal server, but even if you threw significant hardware resources at the server and network, the 8-bit color limitations would still make Terminal Services an inappropriate platform.

ICA, the protocol for Citrix MetaFrame, is also currently limited to 256 colors, but Citrix has indicated that it will be adding support for greater color depths, up to 24-bit. This will, of course, add considerably to the program's CPU and network requirements.

MS-DOS and Win16 Application Misbehaviors

Here are some of the things that MS-DOS applications do which make them unwelcome on a Windows 2000 Terminal Services server.

Some applications enter a tight loop waiting for input from the keyboard, mouse, or some other device. This "going nowhere in a hurry" was no big deal on a single user PC, but it wastes CPU bandwidth in a multiuser environment.

According to Microsoft, FoxPro for MS-DOS applications generate inordinate numbers of CPU interrupts and end up draining performance on a Terminal Services system.

Many MS-DOS programs use printing techniques that don't work well in a Terminal Services environment (such as direct port access). Win16 programs that use standard Windows printing facilities should work without a problem.

Many companies will maintain NetWare servers, even in a Terminal Services environment. In this case, the Terminal server becomes a NetWare client, providing access to NetWare to the Terminal Services users. But MS-DOS and Win16 programs running on Terminal servers that use NetWare functions to mount drives on NetWare servers won't work on Terminal Services. Such programs can use UNC names to shares.

Troubleshooting Server Application Behavior

When multiple users run sessions on the same Terminal server, they get the same IP address (that of the server). This presents a problem for some server and Web-based applications that track users by their IP address, either for licensing reasons or to differentiate communications among users.

It is possible for a Terminal Services-aware application (see "Rules for Terminal Services-Aware Applications" later in this chapter) to detect the IP address and computer name of the Terminal Services client, which is unique, using the WTSQuerySessionInformation API function.

Another, perhaps obvious point: network applications must use TCP/IP and standard interfaces to it, specifically Winsock.

Hardware Dependencies

There are programs, such as barcode-reading software, that are dependent on specific hardware being present in the computer on which the program is run. Sometimes this is a problem for Terminal Services, sometimes not.

Sometimes, if a Terminal server is physically accessible and you can guarantee that only one user at a time will use the application, no harm comes from running such an application on the Terminal server. For example, one of my Terminal servers has my CD-R drive in it, and I run Adaptec Easy-CD on it.

It's important to know that very little hardware connected to the client device is accessible to the Terminal Services session. The keyboard and mouse, of course, are standard devices. RDP5 allows printing to local printers. Beyond that, in order for a local device to be accessible to a Terminal Services session, it must be shared on the network. Local drives may be shared and thereby accessible, although this often presents a security hazard.

Rules for Terminal Services-Aware Applications

When normal programs run under Terminal Services, the operating system usually loads a DLL to intercept and handle some of the special cases that normal programs cause. There is some overhead to this, but it is possible to write Windows programs at the API level that are aware of the presence of Terminal Services and follow rules that eliminate the need to load the compatibility code.

This section is not a programming reference for writing such applications. It describes some of the possibilities and rules for writing such applications and gives references for those who wish to pursue the matter.

Terminal Services recognizes your application as Terminal Services-aware if it sets the IMAGE_DLLCHARACTERISTICS_TERMINAL_SERVER_AWARE flag in the optional header. Visual Studio 7.0 includes a linker option named TSAWARE that sets this feature. Such an application should not use .ini files or write to HKEY_CURRENT_USER during setup.

On the affirmative side, such programs should install themselves into the All Users user environment on the server. They should also create an administrative template file, which allows an administrator to customize features for each user.

Microsoft has a white paper entitled "Optimizing Applications for Windows 2000 Terminal Services and Windows NT Server 4.0, Terminal Server Edition" (available at http://www.microsoft.com/windows2000/library/planning/terminal/tsappdev.asp) which goes into these matters further. Details on the Terminal Services APIs may be found at http://msdn.microsoft.com/library/psdk/termserv/wtsstart_5in9.htm.

Chapter 5

Administrative Tips and Tricks

M ost Terminal Services administration is performed in the main Windows 2000 administration programs, such as Active Directory Users and Computers, plus a few Microsoft Management Console snap-ins for Terminal Services functions. Some more advanced management capabilities, such as relevant registry settings, are covered in Chapter 6.

Terminal Services adds three new administration programs to your Programs | Administrative Tasks menu: Terminal Services Configuration, Terminal Services Manager, and (if you have installed the Terminal Services Licensing server) Terminal Services Licensing. Other Terminal Services administrative tasks take place in Active Directory Users and Computers. Terminal Services also adds Terminal Services Client Creator to the Programs | Administrative Tasks menu. This program, discussed in Chapter 2, creates Terminal Services client installation disks. Finally, there are command-line programs for administering the server, which you may prefer. See Chapter 8 for details on Terminal Services Licensing and other licensing issues.

Customizing the MMC for Terminal Services

Terminal Services Configuration is an MMC snap-in that you can load into any MMC. In fact, if you work frequently enough with Terminal Services, you may find it convenient to create a new MMC with Terminal Services Configuration and your other most commonly used snap-ins, such as Active Directory Users and Computers. (Sadly, the other Terminal Services administration programs are not MMC snap-ins.)

To create a specialized MMC for managing Terminal Services, follow these steps:

1. Choose Start | Run and enter **mmc** in the Run box. Click OK.

2. Choose Console | Add/Remove Snap-in (or press CTRL-M).

3. Click the Add button near the bottom of the Add/Remove Snap-in dialog box.

4. In the Add Standalone Snap-in dialog box, select the snap-ins you want to add to this MMC (see Figure 5-1). Then click Close.

5. Press OK to complete the process.

6. Name the MMC.

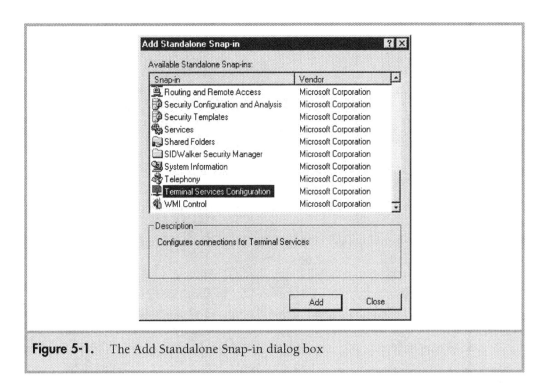

Figure 5-1.   The Add Standalone Snap-in dialog box

Managing Terminal Services Connections

The Terminal Services Configuration program (see the following illustration) has a small number of very important functions. Each network connection to the server has a connection object in this program through which you manage the connections. The program also provides an opportunity to set some server policies.

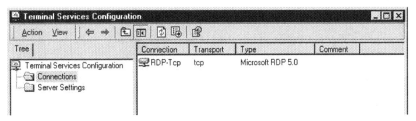

The program has two folders in the left pane: the Connections folder and the Server Settings folder.

The Connections folder contains entries for each network device through which users connect to Terminal Services. When you install Terminal Services, a connection exists by default, almost certainly a TCP/IP connection to your server's network adapter. If you add a new network adapter or some other sort of connection, such as a VPN or RAS connection, you can add a new connection object in this window.

Creating a New Connection

If you have multiple network connections to the server, you can either choose to control them through a single connection object or you can create separate connection objects for each of them. You might use a single object for convenience and simplicity, but there are good reasons to create multiple connection objects.

Sometimes a server has different types of connections, such as an internal network connection or a VPN connection from the outside. You can manage the characteristics of these connections separately, and Terminal Services Configuration lets you do so.

Also, you might want to limit the number of users coming into any one connection to enforce a kind of performance floor on the server or network device to which the connection is attached. By limiting the number of users on a connection, you can limit the number of users accessing the server.

Unfortunately, you can't set up a Terminal server directly as a remote access server. Terminal Services simply doesn't support this. You have to set up a different server to run RRAS (Routing and Remote Access Services, the service that accepts incoming calls to a server in a domain) and connect the RAS server to Terminal Services over a LAN.

To create a new connection, choose Action | Create New Connection to launch the Terminal Services Connection Wizard.

Choose a Connection Type

In the Connection Type screen, choose a connection type, which, in a conventional Terminal Services installation, displays only the choice of Microsoft RDP 5.0. If you are also running Citrix MetaFrame, ICA is also available here.

Choose the Encryption Level

In the Data Encryption screen, choose the encryption level for communication over this connection. See the sidebar "Terminal Services Encryption Levels" for information on the different options.

Terminal Services Encryption Levels

Low encryption means that only data sent from the server to the client is encrypted using the standard key. (The standard key is 56 bits when the client is RDP5 and 40 bits for earlier clients.)

Medium encryption (the default) means that standard encryption is used in both directions between the client and server.

High encryption means that 128-bit encryption is used in both directions. High encryption is available only in the United States and Canada.

Which should you choose? Different people have different philosophies of risk aversion. Clearly, it would be much harder to decrypt data transmitted with high encryption than medium, but decrypting medium-encrypted data is not a trivial task, especially considering the nature of the data (screen images). A reason to avoid high encryption (assuming your users and servers are all in the United States or Canada) is that it imposes some additional processing burden on the client and server. The extent of this burden is difficult to quantify, but it increases in direct proportion to the amount of network traffic between clients and servers. Fundamentally, this is a trade-off you have to decide for yourself.

The Data Encryption screen also has a checkbox labeled Use Standard Windows Authentication. This only really matters on a system where an alternative authentication mechanism, such as a RADIUS server, is installed.

Configure Remote Control Settings

In the Remote Control screen, set the rules for remote control of clients over the connection. Terminal Services allows any user with appropriate rights to remotely control a Terminal Services session from within another Terminal Services session, according to the rules you specify here (see Figure 5-2). See "Configuring Permissions on a Connection" later in this chapter for details on assigning correct permissions.

◆ Use Remote Control With Default User Settings lets you control sessions according to the default user settings. These are the settings in the user's profile as specified in the Remote Control page of their properties in Active Directory Users and Computers.

◆ Do Not Allow Remote Control disallows remote control over this connection.

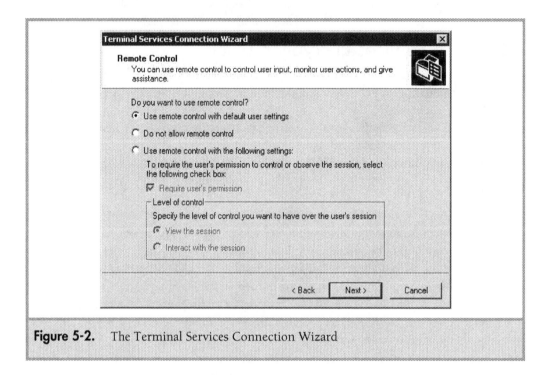

Figure 5-2. The Terminal Services Connection Wizard

✦ Use Remote Control With The Following Settings contains rules for remote control over this connection. Require User's Permission gives users the right to allow or deny remote control when the controlling user attempts to take control.

Specify a level of control to determine whether the administrator can interact with or simply view the session using the radio buttons in the Level of Control box.

Configure the Transport Type

In the Transport Type screen, specify a name for the connection (a task which really belonged earlier in the wizard) and the transport type. Name it something you will recognize, such as LAN2. The name cannot have embedded spaces, and the following characters are forbidden: \ / : * ? # " ' < > % | , . [ ] ( ). Additionally, you can enter a comment for a more verbose description of the connection.

The transport type in a standard Terminal Services installation is always TCP. If you are running Citrix MetaFrame you may have other network protocols available, such as IPX/SPX.

Configure the Network Adapter

On the Network Adapter screen, specify the network device to which this connection applies. All connections must have a unique adapter. The drop-down box lists all your network devices and includes the choice All Network Adapters Configured With This Protocol. That choice, in a normal Terminal Services system, means that all TCP/IP network adapters are grouped into this one Terminal Services connection.

Set the allowed number of concurrent connections either as unlimited or at a specified maximum. When you click Finish to close the wizard, your new connection object appears in the MMC (see the following illustration).

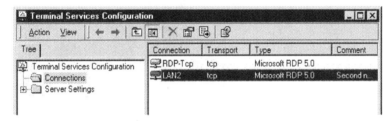

Configuring Existing Connections

After you have created a connection, you can configure many parameters on it that were not available when you created it. With connections selected in the left pane, select a connection in the right pane and open its Properties dialog box (see Figure 5-3).

Most of the settings in this dialog box are similar to user-level settings available in Active Directory Users and Computers. When you make connection-level settings here in Terminal Services Configuration, the settings override any made at the user level.

Set Authentication and Encryption Options

In the General tab, you can change the encryption level and the comment for the connection. See the sidebar "Terminal Services Encryption Levels" for explanations of the encryption levels.

If you have installed an alternative authentication mechanism, such as a RADIUS server, you can override it with the Use Standard Windows Authentication checkbox.

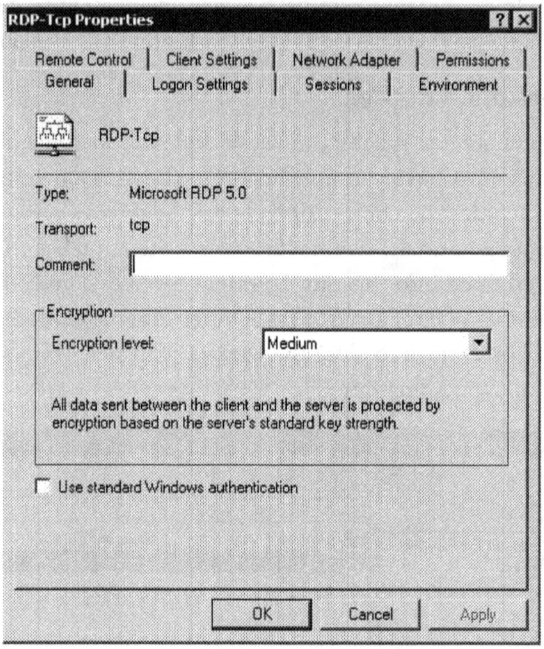

Figure 5-3. The RDP-Tcp Properties box

Change Logon Options for the Connection

Select the Logon Settings tab to specify that all users over this connection log on over a particular username and domain. Include the password in the user logon information and users will be automatically logged on, depending on the setting of the Always Prompt For Password checkbox.

CODE BLUE

If users are being prompted for a password even though they have specified one as part of a connection in Client Connection Manager, the cause is probably that the Always Prompt For Password checkbox is set in the Logon Settings tab of the Connection properties.

Setting Timeout Values for Connections and Logons

Because a connection is a critical shared resource, you may want to set time limits on users'
access to it. Go to the Sessions tab in the Connection Properties dialog box to set timeouts
at a connection level. These settings override identical user-level settings on the user's
Properties page in Active Directory Users and Computers. None of these settings is
available until you check the relevant Override User Settings checkbox.

The rules for all three of these settings are the same. You can specify Never and the
timeout will never kick in. You can drop down the combo box and select one of the
predefined time limits. Or, you can specify the amount of time in days, hours, and minutes.
To specify a value like this, type in the combo box itself, and append **d** for days, **h** for hours,
and **m** for minutes to the numbers. For example, "1d 2h 3m" is 1 day, 2 hours, 3 minutes.

Use the End A Disconnected Session option to specify the maximum amount of time that
a session stays alive on the server after being disconnected. Depending on the value of this
setting, a disconnected session may be available for reconnection from the same or a
different client system for some period of time. When this time limit is reached, the
disconnected session ends.

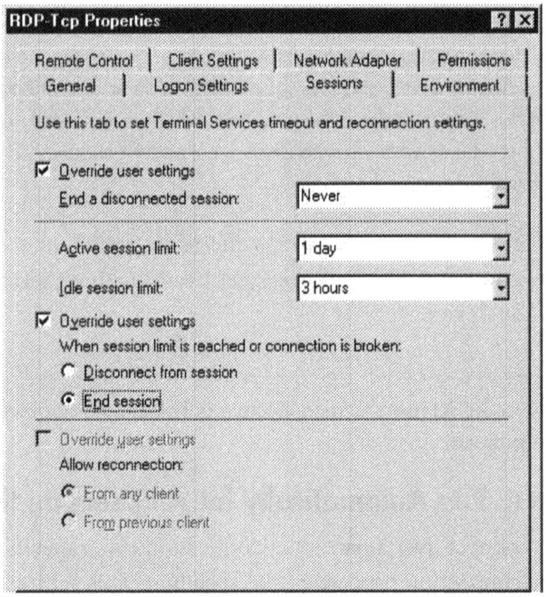

Figure 5-4. Setting time limits on users' access

Use the Active Session Limit to specify the maximum amount of time a session can remain active on the server, even one which is in active use. At the end of the specified time, the session is ended.

Use the Idle Session Limit setting to set the maximum amount of time a session can remain active while there is no user activity, such as keyboard or mouse movement. When the connection is idle for the specified amount of time, the user is disconnected.

The need for this setting is not hard to see: for example, you might have users who connect sometimes from inside the local area network and sometimes through an external VPN, which is more expensive. By changing the properties on the connection, you can allow the user setting to provide a default that they never be disconnected, but specify that connections over the VPN be limited in time and especially limited in idle time. Administrators of very expensive Internet Connector licenses should be especially interested in limiting connection abuse by users.

Further down in the same dialog box you can specify whether sessions should be ended or merely disconnected when these timeouts are reached or when communications are broken.

BUG ALERT If you set the Session properties to end a session when a connection is broken, users who close a Terminal Services client session by closing the window will have their sessions ended rather than disconnected. These users will receive a warning dialog box indicating that the session is being disconnected and that they will be able to reconnect, but in fact the session will end. Microsoft has acknowledged the problem, which is not fixed in Service Pack 1. On a configuration like this, clients who want to disconnect should choose Start | Shut Down and select Disconnect from the combo box.

Below that is another Override User Settings checkbox, which allows you to specify whether a user reconnection should be allowed just from the device from which they were disconnected or from any device.

NOTE: The ability to restrict users to reconnection only from the original client is available only with the Citrix ICA protocol.

Setting a Program to Run Automatically for All Users on the Connection

To make all users who connect over a particular connection run a specific program, go to the Environment tab in the connection properties and specify it. This setting overrides user-level settings, both in Active Directory Users and Computers and Client Connection Manager.

Controlling Client Printer, Drive, and Clipboard Access

To control the client's ability to access their local devices and clipboard, go to the Client Settings tab of the connection properties (see Figure 5-5).

In the upper section, you can control whether clients have access to their local drives and printers from Terminal Services sessions. (Drive access is available only with Citrix MetaFrame.) The settings in this section override those in the Environment tab of Active Directory Users and Computers.

The lower part of the Client Settings tab controls availability of several other client features at the connection level. The first, Drive Mapping, is available only to Citrix ICA clients, and the default is to disable it.

The next three settings are related. Windows Printer Mapping, enabled by default, allows you to map printers configured for Windows on the client to the server applications, and all the Windows printers are automatically connected at logon. But if LPT port mapping or COM port mapping are disabled (checked) and a relevant local printer is connected by one

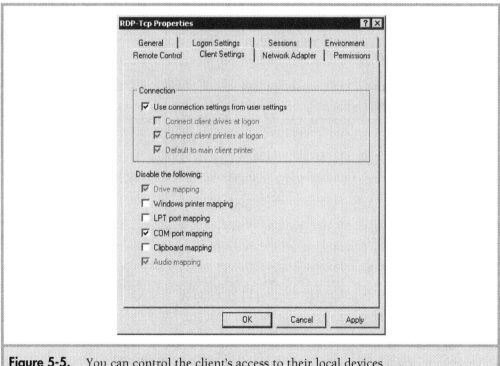

Figure 5-5.   You can control the client's access to their local devices

of them, you won't be able to create new printers manually. If the port mapping selections are unchecked, you can manually create new printers. If Windows Printer Mapping is checked (disabled), Windows printers will not be mapped to the session at logon and users won't be able to map them.

TAKE COMMAND

Use the **change port** command to change COM port mappings for compatibility with MS-DOS applications. This command is most useful if you are using high port numbers (greater than COM4), which MS-DOS applications won't recognize. Remappings live only for the life of the session. They are deleted at logoff. The syntax for **change port** is:

change port [*portx=porty* | **/d** *portx* | **/query**]

where:

portx=porty maps port X to port Y

/d *portx* deletes the mapping for COM port x

/query displays current COM port mappings

Clipboard mapping, enabled by default, lets users swap clipboard data between local and server-based applications. Audio mapping is supported only on Citrix ICA clients.

Assign a Network Adapter to a Connection

Use the Network Adapter tab to specify which network adapter the connection uses. Alternatively, you can select All Network Adapters Configured With This Protocol, which in most cases means all TCP/IP adapters. If you have multiple physical TCP/IP connections over which users may be accessing this Terminal Server, you may assign them to different connections, so that you can separately apply to them all the various settings to which connections are subject.

Limit the Number of User Connections

The bottom part of the Network Adapter tab lets you set up a connection for unlimited connections or limit it to some specific number. You might want to limit a connection to some number of physical connections to ensure that the performance level is always adequate.

Configuring Permissions on a Connection

Finally, the Permissions tab is a standard Windows 2000 permissions tab, which lets you specify which users and groups have access to this connection. One notable point about this particular Permissions tab is that it controls access to remote control. See "Remote Control Permissions" later in this chapter.

CODE BLUE

A user who does not have permission to use this connection and attempts to connect to the Terminal server is denied access at logon time with the following message: "You do not have access to log on to this Session."

Administrators commonly make the mistake of failing to grant users access to the connection. Users may have all the proper non-Terminal Services permissions and permission to log on to the Terminal server itself, but you must grant them access in the connection Permissions tab or they cannot make a successful connection.

Server Settings

Select the Server Settings folder to set configuration options, which are described in this section.

Set Remote Administration or Application Server Mode

The Terminal server mode setting actually is just an indicator of whether the server is running in Remote Administration or Application Server mode. You cannot change the mode in this program. Instead, you must remove and reinstall Terminal Services in the mode of your choice using Add/Remove Programs (see Chapter 3).

Delete Temporary Folders on Exit

The name of this setting is self-explanatory.

Use Temporary Folders per Session

This setting specifies whether Terminal Services creates a temporary folder for each session for each user. The setting is Yes by default, and the temporary folder is

%systemroot%\Documents and Settings\%*username*%\Local Settings\Temp\X, where X is a number corresponding to the session (for instance, 1). Changing this setting to No means that no additional subdirectory is created for the session.

 BUG ALERT If per-user temporary directories are disabled in Terminal Services Configuration and users' TEMP and TMP environment variables have been pointed elsewhere, the new locations must exist. The folders are not created automatically. Applications that depend on these folders may seriously misbehave if proper temporary directories are not configured.

Enable Internet Connector Licensing

The Internet Connector licensing setting specifies whether you've installed an Internet Connector license. This license allows up to 200 anonymous users to connect to the server over the Internet. The default setting is Disable (the license is expensive), and the feature is commonly used by software vendors to demonstrate Windows applications to users over the Internet.

Enable/Disable Active Desktop

Active Desktop is enabled by default. Disabling the feature conserves server resources and potentially large amounts of bandwidth, if users choose multimedia desktop elements. Since Active Desktop was a flop in the real world, users probably won't notice it is missing.

User Permission Compatibility: Windows NT 4.0 or Windows 2000-Compatible

Permission Compatibility sets the permissions of members of the Users group when logged on under Terminal Services. You made this decision when you installed Terminal Services, but you can change it here.

The options are Permissions Compatible With Windows 2000 Users, or Permissions Compatible With Terminal Server 4.0 Users. In the former setting, sessions belonging to members of Users run in a more restricted environment. In the latter, users have access to many areas of the registry and file system which they don't have under Windows 2000.

Many older applications—for instance, those that write to.ini files in %SystemRoot%—require Terminal Server 4.0 permissions to operate. Unfortunately, this is a system-wide setting. You should try to keep the system in Windows 2000 Users mode unless and until you can't because you must run an application that requires otherwise. You might want to consider isolating such applications on their own server.

Finally, if your Terminal servers are running in a Windows NT 4.0 domain or workgroup, you need to use Terminal Server 4.0 permissions because you don't have a Windows 2000 Users group in your domain.

Session Management with Terminal Services Manager

You can use the Terminal Services Manager program to manage live connections to a Terminal Server, remotely controlling the users, sessions, and running applications.

It's a shame that Microsoft didn't make Terminal Services Manager an MMC or snap-in. It would have been convenient to put it together in the same MMC with Terminal Services Configuration, Active Directory Users and Computers, and so on.

Terminal Services Manager Layout

The left pane of the Terminal Services Manager displays a hierarchy of domains, servers, and sessions. Terminal Services sessions appear with an icon of a cable junction, a label that indicates their connection, a session number, and the username. For example, the entry "LAN2#4 (administrator)" indicates that the session is connected on the LAN2 connection, the session ID is 4, and the username is administrator.

Console sessions display a computer icon and the username, such as "Console (administrator)". See the sidebar "Session States" for more types of sessions you might find, and the reference terms for them in the Terminal Services Manager program.

If you run Terminal Services Manager from the server console, as opposed to a Terminal Services session, you receive a warning that some of the program's features, including the Connect and Remote Control features, only work when run from within a Terminal Services session (see the following illustration).

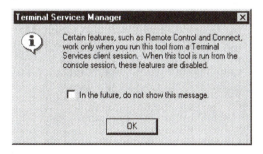

Session States

There are many different session states, although most of the time you'll only see two or three of them. See "Viewing Session Status" for information on the Query Session command, which can display these states using their text names. The name in parentheses is the state as it appears in the Terminal Services Manager program.

- **Active (Active)**   A connected session with a logged-in user.
- **Connected (Conn)**   A connected session without a logged-in user.
- **ConnectQuery (Conq)**   The session is in the process of connecting. If it stays in this state, there is a problem. Consider resetting the connection (see "Resetting Connections") and trying again.
- **RemoteControl (Shadow)**   The session is controlling another session.
- **Listen (Listen)**   A listener session waiting for client connections. You typically see these when more than one connection object is configured in the system.
- **Disconnected (Disc)**   A session is disconnected but still active on the server. Can be reconnected.
- **Idle (Idle)**   A pre-initialized session, ready to accept a connection. Two of these are allocated by Terminal Services in advance of any connections to expedite them.
- **Down (Down)**   A session that failed to initialize or terminate. The session is not available and should probably be reset.
- **Init (Init)**   A session in the process of initializing. If it stays in this state for an extended period, consider resetting it and trying again.

The right pane of the window contains three lists:

- **Users List**   Contains user-oriented information about the current sessions. For example, it includes the logon time and idle time.
- **Sessions List**   Contains session-oriented information about the current sessions. For example, it includes the state and protocol.
- **Processes List**   Displays the processes running in the current sessions.

The Users List and Sessions List have a lot of overlap. In most cases, you can use either for a task, such as disconnecting. The different orientations of the list may make some tasks easier.

You have many (too many!) ways to perform tasks in Terminal Services Manager:

✦ Right-click on the session name in the left pane and select from the menu.

✦ Right-click the username in Users List and select from the menu.

✦ Right-click a session name in the Sessions List and select from the menu.

✦ Select any of these items and then select an action from the Actions menu.

✦ Select any of these items and then click the appropriate icon.

Connecting To and Disconnecting From Servers

If a server appears in your list, but you aren't connected to it, you can do so in many ways. Right-click and choose Connect, or select it and Connect on the Actions menu, or click the Connect icon. You can disconnect with similar operations. From the Actions menu, you can also choose Connect To All Servers, Connect To All Servers In Domain, Disconnect From All Servers, or Disconnect From All Servers In Domain.

CODE BLUE

If you choose the Find Servers In All Domains option on the Action menu and the program fails to find some or all of your servers, it may be because there is no trust relationship between the domains. If you establish a trust relationship between the domains, this menu option will work.

The command-line alternatives to Terminal Services Manager functions, such as **query termserver**, find servers in other domains with or without a trust relationship.

TAKE COMMAND

The **query termserver** command lists Terminal Servers on the network in the current or some other specified domain. You can also get network address information on the servers. The command outputs a list of known Terminal servers. The syntax is:

query termserver [*servername*] [**/domain:***domain*] [**/address**] [**/continue**]

where:

servername is the name of a specific server on which you want information.

/**domain:**domain* is a domain you want to search. The default is the domain to which you are logged on.

/**address** tells the command to output the network and node addresses of the servers.

/**continue** tells the command not to pause between screens if there is more than one screen of output.

Connecting to Sessions

You can connect directly to an existing session using Terminal Services Manager or the command-line program **Tscon**.

Select the session and choose Connect.

TAKE COMMAND

The **tscon** command connects you to a different session. The syntax is:

tscon {*sessionID* | *sessionname*} [/**server:***servername*] [/**dest:***sessionname*] [/**password:***password*] [/**v**]

where:

sessionID is the ID of the session to which you want to connect.

sessionname is the name of the session to which you want to connect.

/**server:***servername* is the name of the server on which the session is running.

/**dest:***sessionname* is the name of the current session to which the new session will be attached. If you have multiple sessions running this parameter will distinguish between them.

/**password:***password* is the password of the user who owns the session to which you are attaching.

/**v** displays verbose information about the operations being performed.

When you connect to the other session, the current session (identified by **/dest**: in Tscon) is disconnected. Likewise, if another user is connected to the session, he is disconnected.

Disconnecting from Sessions

An administrator can disconnect an existing session using Terminal Services Manager or the command-line program **tsdiscon**. If a user is logged on to the session, she may lose data and will see a message box saying, "The Terminal server has ended the connection." But the session remains on the server in a disconnected state and applications in the session continue. You can reconnect (see "Connecting to Sessions" above) from the same or a different system.

You have all the same ways to disconnect in Terminal Services Manager: right-click on the session name in the left pane or the username in the session entry in the right pane, and select Disconnect. Or, you can single-click the entry in either the left or right panes and select Disconnect from the Actions menu. Or, you can select it in the same way and click the Disconnect icon.

TAKE COMMAND

Use the **tsdiscon** command to disconnect a session. The syntax is:

    tsdiscon {*sessionID* | *sessionname*} [**/server**:*servername*] [**/v**]

where:

sessionID is the ID of the session you want to disconnect.

sessionname is the name of the session you want to disconnect.

/server:*servername* is the name of the server on which the session is running.

/v displays verbose information about the operations being performed.

Before you disconnect a session, it's a good idea to send a message warning users about the disconnection (see "Sending Messages to Sessions" in the next section).

It's possible for users to connect and disconnect, change locations, and still work on the same actual session. For example, a user could disconnect from a session, go home, dial in to the network, and reconnect to the same session. The programs running in the original session continue to run. However, the settings for timeout of disconnected sessions (see the section "Setting Timeout Values for Connections and Logons" earlier in this chapter) have an impact on this feature.

Sending Messages to Sessions

You can send a message to a session either from Terminal Services Manager or by using the **msg** command. This can be useful if you need immediacy not available through e-mail, perhaps to warn users that a server or their session will be going down.

In Terminal Services Manager, select a session and choose Send Message. You can specify both a message title and contents. The default message title includes your username and the current date and time. The user sees this message in a popup box.

TAKE COMMAND

The **msg** command sends a popup message to the specified session. This command has many advantages over the Terminal Services Manager. For example, you can send messages to a list of many users and you can wait until they respond. The syntax is:

msg {*username* | *sessionname* | *sessionid* | *@filename* | ***} [**/server**:*servername*]
[**/time**:*seconds*] [**/v**] [**/w**] [*message*]

where:

username is the username of the recipient.

sessionname is the name of the session to send to.

sessionid is the ID of the session to send to.

@filename is the name of a text file containing usernames, session names, and session IDs to send the message to.

* sends the message to all usernames on the system.

/server:*servername* is the name of the server where the session resides. If no server name is specified, the server you are logged on is assumed.

/time:*seconds* is the number of seconds the message should stay on screen before closing itself.

/v displays information about the message (where it's being sent, how long it will appear for, and such).

/w causes the **msg** program to pause until the user clicks OK on the message box.

message is the contents of the message to send.

Resetting Sessions

Reset deletes a session from the server immediately, losing any work in progress. You should only use this function when a session is malfunctioning and cannot be fixed. Select a session and then click the Reset icon.

You are asked to confirm the operation, and then the terminal shows a message box stating, "The Terminal server has ended the connection."

TAKE COMMAND

The **reset session** command deletes a session immediately, without warning the user. It should be used only for malfunctioning sessions. The syntax is:

reset session {*sessionname* | *sessionid*} [**/server:***servername*] [**/v**]

where:

sessionID is the ID of the session to which you want to reset.

sessionname is the name of the session to which you want to reset.

/server:*servername* is the name of the server on which the session is running.

/v displays verbose information about the operations being performed.

If you reset a listener session, all sessions using that connection are also reset. Do this only if absolutely necessary.

Viewing Session Information

You can view session-related data in Terminal Services Manager, or use the **query session** command to view data about a session. The Terminal Services Manager information is richer.

Select a session name in the left pane of the program and then the Information tab in the right pane. Some of the information displayed may be useful, like the IP address and client resolution, and some of it is less useful, like the number and size of buffers on the client and server.

If you have hotfixes applied to the system, they should also appear on this page.

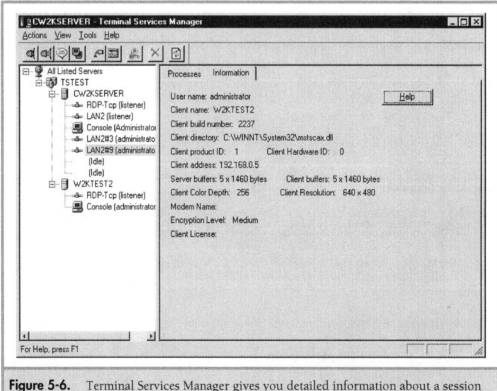

Figure 5-6. Terminal Services Manager gives you detailed information about a session

BUG ALERT According to Microsoft (see Knowledge Base article Q238151), the Information tab can also include a particular hotfix (described in Q147222), even when it is not installed on the system. Strangely, according to Microsoft's descriptions, all my test systems should have had this hotfix appear, but I never saw it. However, be on the lookout for it.

TAKE COMMAND

The **query session** command displays information about a session, although not the same information that Terminal Services Manager displays.

The result is a table of sessions and information about them, including the username, session ID, session state (see sidebar "Session States"), and type of session (such as console or RDP).

The syntax is:

query session [*sessionname* | *username* | *sessionid*] [**/server:***servername*] [**/mode**] [**/flow**] [**/connect**] [**/counter**]

where:

sessionname is the name of the session you are querying.

username is the name of the user whose sessions you want to query.

sessionid is the ID of the session you want to query.

/server:*servername* is the name of the server where the session is running. If no server name is specified, the server you are logged on is assumed.

/mode displays current line settings.

/flow displays current flow control settings.

/connect displays current connect settings.

/counter displays counter information about sessions on the server.

The **query user** command returns session information, much like **query session**, but without some of the useless stuff, and with some additional useful information. Much like Terminal Services Manager, **query user** adds the time the user logged on to the session and the number of minutes a session has been idle. The syntax is:

query user [*username* | *sessionname* | *sessionID*] [**/server**:*servername*]

where:

username is the name of the user whose sessions you want to query.

sessionname is the name of the session you are querying.

sessionid is the ID of the session you want to query.

/server:*servername* is the name of the server where the session is running. If no server name is specified, the server you are logged on is assumed.

You can also view the I/O status of a session that shows the number of bytes transmitted to and from the session. To do so, select a session and select Status (see Figure 5-7).

The information is interesting because it shows how much data transmission actually goes on under Terminal Services.

Logging Sessions Off

An administrator can log a user off of an existing session using Terminal Services Manager or the command-line program **logoff**. Users lose any unsaved work, and see a message box saying, "The Terminal server has ended the connection." It's more considerate to send them a message warning them in advance.

To log the session off, select it in Terminal Services Manager and then select Log Off.

TAKE COMMAND

The **logoff** command logs a user off from a session and deletes the session from the server. The syntax is:

logoff [*sessionid* | *sessionname*] [**/server**:*servername*] [**/v**]

where:

sessionID is the ID of the session to which you want to log off.

sessionname is the name of the session to which you want to log off.

/server:*servername* is the name of the server on which the session is running.

/v displays verbose information about the operations being performed.

Ending Processes in a Server or Session

You can view the processes running on a server or an individual session and end them remotely. Processes may be viewed at the command line with the **query process** command and ended with **tskill**. Ending a process is always a dangerous thing to do, but sometimes it can jar a session back into responsiveness.

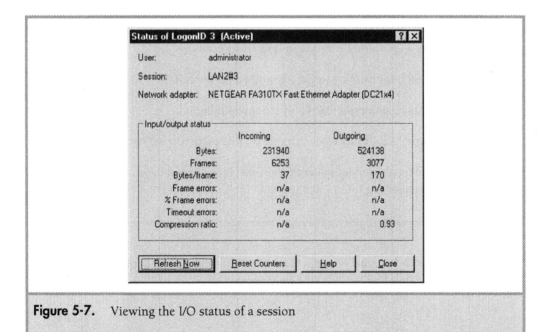

Figure 5-7.   Viewing the I/O status of a session

With either a server or session selected in the left pane of Terminal Services Manager, select the Processes tab of the right pane. You see the session ID, the process ID of each process, and the name of the executable program that launched the process (see Figure 5-8).

| TAKE COMMAND |

The **query process** command lists information about processes running on a server or session with far greater flexibility than in Terminal Services Manager. For example, you can ask for processes associated with a particular executable or username. The syntax is:

query process [* | *processid* | *username* | *sessionname* | **/id**:*nn* | *programname*] [**/server**:*servername*] [**/system**]

where:

* lists processes running in all sessions.

processid lists information on a specific process by ID.

username lists all processes running in *username*'s sessions.

sessionname lists all processes running in session *sessionname*.

/id:*nn* lists all processes running in the session with session ID *nn*.

programname lists all processes started by this executable.

/server:*servername* lists all processes running on this particular server.

/system lists information about system processes (such as ntvdm.exe, as opposed to applications like word.exe).

To kill a process in Terminal Services Manager, right-click on the leftmost column of the processes page and select End Process (the only menu option).

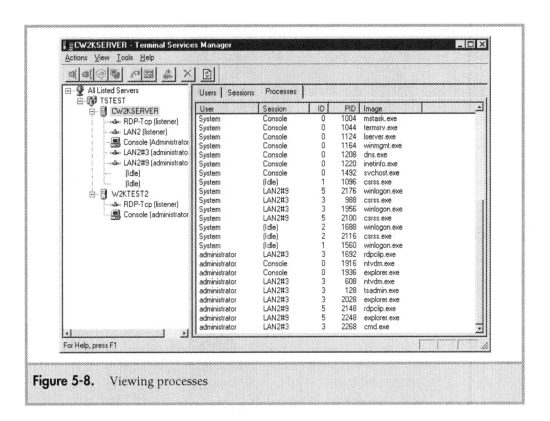

Figure 5-8. Viewing processes

The **tskill** command allows you to end a process with precise control. Unlike the visual method in Terminal Services Manager, you can choose to end all instances of a specific executable. The syntax is:

tskill {*processid* | *processname*} [**/server**:*servername*] [**/id**:*sessionid* | **/a**] [**/v**]

where:

processid ends the process with the specified ID.

processname ends the process with the specified name.

/server:*servername* specifies the server on which the process is running. If none is specified, the server you are logged on is assumed.

/id:*sessionid* specifies a session ID in which the process is running.

/a ends all instances of the process.

/v displays verbose information about the operations being performed.

Remote Control

Terminal Services allows users with appropriate rights from within a Terminal Services session to remotely control a client session. You can use this for support or training purposes. Did you ever have a user call you up and say it was doing A on the screen and you just know it's actually doing B? Terminal Services lets you actually see what's on the user's screen without being there, and also allows you to control the session remotely.

Depending on how the system is configured, Terminal Services may ask permission of the user before you either observe or take control of their session. Connection-level settings for remote control override the user- and group-level settings.

Setting Remote Control Options

You can set remote control options at the user level in Active Directory Users and Computers on the Remote Control tab. You can make almost identical settings at the connection level in the Terminal Services Configuration program on the Remote Control tab.

NOTE: At the connection level you can configure options either to accept or override the user-level settings for any users on that connection.

The Remote Control tab on the connection options lets you choose, globally for the connection, from among these options:

✦ Allow remote control and accept user-level settings for it

✦ Disable remote control on the connection

✦ Allow remote control and override user settings for it

On the Remote Control tab in Active Directory Users and Computers, you merely select whether to enable remote control for the user.

On either level, you can specify two other parameters: whether the user should be asked for permission when another user attempts to take control of his or her system, and whether such users should be able only to view the session remotely rather than take control of it.

Remote Control Permissions

Administrators have the right, by default, to initiate remote control, but other users (helpdesk personnel, for example) can be granted this right. To accomplish this, go into Terminal Services Configuration and open the Properties sheet for the connection over which you wish to grant remote control permission. Select the Permissions tab.

If the user or group to which you wish to grant permission is not on the user list, click Add and select the user or group from the list. Back in the Permissions tab, select the appropriate user or group, and click the Advanced button to enter the Access Control Settings for RDP-Tcp dialog box.

Select the user again and click View/Edit. Here you can explicitly grant permission to the user or group to perform remote control. (As an example, Figure 5-9 shows the Permission Entry for RDP-Tcp dialog box.)

Invoking Remote Control

You can invoke remote control in the Terminal Services Manager program or from the command line.

To start a remote control session in Terminal Services Manager, right-click on the connection and select Remote Control (alternatively, you can click the connection and select Remote Control from the Actions menu, or click the Remote Control icon).

A dialog box appears asking you to select a keystroke to end the session. The default keystroke is CTRL-*, specifically the * on the numeric keypad (see the following illustration).

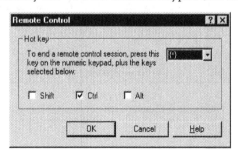

Figure 5-9. You can grant any user the right to perform remote control, but be careful
with this power

Click OK. At this point, if the system is configured to require permission of the user
before allowing you to take control, he receives a warning dialog box (see the following
illustration).

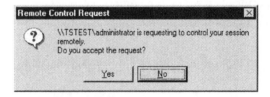

Until the user accepts, you have a message on screen asking you to wait until the session
is established.

At this point you are controlling, or at least observing, the other session. Anything you do, the user sees, and vice versa. If you are only observing, you see exactly what the user does. Things can happen without you initiating them, so don't get spooked. For example, your display may change; you may go into a full-screen mode, even if the remote session is less than your video resolution, with black borders filling to the edge of the screen. If you need to switch back to your own desktop, press CTRL-ESC to do so.

Remembering to switch out of remote control is important, because if you don't, and then you do something silly like locking your workstation, the client won't be able to type.

TAKE COMMAND

The **shadow** command initiates a remote control session, which you specify by the session name or session ID. Unlike the remote control procedures in Terminal Services Manager, you cannot specify the keystroke to end a session. The syntax is:

shadow {*sessionname* | *sessionid*} [**/server:***servername*] [**/v**]

where:

sessionname is the name of the session to control.

sessionid is the ID of the session to control.

/server:*servername* specifies the name of the server on which the session is running.

/v causes the command to output extra descriptive output to the console.

This feature can be really handy to show users exactly how to do something without having to go to their desks and show them. It's nowhere near as powerful as full remote control products, such as Symantec's pcAnywhere, but it's much lighter weight.

Because Terminal Services Manager doesn't see servers in other domains, you cannot control them. The **shadow** command isn't capable of controlling servers outside of a domain either.

Your display must be able to support at least the video resolution of the session you are attempting to control, or the operation will fail.

If the session you are attempting to control is disconnected you can still control it, but only if the system is not configured to require permission of the user before allowing you to take control.

There are privacy implications to the use of this feature. It is possible to configure the feature so that administrators can view other users' sessions without the users' knowledge. Work this out amongst yourselves.

Home Directories

I've already mentioned home directories, but I'm going to discuss them again. They're that important.

It's generally a good idea in a Windows NT or Windows 2000 network to assign home directories to users. In Terminal Services, it's essential. By default, users have home directories assigned with their logon names as subdirectories in the \Documents and Settings directory.

Terminal Services Home Directories

Terminal Services users can have a second home directory. Over time, if you use roaming profiles, using this second home directory can improve system performance, especially at logon time. Remember that users frequently save documents to their home directories. When a user logs on to Windows 2000, and the account is set up for roaming profiles, the operating system copies everything from the user's profile directory to his profile cache. If the home directory is inside the profile directory (which it is by default), logons can slow down a great deal, especially if roaming profiles are used and stored across the network, and profile caches can balloon in size unnecessarily.

Instead, you can specify a separate home directory for Terminal Services on a user-by-user basis. Open Active Directory Users and Computers to find the user for whom you want to specify a home directory or Terminal Services home directory . On the Terminal Services Profile tab of the user's property sheet (see Figure 5-10) specify a profile path, home directory path, and drive letter.

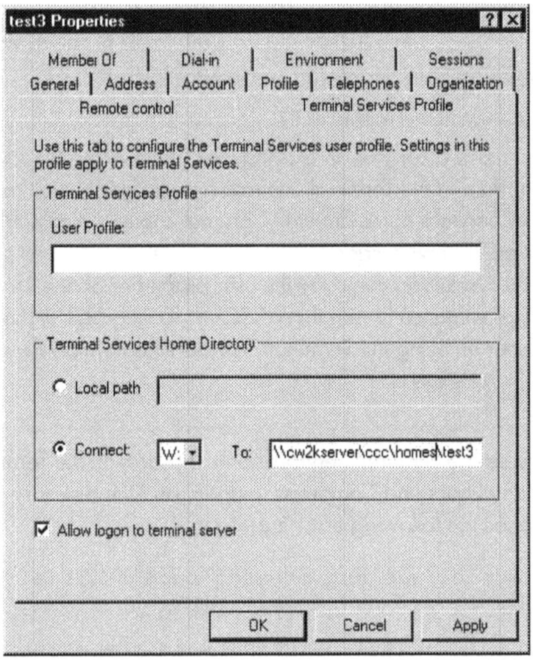

Figure 5-10. You can specify a separate home directory for Terminal Services users

If you specify a Terminal Services home directory, whether or not you specify a regular home directory path in the Profile tab, the user's home directory is the Terminal Services home directory when she logs on using Terminal Services. The settings for home directory and profile in the Profile tab of Active Directory Users and Computers have no effect for users logging on under Terminal Services.

If the user logs on locally to the system, or logs on under Terminal Services and no Terminal Services home directory is specified, the home directory is the %SystemDrive%\ Documents and Settings\%username% folder.

Remember that if the user logs on to the console of the Terminal server, the Terminal Services profile and Terminal Services home directory are not used. Instead, if a normal home directory is specified in the Profile tab, this is used; if none is specified, the home directory is %SystemDrive%\Documents and Settings\%username%.

Terminal Services automatically creates the username subdirectory and gives it appropriate permissions. Users have full access to their own home directories. Administrators can copy files into them, but not read or delete files.

BUG ALERT If you make a copy of an existing user in the Active Directory Users and Computers snap-in, data in the Terminal Services-specific fields, such as the Terminal Services profile and Terminal Services home directory, are not copied. Microsoft has acknowledged this bug, but it is not fixed in Service Pack 1.

If you're up for the work, you can copy the user properties of one user and set the properties of another user programmatically with the WTSQueryConfig and WTSSetUserConfig API calls. There is a white paper on using the Terminal Services APIs at http://www.microsoft.com/ntserver/zipdocs/TseApis.exe.

BUG ALERT If you set the Terminal Services home directory in the Terminal Services Profile tab in the Active Directory Users and Computers snap-in, and the directory you are specifying already exists, you see the following error message:

```
The home directory was not created because it already exists.
You might want to select a different name, or make sure that
the user has full access privileges to the existing one.
```

There isn't really a good reason for this message, but Microsoft has acknowledged that it is a bug. It's just cosmetic though, as you didn't really need to create the directory anyway.
This problem is fixed in Windows 2000 Service Pack 1.

Use a Single RootDrive for Users

The first time you run application compatibility scripts, you are asked to set a drive letter that references what Terminal Services internally calls the RootDrive. This same letter is used for all subsequent application compatibility scripts. Furthermore, when users log on, Windows 2000 executes a batch file named usrlogon.cmd, located in %systemroot%, which does a lot of complicated stuff, including setting the ROOTDRIVE environment variable to a value (%HomeDrive%%HomePath%) expected by many third-party applications. Therefore, it's a really good idea to settle on one letter for all your users for this purpose.

Managing User Profiles

By default, in Terminal Services, the user profile comes from the server the user logs on to, so if a user connects to multiple Terminal servers, he ends up with multiple profiles. A roaming profile, one that is stored in a central location, is the answer to this, just as it is the answer for conventional LAN users who may log on from one of many workstations. No matter which server the user logs on to, he will retrieve the profile from the specified location. Unless the administrator specifies otherwise, a local cached copy remains on the Terminal server on which the user is running. When users log on, the dates of the local cached and server profiles are compared, and if the server profile is newer, the cached version is overwritten.

Terminal Services provides the Terminal Services Profile tab in Active Directory Users and Computers user entries so that you can specify specific profiles for users when logged on under Terminal Services (see Figure 5-11).

If you specify a profile for a user on the Terminal Services Profile tab, that is the profile used when the user logs on under Terminal Services. If you have not specified a Terminal Services profile, but have specified a Windows 2000 roaming profile in the Profile tab in the user's Active Directory Users and Computers property page, that profile is used. If you have

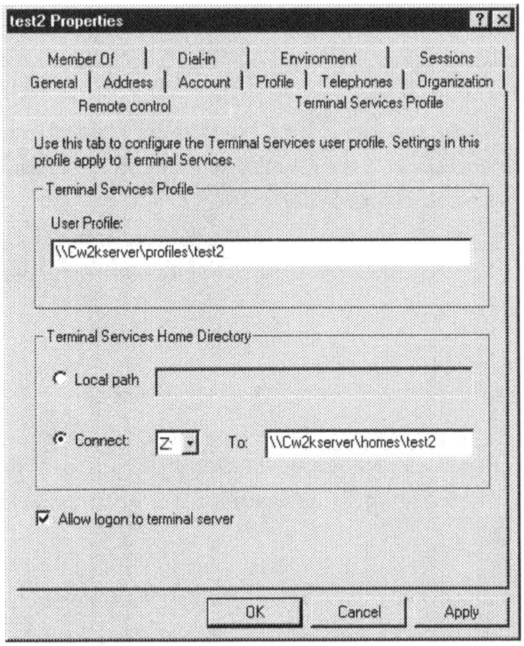

Figure 5-11. You can specify a roaming or mandatory user profile for users logging on to Terminal Services

not specified such a profile, the default user profile is used, which is the user's NTUser.dat file in (usually) \Documents and Settings\%*username*%.

If your users log on to multiple Terminal servers, you almost certainly want to create Terminal Services profiles. Even if you have users who sometimes log on with Terminal Services and sometimes not, their profiles under Terminal Services will likely be different from the non-Terminal Services profile. In that case, specify a standard roaming profile on the Profile tab and a Terminal Services profile on the Terminal Services Profile tab. If your users always use a single, specific Terminal server, you can safely ignore the Terminal Services Profiles tab.

The Terminal Services tab on the user properties in Active Directory Users and Computers has a checkbox labeled Allow Logon To Terminal Server. If it is unchecked for the user, she receives the following message when attempting to log on:

```
Your interactive logon privilege has been disabled. Please
contact your system administrator.
```

Check the box and the user will be able to log on.

A user who does not have rights to log on locally on the server sees an error when logging on to that server with Terminal Services: "The local policy of this system does not permit you to log on interactively."

To fix this, go to the Local Security Policy program in Administrative Tools. Expand Local Policies on the left and select User Rights Assignment. In the right pane, find Log On Locally and double-click it (see Figure 5-12).

In the Select Users of Groups window, click the Add button, select your user and click Add to put him in the lower list. Click OK and then OK again. The user can now log on.

TAKE COMMAND

The **tsprof** command copies user profile information from one user to another. It can also set the profile path for a user. You must have administrator rights to use **tsprof**.

The syntax for **tsprof** is:

tsprof /update [**/domain**:*domainname*|**/local**] **/profile**:*path username*

tsprof /copy [**/domain**:*domainname*|**/local**] [**/profile**:*path*] *src_usr dest_usr*

tsprof /q [**/domain**:*domainname*|**/local**] *username*

where:

/update updates the profile path in domain *domainname* to *path*.

/copy copies user profile from *src_usr* to *dest_usr*. Update profile path information for *dest_usr* to *path*.

/q displays the current profile path for *username*'s profile.

/domain:*domainname* is the name of the domain in which the profiles exist.

/local applies only to local user accounts.

/profile:*path* is the location of the profile.

src_usr is the name of the user whose profile you want to copy.

dest_usr is the name of the user whose profile you want to overwrite.

username is the name of the user whose profile you want to query or update.

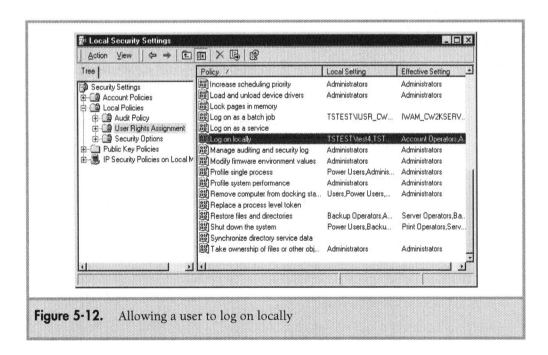

Figure 5-12.   Allowing a user to log on locally

TAKE COMMAND

The **cprofile** command cleans user profiles to get rid of wasted space. You need administrator rights to run it. Profiles that are in use are not affected, so you may want to schedule it to run at a time when the server is least busy. This program also removes user-specific file associations that are disabled. The syntax is:

cprofile [/i] [/l] [/v] *filelist*

where:

/i interactively prompts the user to confirm cleaning each profile.

/l cleans all local profiles. You can still add other files in the file list.

/v displays verbose information about the operation.

filelist specifies a list of files to clean.

TAKE COMMAND

The **flattemp** command enables or disables flat temp folders for users. You must have administrator rights to execute this command.

By default, users' temporary folders are in a separate directory relative to their profile directory. Each session for Terminal Services creates a new subdirectory in this temporary directory with a name based on the session ID. This command lets you specify that the temp folder for Terminal Services should be the user's temp directory, not a temporary subdirectory of the temp directory.

This command is analogous to the Use Temporary Folders Per Session policy in Terminal Services Configuration. The syntax is:

flattemp {/query | /enable | /disable}

where:

/query displays the current setting.

/**enable** sets the system to use flat temporary folders.

/**disable** sets the system not to use flat temporary folders.

Restricting User Capabilities

It's always a good idea to look at what features users *shouldn't* have, but on Terminal Services you should be even more restrictive. Many features of Windows, especially cosmetic desktop options, can have an inordinate impact on server and network bandwidth. Other features, such as registry access, are more dangerous when the user is running on the server than on their own client machine.

Disable Menu Options

There are a number of menu options you can and should disable for Terminal Services users. Most of this can be done through Group Policy, which is the preferred method for anything in Windows 2000.

Peruse the Group Policy objects for policies you feel are necessary. Better yet, read *Admin911: Windows 2000 Group Policies*, by Roger Jennings (Osborne/McGraw-Hill, 2000). You can enter the Group Policy Editor in Active Directory Users and Computers by right-clicking on either the domain or, if you have created any, a relevant organizational unit (OU).

Select the Group Policy tab on the dialog box that appears (see Figure 5-13). At this point, you probably have only a single entry in the list, Default Domain Policy (if you have more than that, you're a Group Policy pro, and you don't need my help getting into the editor). Select Edit to open the Properties dialog box.

Some of the policies that look like drop-dead obvious candidates for Terminal Services are the following:

❖ In Group Policy\Computer Configuration\Administrative Templates\System, the policy **Remove Security Option From Start Menu (Terminal Services only)**. Enabling this policy removes the Windows Security option from your users' Start | Settings menu.

❖ In Group Policy\User Configuration\Administrative Templates\Start Menu and Taskbar, the policy **Disable and Remove Shut Down Command**. Do you really want your Terminal Services users to have a Shut Down command? Why would Microsoft put it in the default Start menu for Terminal Services users to begin with?

◆ In Group Policy\User Configuration\Administrative Templates\System, the policy **Disable Registry Editing Tools**. Terminal Services users don't usually have a need for Regedit and Regedt32.

◆ In Group Policy\User Configuration\Administrative Templates\Control Panel\Display, use this group of policies to disable features such as screen savers and the settings tab of the Control Panel Display applet (see Figure 5-14). Nothing good can come of Terminal Services users having access to these features.

Set User Time Limits

Terminal Services sessions aren't like regular PCs that are left on all night. They consume server resources and thereby impede performance for other users. You can use the Sessions tab in Active Directory Users and Computers to restrict the damage.

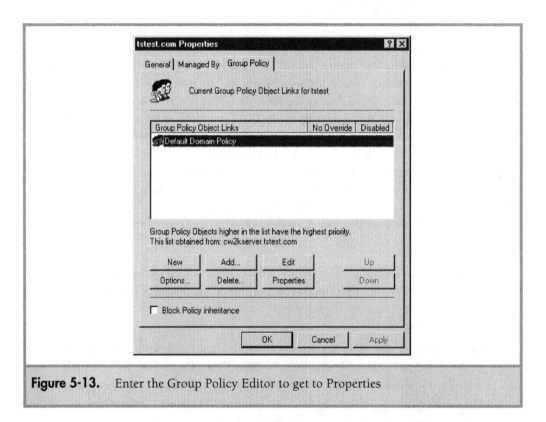

Figure 5-13. Enter the Group Policy Editor to get to Properties

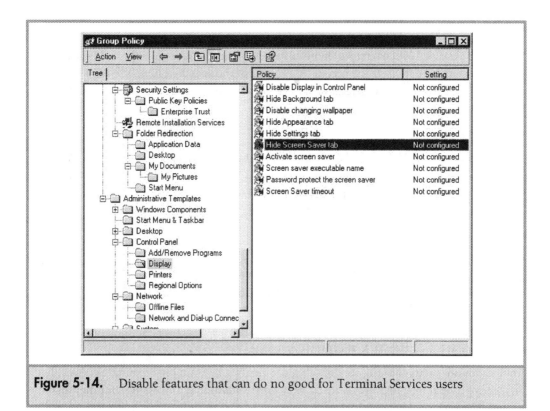

Figure 5-14.   Disable features that can do no good for Terminal Services users

Automatically End Disconnected Sessions

End A Disconnected Session lets you specify an override for the maximum amount of time that a session stays alive on the server after being disconnected. Depending on the value of this setting, a disconnected session may be available for reconnection from the same or a different client system for a specified period of time. When this time limit is reached, the disconnected session ends.

✦   Choose Never to keep the connection alive indefinitely.

✦   Choose a time limit from the drop-down list to specify the maximum time before disconnection.

✦   Specify an amount of time in days, hours and minutes by entering a value in the combo box. Append **d** for days, **h** for hours, and **m** for minutes to the numbers. For example, "1d 2h 3m" is 1 day, 2 hours, 3 minutes.

Set Active Session Limits

The Active Session Limit overrides the user value for the maximum amount of time a session can remain active on the server. At the end of the specified time, the session is ended. You can specify the time for the Active Session Limit in the same manner as with End A Disconnected Session.

Set Idle Session Limits

The Idle Session Limit setting overrides the user value for the maximum amount of time a session can remain active while there is no user activity (keyboard or mouse movement). When the specified time elapses, the user is either disconnected or the session ended, depending on the state of the checkbox immediately below the Idle Session Limit setting.

NOTE: In Terminal Services Configuration, you can set an override for these user settings for an entire connection. On that program's Sessions tab are identical controls with identical mode of operation for configuring options. This is a coarser level of control, as it applies to all users over that connection, so you may want to use the user-level settings described above.

Minimizing Client Graphics Use

Animations are pretty, but they are much more costly when run on Terminal Services than on a conventional machine. Not only do they create additional processing, but they also increase the amount of network bandwidth used by the session.

You can use the registry to minimize the animation effects in the Windows 2000 shell. To do this for a single user, log on to the server as that user and go to HKEY_CURRENT_USER\ControlPanel\Desktop\WindowMetrics. Add a REG_SZ key named MinAnimate, and set the value to 0.

You can also create a general system override for settings users can make to their own desktops. On the server, go to HKEY_LOCAL_MACHINE\System\CurrentControlSet\ Control\TerminalServer\WinStations\RDP-tcp\UserOverride\ ControlPanel\ Desktop\ WindowMetrics and create a REG_SZ data item named MinAnimate. Set the value to 0. If this registry subkey doesn't exist, add the necessary subkeys to create this registry path.

You can, in fact, duplicate the entries in any of the subkeys of HKEY_CURRENT_USER\ ControlPanel\Desktop\WindowMetrics under the UserOverride subkey to prevent implementation of user entries in favor of the settings you establish.

You can also disable client wallpaper, which should improve screen redraw time and conserve some memory and processing on the server. In the Terminal Services Configuration program on the Environment tab, you can disable wallpaper for all users connecting over that connection. You'd think there would be a group policy for such a thing, but apparently not.

Shutting Down a Terminal Server

When you shut down a Terminal Server it is best to use the **tsshutdn** command instead of the conventional Shut Down in the Start menu. A conventional shut down just shuts things down without any warning to the users, which may result in loss of data.

The **tsshutdn** command notifies all connected sessions of the impending shut down (see the following illustration).

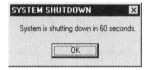

Sessions that have applications with open files automatically prompt the user to save the files.

TAKE COMMAND

The **tsshutdn** command shuts down a Terminal Services server in an orderly manner. The syntax is:

tsshutdn [*wait_time*] [**/server**:*servername*] [**/reboot**] [**/powerdown**] [**/delay**:*logoffdelay*] [**/v**]

where:

wait_time specifies the number of seconds to wait, after notifying users of the impending shut down, before logging users off from sessions. The default value is 60 seconds. The administrator running the command has this amount of time to press ^C to abort the shut down.

/server:*servername* specifies the name of the server to shut down.

/reboot tells the command to reboot the server after the shut down.

/powerdown tells the command to power the server off after the shut down, assuming the hardware in the server supports software power-down.

/**delay**:*logoffdelay* specifies the number of seconds to wait, after logging all users off from their sessions, before shutting server processes to finish the system shut down. The default value is 30 seconds.

/**v** displays verbose information at the console about the operation. This command echoes to the console each shut down message that it sends to each session.

TAKE COMMAND

The **change logon** command enables or disables logons from a Terminal server. You must have administrator rights to use this command.

If you disable logons while logged on from a remote session and then log off, you won't be able to get back in from a remote session. You will have to log on locally at the server console to re-enable logons. The syntax for **change logon** is:

change logon [/enable | /disable | /query]

where:

/**enable** enables logons to the server.

/**disable** disables logons to the server.

/**query** displays the current logon status.

Printing from Terminal Services

When any Win32 RDP5 Terminal Services client connects to a Terminal Services server, the two automatically make the user's local printers available to server-based applications. This applies to all local printers, whether they are connected to parallel, serial, or USB ports.

Windows 3.x clients and Windows-Based Terminals (WBT) must use manual printer redirection. To do this, they must share their printer on the network. Then, when logged on to the server, they can use the Add Printer Wizard to connect to it just as with any network printer.

NOTE: If users are printing to a local printer and are connected over a slow link, printing could take a long time and consume large amounts of bandwidth. Even though normally only RDP5 communications take place over the line, when you redirect to a local printer the actual print image is sent back over the line to the client.

If you have experience with Terminal Server 4.0, you may have bad memories of blue-screened servers that bombed out because of a bad printer driver. This problem turned out to be unusually common in Terminal Server 4.0. Because of the mini-driver model in Terminal Services in Windows 2000, which requires only a small amount of development on the part of the driver writer, print drivers are much more stable than they used to be.

Even though I have no reason to think that Terminal Services under Windows 2000 is subject to this sort of error, it is something you should pay attention to, especially when you use third-party drivers.

CODE BLUE

If you are using certain obscure printers or print drivers on a Win9x client, printer redirection from Terminal Services to your local printer ports may not work. You may notice errors in the server's system event log indicating that the printer driver was unknown, the printer security information could not be set, or the printer could not be installed.

This is because Terminal Services maintains a list of printers in \winnt\inf\ntprint.inf. The list is not as exhaustive as it might be, but you can add lines to it to support your own printer.

Open ntprint.inf and look for the [Previous Names] section. You'll see a number of entries for printer models:

[Previous Names]
"Apple LaserWriter v23.0"   =   "Apple LaserWriter"
"Apple LaserWriter II NT v47.0"   =   "Apple LaserWriter II NT"
"Apple LaserWriter II NTX v47.0" =   "Apple LaserWriter II NTX"

The left column is the name of a Windows 2000 print driver and the right column is the name of the driver used on the client. First, you need to install the Windows 2000 driver for the printer and determine its name, then determine the name of the print driver on the Win9x system. You can determine this either from the printer properties on the system or from other entries in the ntprint.inf file. Add a line to the [Previous Names] section of the file with the Windows 2000 driver name on the left and the Windows 9x driver name on the right.

BUG ALERT Windows 2000's support for printing over the Internet to a printer at a URL using the Internet Printing Protocol (IPP) is buggy under Terminal Services. When combined with roaming profiles (including profiles set in the Terminal Services Profile tab of Active Directory Users and Computers), print jobs can fail, changes to roaming profiles can be discarded, and a memory leak in a system process can result.

IPP keeps a registry entry in HKEY_CURRENT_USER open, so if a user attempts to log off during the printing process, the Winlogon service is unable to unload the registry and write the profile back to the specified location on the server. Parts of the registry remain in memory, hence the memory leak.

This problem is not specific to Terminal Services, but is exacerbated by it because of the large number of users who might be logging on and off locally, creating leaks.

Essentially, you have to make a choice between roaming profiles and IPP.

The system log on a busy Terminal server is liable to fill up because of informational events for print jobs. The event log stores print events even when the job is to a local printer attached to the client (see the following illustration).

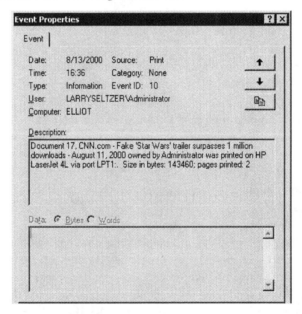

The best solution is to set the event log to overwrite old events more frequently. In Event Viewer, right-click on System Log and select Properties. Then take one of these actions:

✦ Choose Overwrite as needed.

✦ Increase the maximum log size.

✦ Decrease the number of days before events are overwritten.

Chapter 6

Advanced Management Techniques

C hapter 5 dealt with common administration issues, especially those involving the main administration programs, Terminal Services Manager and Terminal Services Configuration. In this chapter, I attempt to deal with more obscure problems, and more obscure details of configuration, such as the registry entries behind the settings in the programs. If you prefer, you can create .reg files to distribute registry changes, rather than make them on individual servers.

Troubleshooting Roaming Profile Inconsistencies

Roaming user profiles may become inconsistent if you use the same profile for the standard roaming profile (on the Profile tab in Active Directory Users and Computers) and the Terminal Services profile (on the Terminal Services Profile tab).

The problem arises if the user logs on as both a regular user and Terminal Services user, which is actually quite common. To access the Terminal Services client software, they first need to log on to the network.

If the user were to make profile changes in the Terminal Services profile (such as changing a persistent drive mapping), log off from their Terminal Services session (uploading the profile back to the server), and then log off from the Windows 2000 workstation, the roaming profile on the workstation wouldn't overwrite the server profile.

Change Your Thinking on User Profiles— It's Terminal Services

Roaming profile management in a Windows NT or Windows 2000 network often centers on the implications of users logging on and off the network, and the movement of profile data at those times between the client and server.

It's worth reminding yourself that, in Terminal Services, the Terminal server is the "client," and therefore that is where the profile information resides while the session is open. The Terminal Services profile never gets transferred to the original client system, meaning the computer at which the user is working.

This is one of the magical things about Terminal Services, and one of the things that makes it ideal for supporting remote users over slow dial-up links. User profiles in Terminal Services can get complex and large, but they will not need to download to the client system.

At the heart of this is the issue of time: when you log on or log off, Windows compares the timestamp of the local profile with that of the roaming profile. If the roaming profile on the network server is more recent than the local profile, it is downloaded and becomes the local profile. If the local profile is more recent, the roaming profile is not downloaded. At logoff time, the same type of comparison is made: if the local profile is more recent than the roaming profile, the local profile is uploaded.

Because of this, if you use roaming profiles (or Terminal Services profiles, which are just another type of roaming profile), it is imperative that you use the Windows Time service and have all systems periodically synchronize computer time with the **net time** command.

The complicated implications also make it hard to make a case for using the same roaming profile both for the Windows 2000 logon and the Terminal Services profile. Perhaps it's not worth whatever convenience it may bring. Conceivably it could work if both profiles were made mandatory, because there would be no uploading of changed profiles.

Restricting User Application Access

Very often you want to restrict users' access to applications. This can be done through normal file and directory rights, but that can be time consuming and cumbersome. Windows 2000 and the Windows 2000 Resource Kit have specific facilities for creating both permitted application lists (applications that users are allowed to run) and denied application lists (applications that users cannot run).

CODE BLUE

If you install the Windows 2000 Server Resource Kit to a Terminal server using a mapped drive path to the install source, you may receive an error message: Internal Error 2755. 3 %path%\w2000rk.msi.

You can work around the problem by using a full UNC name to the install source (for example, \\servername\sharename\w2000rk.msi as opposed to z:w2000rk.msi). This problem can occur whether you use setup.exe or w2000rk.msi to install the Resource Kit.

The two methods I discuss here take different approaches and are useful for different circumstances. You can conceivably mix them. That might make your life more difficult, but if something's worth doing, it's worth doing right.

Appsec

Appsec is a Windows 2000 Server Resource Kit utility that creates a permitted application list. Appsec's main advantage is that it makes settings machine-wide. With this program, you can control program execution by any user (except administrators) on the machine.

NOTE: Microsoft has a hotfix for this tool at http://www.microsoft.com/windows2000/ library/resources/reskit/tools/hotfixes/appsec-o.asp.

Appsec works on a machine basis: only applications that run on that machine are affected. Note that this doesn't mean programs *stored* on that machine, but programs *run* on that machine. Contrary to its Windows NT 4.0-era documentation, Appsec can be used to grant permission to run programs stored on other servers.

To use Appsec, it must first be installed on the machine. Run instappsec.exe to do this. Then you can run appsec.exe from the command line or Start | Run. Don't be fooled by the fact that appsec.exe (which is installed when you install the Resource Kit) appears to run correctly before you run instappsec.exe; it may run, but it won't actually do anything.

BUG ALERT The first release of the Windows 2000 Server Resource Kit has a bug that's so extreme, it's almost funny. The Resource Kit is missing three files necessary for Appsec to function, including instappsec.exe. Luckily, the solution is as easy as the bug is unforgivable: download ftp://ftp.microsoft.com/reskit/win2000/appsec.zip. It contains not only the missing files (appsec.cnt, appsec.dll, instappsec.exe), but also current versions of the files Microsoft remembered to include with the Resource Kit. Future updates to the Resource Kit will likely fix this problem.

As the program's title bar indicates, the list of programs in the window (see Figure 6-1) is a list of programs that users are authorized to run. They are not allowed to run anything else while logged on to that server.

The Security Enabled/Disabled setting at the bottom of the window turns the program's features on and off for the server on which it runs. At the time you make the switch from Disabled to Enabled, the change has no any effect on currently logged-on users. Users have to log off (or you can kill their sessions) and when they log back on, the Appsec restrictions take effect. But from that point, you can make live changes to the list of Authorized Applications and they have immediate effect, even for logged-on users.

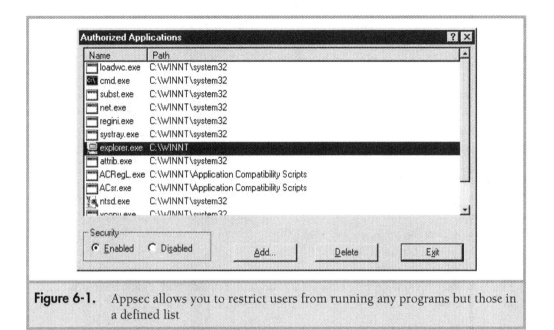

Figure 6-1. Appsec allows you to restrict users from running any programs but those in a defined list

When Appsec security is enabled, the data item fEnabled at HKEY_LOCAL_MACHINE\ SYSTEM\CurrentContolSet\Control\Terminal Server\ AuthorizedApplications is set to 1, and to 0 when it's disabled. The data item ApplicationList in HKEY_LOCAL_MACHINE\ SYSTEM\CurrentContolSet\Control\Terminal Server\ AuthorizedApplications contains the list of authorized applications.

Application Tracking

Remember, Appsec works by denying user access to everything *except* what's in the authorized application list. This is one of those tools, like most of Terminal Services, that requires testing before you use it in a production environment. Simply apply it to an existing Terminal server and something will go wrong, almost guaranteed. Usually the problem is that some unauthorized programs are also being run, either by Windows or by authorized programs.

Appsec helps somewhat with the testing. When you add a new program to the list, you have the opportunity to use the Tracking feature to monitor which programs are being loaded. After you click Add to add a program to the list, click the Start Tracking button. Then run the program you want to add to the list and perform functions that you want to allow users to perform. This can be tough if you're a network administrator and haven't had the pleasure of learning everything there is to do in Microsoft PowerPoint, for instance, but do what you can. At least run the program and open a document, but if you can't give it a thorough workout you can expect support calls later.

When you are done testing, click the Stop Tracking button, and a list of processes launched from within the program appears. Figure 6-2 shows the results of running Microsoft Word and then System Information from within the Word About box.

When you click OK in the Add Authorized Application dialog box, all the tracked programs, in addition to the one you ran yourself, are added to the authorized list.

Restrictions in Appsec

There are only two types of users to Appsec: administrators and non-administrators. If you need to make finer distinctions in your application permissions, look for another method. The setting is machine-wide; all users are subject to the restriction, and not just when connected through Terminal Services.

One big advantage of Appsec is that it places no restrictions on administrators. Group policies can have the unfortunate effect of locking out all users, including administrators, from key features, if you use them without proper caution.

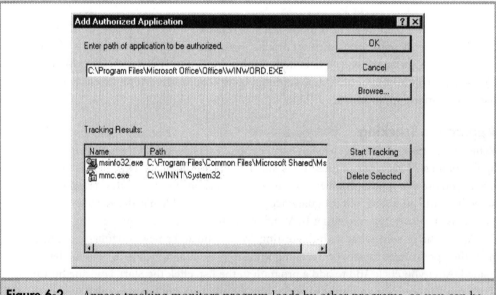

Figure 6-2.   Appsec tracking monitors program loads by other programs, so you can be sure to authorize all the necessary programs

Appsec can block most but not all applications from running. It works by monitoring calls to the Windows 2000 CreateProcess() API call, which is the main (not exclusive) call for executing programs. For example, if a program executes another program using the NTCreateProcess() call (which is actually an NT kernel call, not a Win32 API call), Appsec would miss it. Also, Appsec cannot restrict execution of a DLL, just full .exe files.

Similarly, since Appsec monitors the Win32 CreateProcess() call, it can't allow/disallow specific Win16 programs. You can use it to allow or disallow access to ntvdm.exe, the Win32 program that launches Win16 programs, but this is a global switch on Win16 programs.

CODE BLUE

After you apply Appsec, you may notice errors at logon time (see the following illustration). These errors occur because many programs load at logon time, and you may not have authorized them.

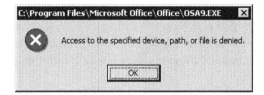

When this happens, fortunately, Windows 2000 tells you which programs are affected by raising error messages. Since the error message gives you the full path of the program, you can easily add it to the authorized list (or delete the call to it).

Remember that programs like this can be run from any number of locations, including the Startup folder, the Run keys in the registry, and logon scripts.

Another problem with Appsec is that it is difficult to fully exercise a program to the point of being sure that you have configured Appsec correctly for it. If you miss a feature in your testing that runs an external EXE, some user will invoke it and get a security-related error and call the helpdesk. The only way to deal with this is to be as thorough in your testing as possible. You might also try asking the application vendor for a list of executables that they invoke.

Group Policy Restrictions on Applications

If you need to take a more user-oriented approach, you can use a couple of Windows 2000 Group Policies to restrict individual users from running specific programs, or give them a list of programs they may run to the exclusion of all others.

In Group Policy\User Configuration\Administrative Templates\System, note the following polices:

◈ Run Only Allowed Windows Applications

◈ Don't Run Specified Windows Applications

Run Only Allowed Windows Applications lets you create a list of applications that are the only ones the user is allowed to run. Don't Run Specified Windows Applications lets you create a list of applications that users are not allowed to run.

As with Appsec, the list of applications you create for Run Only Allowed Windows Applications may miss some necessary programs called by permitted programs if your testing doesn't fully exercise the program features.

These policies only apply to programs run through Windows Explorer facilities. If users run the programs at the command line, this policy won't stop them. Of course, the convenient Disable The Command Prompt policy can deal with that little problem, should you want to go that far.

There are two reasons to use group policies instead of Appsec (maybe there are more reasons, but I can think of two). First, Appsec is machine-wide, and the policies cannot be applied to individual users. So if, for example, you have a single user who is addicted to solitaire, you can restrict him, and just him, from using it, through group policies. With Appsec you have to punish everyone. The second reason is that Appsec is machine-specific. If you have multiple servers, or any kind of complex network, group policies are appealing because they propagate through the entire domain. With Appsec, you must maintain each server individually, potentially duplicating a lot of work.

Changing File Associations

One of the smart things Microsoft did when they set the rules in Terminal Services was to lock out the user functionality for changing file type associations. No users, *not even administrators*, can change associations on a Terminal Services server in Application Server mode (this rule does not apply to Remote Administration mode). Go into the Open With dialog box or Explorer's Folder Options | File Types dialog box and you'll see that all the relevant buttons and checkboxes are grayed out.

Before Windows 2000, associations were always global to the system (stored in HKEY_LOCAL_MACHINE). Fouling up file associations is a very, very common source of application problems, and on a Terminal server the problems would affect all users.

Ironically, Microsoft created a new place in the registry to store user-specific file type associations (HKEY_CURRENT_USER\Software\Classes), but provided no user interface for accessing them! It is possible for programs to access them using documented facilities in the Windows 2000 SDK.

It is possible to unlock the access in the user interface to global changes to file associations by changing the data item NoFileAssociate in HKEY_LOCAL_MACHINE\ Software\Microsoft\Windows\CurrentVersion\Policies\Explorer from 1 to 0. Beware: Doing this means that any user on the Terminal server can make a change to file associations that might cripple applications for all users on the server!

NOTE: If you think a user interface should be available to allow users to change their individual file associations under Windows 2000, including under Terminal Services, you can send a request for this feature to mswish@microsoft.com. (No, I'm not kidding, they're actually taking a vote on the matter.)

Make User Local Drives Accessible

While users are logged on to Terminal Services, they do not normally have access to their local drives. Citrix MetaFrame has a built-in feature to allow it. On plain Terminal Services, users can use the **net share** command on the client and **net use** on the Terminal server to make their drives available.

The Windows 2000 Resource Kit comes with a utility called Drive Share that automates the latter process. Install the client and server portions, run drmapsrv on the client, and the drives appear automatically as network shares.

NOTE: Microsoft has a hotfix for this tool at http://www.microsoft.com/windows2000/ library/resources/reskit/tools/hotfixes/drmapsrv-o.asp.

To install it:

1. On the server side, copy drmapsrv.exe from the Resource Kit directory to %systemroot%\system32.

2. On the server, run the drmapsrv.reg file from the Resource Kit directory.

3. On the client, copy drmapclt.dll from the Resource Kit directory to the Terminal Services client directory (usually \Program Files\Terminal Services Client\).

4. On the client, run the drmapclt.reg file.

BUG ALERT Drive Share works by creating network shares. If the client system is a Windows 9x system using share-level security and they share their drives to the Terminal server, other Terminal Services users on that server will be able to connect to the share without needing a password, even if a password was specified for the share. Microsoft has confirmed that this is a bug.

Copy and Paste Functions

The default Terminal Services client allows users to copy and paste text and graphics between the client and server sessions. This is handled by the rdpclip.exe program, which runs in all Terminal Services sessions. The Windows 2000 Resource Kit has an enhanced rdpclip.exe, referred to as File Copy in the documentation, which also allows users to copy and paste files between the client and server session.

NOTE: Microsoft has a hotfix for this tool at http://www.microsoft.com/windows2000/ library/resources/reskit/tools/hotfixes/rdpclip-o.asp.

To install it on the server, run the fxfrinst.bat file from the Resource Kit directory. To install on the client, copy the fxfr.dll and rdpdr.dll files from the Resource Kit directory to the Terminal Services client directory (usually \Program Files\Terminal Services Client\). The rdpdr.dll overwrites the one included with the standard Terminal Services client.

Subsequent logons use the new clipboard facilities. There's no explicit UI for it, you just use normal clipboard operations. With the standard client, these would fail on large content, but File Copy uses Terminal Services' virtual channel feature to stream data between the two systems.

Restricting Terminal Services Client Versions

The Tsver (Version Monitor Configuration Wizard) utility in the Windows 2000 Server Resource Kit lets you restrict, at the server, the Terminal Services client versions that are allowed to run and those which are not.

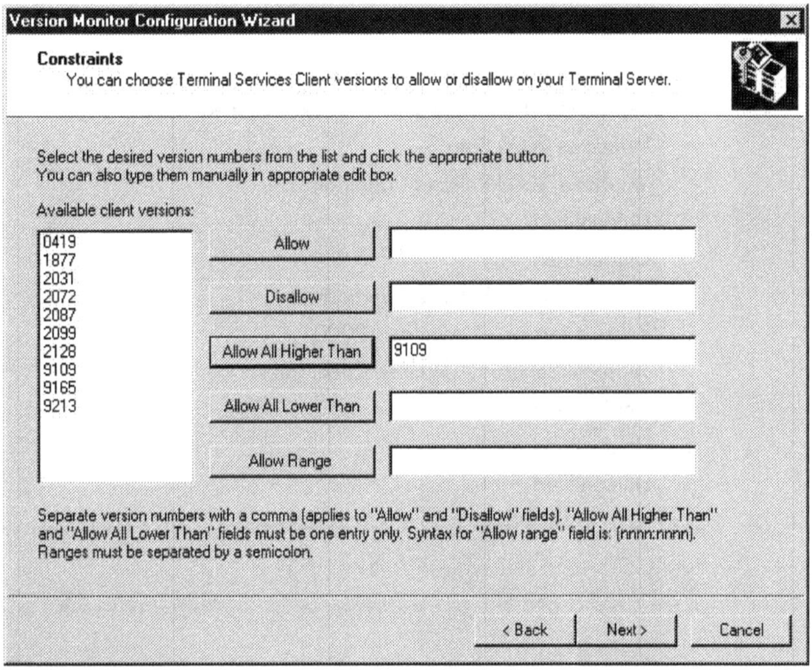

Figure 6-3.   Tsver lets you set complex rules for which Terminal Services clients are allowed to run

As Figure 6-3 shows, you can allow and disallow specific version numbers or ranges of numbers. In the next screen of the wizard, you can specify a customized error message to send to the client in case they attempt to connect with an unapproved client version. An event containing the customized message, if one were defined, and the client station name and IP address, is written to the System event log.

You must copy the tsver.dll file from the Resource Kit directory to %systemroot%\ system32.

To determine your client build number, check the About box in the client.

The list of versions in the program contains many beta versions of Windows 2000, versions of Windows NT 4.0 Terminal Server Edition, and a number of unidentified numbers. Incredibly, the list in the program appears to be hard-coded in it and does not contain the shipping version of Windows 2000, although you can manually add version numbers to track. Table 6-1 shows what I have been able to track down so far.

Version Number	Name
0419	Windows NT 4.0 Terminal Server Edition
1877	Windows NT 5.0 beta 2 (soon to be renamed Windows 2000)
2031	Windows 2000 Beta 3
2072	Windows 2000 Release Candidate 1
2087	Unidentified
2099	Unidentified
2128	Windows 2000 Release Candidate 2
2195	Release version of Windows 2000
2237	Terminal Services Advanced Client (all variations)
9109	Unidentified
9165	Unidentified
9213	Unidentified

Table 6-1.   Terminal Services Client Version Numbers

Registry Information for Terminal Services

The normal, obvious way to determine if a server is running Terminal Services is to see if you can connect to it. The normal, obvious way to determine if a Terminal server is running Remote Administration mode as opposed to Application Server mode is to check the setting in the Terminal Services Configuration program.

But if you need another method, perhaps to use for scripting, or for making the determination from a remote computer, there are registry keys you can check. If Terminal Services is installed on the system, the data item ProductSuite in HKEY_LOCAL_MACHINE\SYSTEM\CurrentContolSet\Control\ProductOptions has the value Terminal Server.

The version of Terminal Services may be retrieved from the data item ProductVersion in HKEY_LOCAL_MACHINE\SYSTEM\CurrentContolSet\Control\Terminal Server (the default in Windows 2000 is 5.0).

If Terminal Services is enabled, the value of TSEnabled in HKEY_LOCAL_MACHINE\SYSTEM\CurrentContolSet\Control\Terminal Server is 1, or 0 if it's not enabled.

To determine whether Terminal Services is running in Remote Administration mode or Application Server mode, check the value of TSAppCompat in HKEY_LOCAL_MACHINE\

SYSTEM\CurrentContolSet\Control\Terminal Server. 0 is Remote Administration; 1 is Application Server.

To determine the permission compatibility, check the value of TSUserEnabled in HKEY_LOCAL_MACHINE\SYSTEM\CurrentContolSet\Control\Terminal Server. 0 is Windows 2000 Users; 1 is Terminal Server 4.0 Users.

To determine how Terminal Services is treating temporary directories on exit, check the value of DeleteTempDirsOn Exit in HKEY_LOCAL_MACHINE\SYSTEM\CurrentContolSet\ Control\Terminal Server. 0 is No; 1 is Yes.

To determine whether Terminal Services is using temporary folders per session, check the value of PerSessionTempDir in HKEY_LOCAL_MACHINE\SYSTEM\CurrentContolSet\ Control\Terminal Server. 0 is No; 1 is Yes.

To determine whether a flat temporary directory structure is used, rather than giving users a unique temporary directory, check the value of FlatTempDir in HKEY_LOCAL_MACHINE\SYSTEM\CurrentContolSet\Control\Terminal Server. By default, the value does not exist, you must add it to the registry manually or via the **flattemp** command-line utility. A value of 0 (the default) indicates the feature is disabled and per-user temporary directories are used; a value of 1 indicates the feature is enabled.

CODE BLUE

The two keys above, PerSessionTempDir and FlatTempDir, both control the same feature. PerSessionTempDir corresponds to the Use Temporary Folders Per Session option in the Server Settings window of Terminal Services Configuration. FlatTempDir corresponds to the **flattemp** command-line program (see Chapter 5). It's not unusual for a GUI tool to have a corresponding command-line option, but it is unusual for them not to change the same registry value.

If either of these keys is set for flat/non-user temp directories, temp directories will be flat. In other words, if FlatTempDir is 1 *or* PerSessionTempDir is 0, there will be one temp folder.

IdleWinStationPoolCount in HKEY_LOCAL_MACHINE\SYSTEM\CurrentContolSet\ Control\Terminal Server\: defines the number of idle sessions set up by Terminal Services at boot time. By default, in Remote Administration mode, this value is 0. In Application Server mode, it defaults to 2. To improve connection performance on lightly loaded servers, you can increase the number.

Microsoft does not document an allowed range for this value, but the maximum would likely be a trade-off involving your CPU and memory capacity; the more you have, the more idle sessions you can afford to allocate. If your server ever gets starved for CPU or memory, allocating idle sessions is just going to slow things down.

FirstCountMsgQPeeksSleepBadApp in HKEY_LOCAL_MACHINE\SYSTEM\ CurrentContolSet\Control\Terminal Server defines the number of times a program must query the message queue before Terminal Services decides that it is an ill-behaved application and suspends it for a period of time defined by the MsgQBadAppSleepTimeInMillisec value (discussed next). The default value is 0xF and the legal range is 0xF-0xFF. If you increase the number, you make the system more tolerant of CPU cycle-sucking programs at the expense of everyone's performance. If you make the number lower, you make Terminal Services more likely to kill applications that misbehave.

MsgQBadAppSleepTimeInMillisec in HKEY_LOCAL_MACHINE\SYSTEM\ CurrentContolSet\Control\Terminal Server defines the number of milliseconds a program is suspended when Terminal Services decides that it is ill behaved, according to the criteria defined in the FirstCountMsgQPeeksSleepBadApp data item.

NthCountMsgQPeeksSleepBadApp in HKEY_LOCAL_MACHINE\SYSTEM\CurrentContolSet\Control\Terminal Server defines the number of times that the program must query the message queue before Terminal Services suspends it again, after Terminal Services determines that an applications is ill behaved. In other words, this is the setting for programs that already have a bad rep.

Delegating Administration

Users who don't have administrator rights cannot log on to a Terminal server in Remote Administration mode by default. If they attempt to connect, they receive the following message: "You do not have access to log on to this Session."

If you want to delegate administrative responsibility for some servers to users to whom you don't want to grant administrator rights, you can do so for each Terminal Services connection. Go to the Terminal Services Configuration program, select the Properties sheet for the connection, and go to the Permissions tab.

By default, you should see Administrators and SYSTEM in this list. To add another user or group, click Add and add the users to whom you want to grant rights.

NOTE: This permissions dialog applies only to Terminal Services permissions, not other permissions.

Back in the permissions tab, the user(s) or groups(s) are added, but only with Guest Access rights, which is enough to log on to the server, but not enough to do anything administrative. In fact, if you select Advanced and then choose View/Edit (the Permission Entry for RDP-Tcp dialog) for the user, you'll see that Logon rights are all they have for the connection. Their rights for other operations, such as deleting files and creating directories, are separate from this operation, so if you don't want the user to be performing Terminal Services administration, Guest Access may be adequate.

If you apply User Access, the users/groups also get permissions to Query Information, Send Messages, and Connect To Sessions. If you grant Full Access, users gain full permissions to administer Terminal Services on that server. Of course, through the Permission Entry for RDP-Tcp dialog you can grant any custom mix of permissions to users.

NOTE: Even though non-administrators may use Terminal Services in Remote Administrative mode, the server is still restricted to two concurrent Remote Administration sessions. Many applications still do not run because necessary components are only installed when the server is in Application Server mode.

Peer-to-Peer and Windows NT 4.0 Networks

If your network is not a Windows 2000 domain, you can still run Terminal Services. Administration is somewhat different and, depending on your configuration, may be more cumbersome.

For example, in Windows 2000 if you have many Terminal servers, Active Directory makes administration of users a breeze, because you can set your policies centrally in the directory and they replicate throughout the domain. If your Windows 2000 Terminal servers are member servers in a Windows NT 4.0 domain, you can use Windows 2000 versions of User Manager and Server Manager to administer them. If you're in a peer-to-peer network, you have to do your Terminal Services administration locally on each of your Terminal servers.

Peer-to-Peer Networks

In a peer-to-peer network, also known as a workgroup, all servers must be administered individually. If you have more than one server, you must maintain user accounts and settings, including Terminal Services settings, on all of them.

NOTE: Just as with Active Directory, the user must have appropriate permissions to the Terminal Services Connection as well as to the server. See "Managing Terminal Services Connections" in Chapter 5.

To administer users, open the Computer Management MMC (Start | Programs | Administrative Tools | Computer Management). Under System Tools in the left pane, expand Local Users and Groups to see folders for Users and Groups.

Select a user and bring up the Properties page. If you are running Terminal Services on the server, you see (just as Active Directory Users and Computers users see) tabs on the Properties sheet for Terminal Services Profile and Remote Control. See "Home Directories and Profiles" later in this chapter for details on these settings in a peer-to-peer network.

Setting Remote Control Options

You can set remote control options on a user-level in Local Users and Groups on the Remote Control tab. You can make almost identical settings at the connection level in the Terminal Services Configuration program on the Remote Control tab (see "Remote Control" in Chapter 5).

NOTE: At the connection level, you can configure options to either accept or override the user-level settings for any users on that connection.

The main decision you need to make on this tab is whether to enable remote control when this user is logged in. You may specify two other parameters: whether the user should be asked for permission when another user attempts to take control of their system, and whether such controlling users should be able only to view the session remotely or to take actual control of it.

Set User Time Limits

Terminal Services sessions aren't like regular PCs that are left on all night. They consume server resources and thereby impede performance for other users. You can use the Sessions tab in Local Users and Groups to limit the impact.

End A Disconnected Session lets you specify the maximum amount of time that a session stays alive on the server after being disconnected. Depending on the value of this setting, a disconnected session may be available for reconnection from the same or a different client system for a specified period of time. When this time limit is reached, the disconnected session ends.

◆ Choose Never to keep the connection alive indefinitely.

◆ Choose a time limit from the drop-down list to specify the maximum time before disconnection.

◆ Specify an amount of time in days, hours, and minutes by entering a value in the combo box. Append d for days, h for hours, and m for minutes to the numbers. For example, "1d 2h 3m" is 1 day, 2 hours, 3 minutes.

The Active Session Limit overrides the user value for the maximum amount of time a session can remain active on the server. At the end of the specified time, the session is ended. You can specify the time for the Active Session Limit in the same manner as with End A Disconnected Session.

The Idle Session Limit setting controls the maximum amount of time a session can remain active while there is no user activity (keyboard or mouse movement). When the specified time elapses, the user is either disconnected or the session ended, depending on the state of the checkbox immediately below the Idle Session Limit setting.

NOTE: In Terminal Services Configuration, you can set an override for these user settings for an entire connection. On that program's Sessions tab are identical controls with identical mode of operation for configuring options. This is a coarser level of control, as it applies to all users over that connection, so you may want to use the user-level settings described above.

Starting Programs Automatically When Users Log On

On the Environment tab of Local Users and Groups, you can specify a program to run when the user logs on to Terminal Services, and enter the starting directory for the program. This setting overrides any user settings, such as when a user specifies a program to run in Client Connection Manager.

Connecting Client Devices to Terminal Services Sessions

On the Environment tab of Local Users and Groups you can also specify whether the client printers are made available to the Terminal Services session, and whether the default client printer is made the default printer for the Terminal Services session. There is also a setting for connecting client drives, but this is available only when Citrix MetaFrame is installed.

Windows NT 4.0 Domains

On Windows 2000 Server, Microsoft provides versions of the Windows NT 4.0 User Manager and Server Manager programs to administer network user access to the Terminal server and their capabilities on the server. Providing for Windows 2000 member servers adds about 1K to the SAM for each user.

Windows 2000 does not put a shortcut in the Programs menus to User Manager or Server Manager. Find %systemroot%\system32\usrmgr.exe and %systemroot%\system32\srvmgr.exe and create shortcuts to them so that you can call them up easily.

User Manager

For the most part, User Manager is identical to the NT 4.0 version, although there is a new button labeled TS Config (see Figure 6-4). To administer the Windows 2000 Terminal server, you must run the local version on the Windows 2000 server (see "Use Windows NT 4.0 Terminal Services Tools" later in this chapter for a way to use the Windows NT 4.0 Terminal Server Edition version).

The User Manager for Domains on your Windows NT 4.0 Server won't have the TS Config button, so you'll have to do all Terminal Services configuration on the Windows 2000

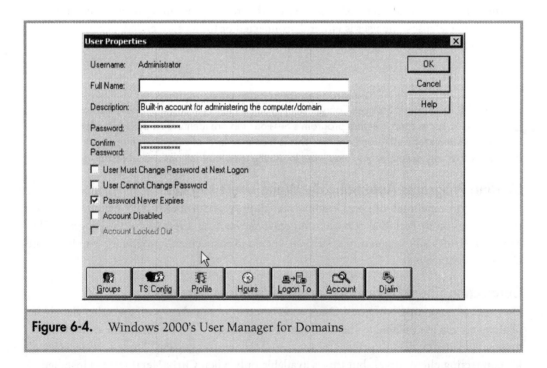

Figure 6-4. Windows 2000's User Manager for Domains

Server, which, luckily for you, is a Terminal server, so you can administer it remotely. Since you would only run the Windows 2000 User Manager on a member server in a domain, it is the equivalent of running User Manager for Domains. All your domain users appear in the user list.

Select a user and click on the TS Config button to see the User Configuration dialog box (see Figure 6-5). In this dialog box you will find settings that, on a Windows 2000 domain, would be spread out among many property sheets in Active Directory Users and Computers. This makes administration easier in some small ways for Windows NT 4.0 domains than for Windows 2000 domains.

At the top of the dialog box, specify whether the user should be allowed to log on to the Terminal server. In the Timeout Settings section, set the maximum time that a user can be connected, the maximum time that a disconnected session is maintained on a server before

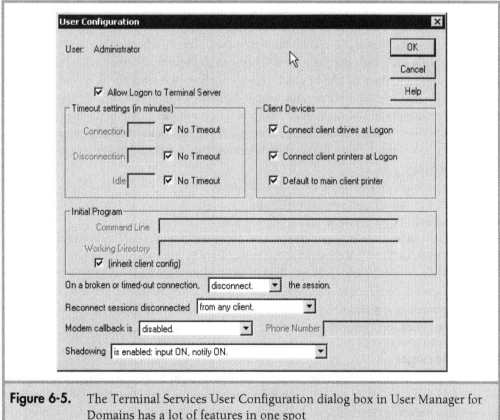

Figure 6-5.   The Terminal Services User Configuration dialog box in User Manager for Domains has a lot of features in one spot

being dropped, and the maximum amount of idle time in a session before it is disconnected. All times are in minutes and all the timeouts default to off.

In the Client Devices section, specify whether users can have client drives and printers connected at logon, and whether the main client printer is set as the default printer.

NOTE: The ability to connect client drives at logon is available only with the Citrix MetaFrame add-on software. In a Windows 2000 domain, this checkbox is grayed out if MetaFrame is not installed. The Drive Share utility in the Windows 2000 Server Resource Kit (see "Using Drive Share to Make Users' Local Drives Accessible" earlier in this chapter) provides a similar facility, although it does so by creating network shares on the clients.

In the Initial Program section, you can specify a program that the client should load automatically upon logon, and a working directory for the program. By default, this section is set to use the setting the user specifies in Client Connection Manager. If you make a setting here in User Manager, it overrides the client setting.

Below that section, you can specify behavior in the event of a broken or timed-out connection, either to disconnect or reset it. Then you can specify whether a disconnected session belonging to the user can be reconnected only from the same client system or from any client. Then, if you have MetaFrame installed and are using Citrix ICA clients, you can say whether modem callback is disabled, and whether the server prompts the user for a phone number or to a fixed number. If you are specifying a default or fixed number, there is a space for it to the right. You can specify callback options for Terminal Services users using the RAS service.

Finally, you can make remote control (shadowing) settings. You can disable it, specify whether the controlling user can control or only view the session, and specify whether the client is notified that someone is attempting to shadow the session.

Back in the main User Manager screen, select a user and click the Profile button to see a few new fields for Terminal Services users. In the User Profiles section you can specify a Terminal Services profile, which, if specified, is used when the user connects via Terminal Services. There is also a Terminal Services Home Directory section that can be used to specify a separate home directory and mapped drive if the user connects via Terminal Services. See the "Home Directories and Profiles" in this chapter.

Server Manager

Server Manager (see Figure 6-6) has no new features relevant to Terminal Services. It is provided so that you can do domain administration from the Terminal server just as with any member server in the Windows NT 4.0 domain.

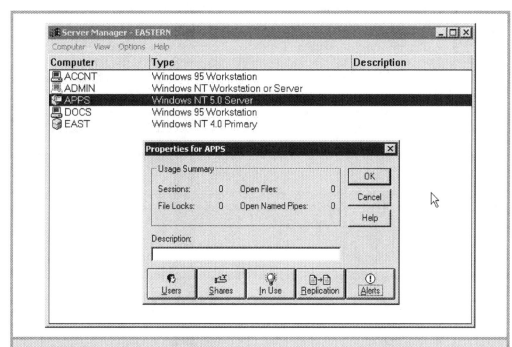

Figure 6-6. Windows 2000's Server Manager for Windows NT 4.0 domains

CODE BLUE

If you attempt to connect to Terminal Services, you may be denied logon and see an error message: "Your interactive logon privilege has been disabled. Please contact your system administrator."

There are several possible causes of this problem. According to Microsoft, this error may occur more frequently when the Terminal server is a member server in a Windows NT 4.0 domain. The first place to check, especially if the problem is occurring only with some users, is whether the Allow Logon To Terminal Server checkbox is checked. In a Windows NT 4.0 domain, this option is in User Manager for Domains. In a Windows 2000 domain, the option is in Active Directory Users and Computers. In a workgroup, the option is in Computer Management, under Local Users and Groups.

If the Allow Logon To Terminal Server checkbox is not the problem, you should check that all the relevant users have appropriate permissions for the connection. If the problem is widespread, affecting large numbers of users, this is the more likely cause. To check this, go to Terminal Services Configuration and open the Properties sheet for the connection. On the Permissions tab, make sure that all the users have at least User Access to the connection.

NOTE: Some of these errors may not be recorded in the event logs of the clients or servers.

Use Windows NT 4.0 Terminal Services Tools

If you have access to a copy of Windows NT 4.0 Terminal Server Edition (TSE), you can copy the User Manager files from it to your Windows NT 4.0 Server, specifically the domain controller, and use it to administer Terminal Services features on the Windows NT 4.0 box. The files you need are:

◆ regapi.dll

◆ usrmgr.exe

◆ utildll.dll

◆ winsta.dll

You can retrieve these files from an existing installation of TSE by copying them from the %systemroot%\system32 directory (which, in TSE, is likely \WTSRV\System32). You can retrieve then from the TSE CD from the \i386 directory, but they will be compressed files with underscores replacing the last letter of file extension (for example, usrmgr.ex_). You will need to expand them with the Microsoft Expand utility. Place them in the %systemroot%\system32 directory of the domain controller and create a link to usrmgr.exe.

It's probably better to use a version from an installed and up-to-date version of TSE, if that installation has the most recent service packs applied.

Home Directories and Profiles

It's generally a good idea in a Windows NT 4.0 or Windows 2000 network to assign home directories to users. In Terminal Services it's basically mandatory. By default, users have home directories assigned as the *<LogonName>* subdirectory under the Documents and Settings directory.

Terminal Services Home Directories

Terminal Services users can have a special home directory for when they are logged in under Terminal Services. Over time, if you use roaming profiles, using this second home directory can improve system performance, especially at logon time. Remember that users frequently save documents to their home directories. When a user logs on to Windows 2000, and the account is set up for roaming profiles, the operating system copies everything from the user's profile directory to their profile cache. If the home directory is inside the profile directory (which it is by default), logons can slow down a great deal, especially if roaming profiles are stored across the network, and profile caches can balloon up unnecessarily.

Instead, you can specify a separate home directory for Terminal Services. On a user-by-user basis you can go in Local Users and Groups or User Manager for Domains and find the user for whom you want to specify a home directory or Terminal Services Home Directory. For a workgroup, in Local Users and Computers, this setting is on the Terminal Services Profile tab of the user's property sheet (see Figure 6-7). For a Windows NT 4.0 domain, select the Profile button in User Manager for Domains.

If you specify a Terminal Services Home Directory, whether or not you specify a regular home directory path in the Profile tab or Local Users and Groups or the Profile dialog of User Manager for Domains, the user's home directory is the Terminal Services home directory when he logs on using Terminal Services. These settings for non-Terminal Services home directory and profile in the Profile tab of Local Users and Groups and the Profile dialog of User Manager for Domains have no effect on users logging on under Terminal Services.

If the user logs on locally to the system, or if he logs on under Terminal Services with no Terminal Services Home Directory specified, the home directory is the %SystemDrive%\ Documents and Settings\%username% folder.

Remember that if the user logs on to the console of the Terminal server, the Terminal Services profile and Terminal Services Home Directory are not used. Instead, if a normal home directory is specified, this is used; if none is specified, the home directory is %SystemDrive%\Documents and Settings\%username%.

When you specify a Terminal Services home directory and use %username% in the name, Terminal Services automatically creates the username subdirectory and gives it appropriate permissions. Users have full access to their own home directories. Administrators can copy files into them, but not read or delete files.

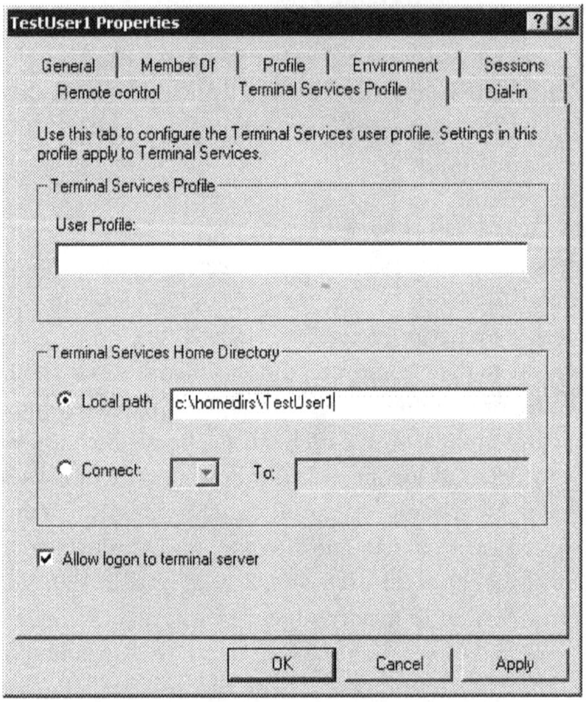

Figure 6-7. You can specify a separate home directory for users when they log on under Terminal Services

Use a Single RootDrive for Your Users

The first time you run application compatibility scripts, you are asked to set a drive letter that references what Terminal Services internally calls the RootDrive. This same letter is used for all subsequent application compatibility scripts. Furthermore, when users log on, Windows 2000 executes a batch file named usrlogon.cmd, located in %systemroot%, which does a lot of complicated stuff, including setting the ROOTDRIVE environment variable to a value (%HomeDrive%%HomePath%) expected by many third-party applications. Therefore, it's a really good idea to settle on one letter for all your users for this purpose.

See Chapters 4 and 9 for more on application compatibility scripts.

Managing User Profiles

By default, in Terminal Services, the user profile comes from the server the user logs on to, so if she connects to multiple Terminal servers, she ends up with multiple profiles. A roaming profile, one that is stored in a central location, is the answer to this, just as it is the answer for conventional LAN users who may log on from one of many workstations. No matter which server the user logs on to, she will retrieve the profile from the specified location. Unless the administrator specifies otherwise, a local cached copy will remain on the Terminal server on which the user is running. When users log on, the dates of the local cached and server profiles are compared, and if the server profile is newer, the cached version is overwritten.

Terminal Services provides user entries in the Terminal Services Profile tab in Local Users and Groups and the Profile dialog box in User Manager for Domains so you can specify specific profiles for users when logged on under Terminal Services.

If you specify a Terminal Services profile for a user, that profile is used when the user logs on under Terminal Services. If you have not specified a Terminal Services profile, but have specified a roaming profile, that profile is used. If you have not specified a roaming profile, the default user profile is used, which is the user's Ntuser.dat file in (usually) %SystemDrive%\Documents and Settings\%username%.

If your users log on to multiple Terminal servers, you almost certainly want to create Terminal Services profiles. Even if you have users who sometimes log on with Terminal Services and sometimes not, their profiles under Terminal Services will likely be different from the non-Terminal Services profile. In that case, specify a standard roaming profile and a Terminal Services profile. If your users only ever use a single Terminal server, you need not be concerned with Terminal Services profiles.

TAKE COMMAND

The **tsprof** command copies user profile information from one user to another. It can also set the profile path for a user. You must have administrator rights to use **tsprof**.

The syntax for **tsprof** is:

tsprof /update [**/domain**:*domainname*|**/local**] **/profile**:*path username*

tsprof /copy   [**/domain**:*domainname*|**/local**] [**/profile**:*path*] *src_usr dest_usr*

tsprof /q   [**/domain**:*domainname*|**/local**] *username*

where:

/update updates the profile path in domain *domainname* to *path*.

/copy copies user profile from *src_usr* to *dest_usr*. Update profile path information for *dest_usr* to *path*.

/q displays the current profile path for *username*'s profile.

/domain:*domainname* is the name of the domain in which the profiles exist.

/local applies only to local user accounts.

/profile:*path* is the location of the profile.

src_usr is the name of the user whose profile you want to copy.

dest_usr is the name of the user whose profile you want to overwrite.

username is the name of the user whose profile you want to query or update.

TAKE COMMAND

The **cprofile** command cleans user profiles to get rid of wasted space. You need administrator rights to run it. Profiles that are in use are not affected, so you may want to schedule it to run at a time when the server is least busy. This program also removes user-specific file associations that are disabled. The syntax is:

cprofile [/i] [/l] [/v] *filelist*

where:

/i interactively prompts the user to confirm cleaning each profile.

/l cleans all local profiles. You can still add other files in the file list.

/v displays verbose information about the operation.

filelist specifies a list of files to clean.

Licensing

In a Windows 2000 domain, the licensing server must run on a domain controller. In a Windows NT 4.0 domain or peer network, the licensing server may run on any Windows 2000 member server. Apart from that, the behavior of the licensing service is identical to that in a Windows 2000 domain. See Chapter 8 for more detail on licensing.

Windows Scripting Host

Windows 2000 is a powerful administration environment, but you're not really free to do whatever you want unless you can write scripts. In the case of Windows 2000, Windows Scripting Host (WSH) is an ideal scripting environment. It's available by default in all Windows 2000 systems.

In this section, I won't teach you programming or even WSH. I will discuss some of the more relevant features of WSH and provide a couple of useful examples. WSH is definitely a topic you should investigate further, and the place to begin is the Microsoft Scripting Technologies Web site at http://msdn.microsoft.com/scripting/.

The WshNetwork Object

In the context of Terminal Services, the most interesting administrative feature of Windows Scripting Host is the WshNetwork object. It contains three properties, ComputerName, UserDomain, and UserName (the names are, I hope, sufficiently self-explanatory). There are also methods for managing printer connections and network drives.

AddPrinterConnection

This method creates a new printer connection. The syntax for the method is:

object.**AddPrinterConnection** *LocalConnectionName,*
RemoteConnectionName[,*UpdateUserProfile*][,*UserName*][,*Password*]

where:

object   The instance of the WshNetwork object.

LocalConnectionName   The local name of the printer (for example, LPT1).

RemoteConnectionName   The network name of the printer (for example, \\server1\HPLJ4MV).

UpdateUserProfile   True or false; if supplied and true, the printer connection is added to the user profile.

UserName, Password   If the printer mapping must be done by an account other than the user's (presumably because the user lacks adequate permissions), these are the username and password.

Note that the PrinterDriver name has to be exactly as it appears for that printer in the %SystemRoot%\inf\ntprint.inf file.

EnumPrinterConnection

This method enumerates the current printer mappings. The syntax for the method is:

*Printers = object.***EnumPrinterConnections**

where:

Printers   A collection of printer mapping objects.

object   The instance of the WshNetwork object.

RemovePrinterConnection

This method removes a current printer connection. The syntax for the method is:

*object.***RemovePrinterConnection** *PrinterName* [*,ForceRemoval*] [*,UpdateUserProfile*]

where:

object   The instance of the WshNetwork object.

PrinterName   The name of the printer connection to remove. If the connection is a mapping to a local printer, *PrinterName* should be a local printer name, such as LPT1:. If the connection is not mapped to a local port, the network name of the printer should be used (for example, \\server1\HPLJ4MV).

ForceRemoval   True or false; if supplied and true, the connection is removed whether it is used or not.

UpdateUserProfile   True or false; if supplied and true, the printer connection is removed from the user profile.

SetDefaultPrinter

This method sets a printer connection as the default printer. The syntax for the method is:

   object.**SetDefaultPrinter** *PrinterName*

where:

   object   The instance of the WshNetwork object.

   PrinterName   The name of the printer connection to set as default. This should be a remote network name, such as \\server1\HPLJ4MV.

MapNetworkDrive

This method creates a new network drive mapping. The syntax for the method is:

   object.**MapNetworkDrive** *LocalDriveName, RemoteShareName* [,*UpdateUserProfile*] [,*UserName*] [,*Password*]

where:

   object   The instance of the WshNetwork object.

   LocalDriveName   The local name of the share (for example, F:).

   RemoteShareName   The network name of the share (for example, \\server1\sharename).

   UpdateUserProfile   True or false; if supplied and true, the drive mapping is added to the user profile.

   UserName, Password   If the drive mapping must be done by an account other than the user's (presumably because the user lacks adequate permissions), these are the username and password.

EnumNetworkDrives

This method enumerates the current drive mappings. The syntax for the method is:

   Drives = *object*.EnumNetworkDrive

where:

   Drives   A collection of drive mapping objects.

   object   The instance of the WshNetwork object.

RemoveNetworkDrive

This method removes a current drive mapping. The syntax for the method is:

object.**RemovePrinterConnection** *DriveName* [*,ForceRemoval*] [*,UpdateUserProfile*]

where:

object   The instance of the WshNetwork object.

DriveName   The name of the drive mapping to remove. If the connection is a mapping to a local drive letter, *strName* should be a local drive letter, such as Z:. If the connection is not mapped to a local drive, the network name of the share should be used (for example, \\server1\sharename).

ForceRemoval   True or false; if supplied and true, the connection is removed whether it is used or not.

UpdateUserProfile   True or false; if supplied and true, the connection is removed from the user profile.

Scripting Examples for Terminal Services

The best examples of scripting with respect to Terminal Services have to do with logon scripts and other scripts that run when a user logs on. There are actually a number of places from which you can run scripts when a user logs on. Here are just a few examples:

+ You could put a shortcut to the script in the startup folder for the All Users profile.

+ You could add it as an actual logon script in Group Policy\User Configuration\Windows Settings\Scripts (Logon/Logoff).

+ You could add it to the list of scripts in the value of AppSetup in the key HKEY_LOCAL_MACHINE\Software\Microsoft\Windows NT\CurrentVersion\ Winlogon. This data value is added by Terminal Services, and by default contains usrlogon.cmd, which makes environment changes related to application compatibility scripts. You can add other programs to the data item by separating them with commas (for example, "usrlogon.cmd, mysettings.vbs"). All programs in the list will be run when you log on to Terminal Services.

I'll give two examples: adding a printer mapping and adding a drive mapping. In each case, you could tediously add these setting to user profiles manually, but a central script, as you will see, has some amazing advantages. For example, you can add the settings for individual users by testing for them in the script.

In the examples below, I make a point of testing the UserName and other properties of the WshNetwork object.

This lets you write one script that deals with everyone. Even if you just want to make a change on a single user or computer, you can make it in a central script like this. Note that you could make decisions just as easily based on the computer name by using the ComputerName property or the domain name with the DomainName property.

Adding a Printer Mapping in a Script

```
Set WshNetwork = CreateObject("WScript.Network")
Select Case WshNetWork.UserName
Case "UserA"
    PrinterPath = \\Server\PrinterShareName1
    PrinterDriver = "HP LaserJet 5MP"
    WshNetwork.AddWindowsPrinterConnection PrinterPath, PrinterDriver
    WshNetwork.SetDefaultPrinter \\Server\PrinterShareName1
Case "Username2"
    PrinterPath = \\Server\PrinterShareName2
    PrinterDriver = "Canon LBP-1260 PS"
    WshNetwork.AddWindowsPrinterConnection PrinterPath, PrinterDriver
    WshNetwork.SetDefaultPrinter \\Server\PrinterShareName2
End Select
```

Adding a Drive Mapping in a Script

```
Set WshNetwork = CreateObject("WScript.Network")
Select Case WshNetWork.UserName
Case "UserA"
    LocalDriveName = "Z:"
    RemoteShareName = \\Server\FolderShareName1
    WshNetWork.MapNetworkDrive LocalDriveName, RemoteShareName
Case "Username2"
    LocalDriveName = "Z:"
    RemoteShareName = \\Server\FolderShareName2
    WshNetWork.MapNetworkDrive LocalDriveName, RemoteShareName
End Select
```

Determining a User's Group Memberships in a Script

If you want to determine whether a user is a member of a particular group, you have to get a little fancier and involve the Active Directory Services Interface (ADSI). ADSI is standard in Windows 2000. If you want to run this on a non-Terminal Services, potentially non-Windows 2000 system, make sure the system has ADSI installed.

Consider the following script:

```
set wshShell = Wscript.CreateObject("Wscript.Shell")
Set WshNetwork = CreateObject("WScript.Network")
dsRoot = "WinNT://" & WshNetWork.UserDomain & "/" & WshNetWork.UserName
set dsObj = GetObject(dsRoot)
For Each Prop In dsobj.groups
    if Prop.Name = "Domain Admins" then
        wshshell.popup "I'm A Domain Admin!"
    End If
Next 'Prop
```

The script creates a WshNetwork Object (see "Windows Scripting Host" earlier in this chapter) and uses it to determine the user's domain and username. It then creates an ADSI dsRoot object using the username and domain name in the form: WinNT://DomainName/UserName.

That object has a collection called "groups" which are all the groups the user belongs to. The script cycles through the groups, testing to see if the user is a member of Domain Admins and brings up a message if she is. The script could just as easily map drives, copy files, or anything else.

Chapter 7

Optimizing Performance

P erformance optimization of Terminal Services is a complicated issue, one which, of necessity, requires analysis by you, the administrator, and which cannot always be put into clearly defined, ordered steps.

Still, you have many tools at your disposal to avoid and solve performance problems, and I'll describe them in this chapter.

Avoid Problems by Testing

I hope I've gotten this point across in previous chapters, but it's an important one and cannot be over-emphasized: the best way to avoid problems in a Terminal Services installation is to test your software before actually deploying it to your poor, suffering users.

The support people at Microsoft are of one mind on this, and have told me that if customers would test their applications appropriately before deployment, especially large deployments, those deployments would go more smoothly. Both incompatibility and performance problems could be avoided. A good test can also provide some baseline information for administrators to use for judging whether applications are performing acceptably in the deployment.

Design a Good Test Lab

As with your applications, it is best to design your test lab with a hardware inventory as close as possible to that which will be used in deployment.

Try to use a server system as close in configuration as possible to the deployment server, and try to use one from the same vendor. The server is (obviously, I hope) the most important factor in judging Terminal Services performance.

Network organization is also very important to testing Terminal Services. Try, as best you can, to duplicate the organization's network configuration in your test lab. If performance is a significant consideration, you should test on an isolated network segment so you can accurately judge whether network bandwidth is acceptable (and so that other users aren't affected by the test). If you have a WAN connecting two offices or even connecting Terminal Services clients to servers, use a link simulator to generate the latency of the slow lines.

If you have multiple networks for multiple offices, or other organizational divisions in your company, you can usually get away with one test network, adjusting it as appropriate to the circumstances. For example, one office might have more physical network segments than another; this could affect performance, so you should try to adjust your test network to represent that configuration.

In Terminal Services, the actual client systems are not as important as the rest of the configuration, but you should try to have clients in the test representative of those that will be used in deployment, both in terms of hardware configuration and software. Some features, such as the version of the client operating system and any network-related software,

are more important than others—for example, whether a CD-ROM drive is available. Consider the implications for Terminal Services.

Design Good Tests

The key to a successful and proper test, and the hardest part to do, is to identify just what users will be doing on the Terminal servers and set up tests to replicate those tasks. Even a simple manual replication of the tasks will uncover some non-performance issues. For instance, if an application performs operations incompatible with Windows 2000 or Terminal Services, you'll know immediately. But if you set up a series of automated tasks, you can also uncover performance problems before you deploy to production servers.

Appendix A describes the Terminal Services Capacity Planning tools which you can use to automate tests of applications, including emulating users typing and pausing for periods of time. You can use the tools to run multiple client sessions so that you can simulate many more client systems than you actually have. See the section "Using Windows Network Load Balancing Services" later in this chapter for complications that may arise when using these tools.

There are simpler ways to test as well. If you can represent a real workload using a batch file that runs on the server, there are any number of ways you can set up that batch file to run automatically when the user logs on (see the sidebar in this section on automatically running programs when a user logs on to the server). Simply by putting **logoff** at the end of the batch file you can end the client session. You can also use the **sleep** command-line command to put pauses in the test. Then create batch files on the client that launch the Terminal Services client and load the right session.

TAKE COMMAND

The **sleep** command pauses the console or batch file for the specified number of seconds. This command can be useful in test scripts. By creating pauses, you can make more realistic patterns of program execution.

The syntax for **sleep** is:

> **sleep** *num_seconds*

where:

> *num_seconds* is the number of seconds to pause.

TAKE COMMAND

The **logoff** command logs the user off of a session. In the case of Terminal Services, it also disconnects the session.

The syntax for **logoff** is:

logoff [**/server**:*servername*] [*sessionname* | *sessionid*] [**/v**]

where:

/server:*servername* specifies the Terminal server to log off of (the default is the current server).

sessionname specifies the name of the session to log off of.

sessionid specifies the ID of the session to log off of.

/v causes the command to display verbose information about the logoff as it happens.

The applications you test need to be representative of what the real users will be using. To add a human touch, bring in a few unsophisticated users and have them work for a little while, asking them whether this works for them. Bribe them with a t-shirt you got from a vendor.

Automatically Running Programs When a User Logs On

Sometimes you'd think that Microsoft has a whole department dreaming up ways you can automatically launch programs when a user starts Windows or logs on to a computer.

In the context of a user logging on to a Windows 2000 Server, which is the case for Terminal Services users, there are many options. By creating a batch file with the **logoff** command at the end, you can fully automate a user session.

In such cases, where you are automating for test purposes, you need to define a connection that automatically logs the user on. Remember that this is not usually a good idea in production environments.

The available automation methods are:

✦ In the Client Connection Manager Wizard, on the Starting a Program screen, you can specify the location of a program on the server that will execute after the user connects and logs on.

✦ Put a program or a shortcut to a program in the user's Startup folder.

✦ Run a program from the domain or OU logon script, which you can specify in Group Policy\User Configuration\Windows Settings\Scripts (Logon/Logoff).

✦ Group Policy gives you an extra policy from which to specify programs to run at logon: Group Policy\Administrative Templates\System\Logon/Logoff (the policy is named Run These Programs At User Logon).

✦ Specify the command line in a string value in the registry key HKEY_CURRENT_USER\Software\Microsoft\Windows\CurrentVersion\Run.

✦ Specify the command line in the Environment tab of the user's property sheet in Active Directory Users and Computers.

✦ Specify a user logon script in the Profile tab of the user's property sheet in Active Directory Users and Computers. This script must be located in the NETLOGON share which, by default, is in %SystemRoot%\SYSVOL\sysvol\DNS Domain Name Of The Server>\scripts, where "Domain Name Of The Server" is literally the domain name of the server. If the DNS domain name of the server is "wackawacka.foo.com," the key is %SystemRoot%\SYSVOL\sysvol\ wackawacka.foo.com\scripts.

Tuning DOS and Win16 Programs

DOS and 16-bit Windows programs present special performance problems for Terminal Services. Such programs tend to slow down everything else that runs on the system.

Even though they use only 16-bit instructions, as opposed to standard 32-bit instructions, these programs require about 25 percent more memory than 32-bit applications, mostly because of the overhead of NTVDM, the program that creates the 16-bit DOS and Windows environment in which the programs run.

Furthermore, most operating system calls from these programs must be passed through a translation layer (called a thunk) to the Win32 operating system facilities, another source of performance distress.

Finally, the memory and processing burden of these applications is increased even further if you set them up, as you probably should, to run in separate 16-bit sessions. By default, all 16-bit programs run in the context of a single ntvdm.exe session. But 16-bit programs can more easily interfere with each other than 32-bit programs, so there's an increased risk that one of your 16-bit programs will bring another program down and lose work for many users.

The best solution is not to use 16-bit programs, but the feature is available because some people need it. If you need to use 16-bit programs, be sure to protect yourself from their weaknesses.

A common technique is to isolate all DOS and Win16 programs on a single Terminal server or set of Terminal servers so they don't interfere with the performance of the Win32 programs. You may actually need to use more memory in these servers, depending on the number of users accessing them.

In a multiserver environment such as this, another common technique to make things easier for users is to let them run the legacy applications through a Terminal Services client on the main Terminal server. In other words, if the users normally log on to one server and get their desktop there, some of the icons on that desktop should be connections made in Client Connection Manager (see Chapter 3) directly to the legacy applications on the other Terminal server that runs the 16-bit applications.

Avoid Inappropriate Applications

In earlier chapters, we discussed how you should avoid some applications in a Terminal Services environment because they may make the system unstable. In terms of performance, some applications can be a special burden on overall system performance beyond the extra CPU and memory needs of DOS and Win16 programs. See Chapter 4 for a discussion of these issues and how you can mitigate the performance implications in some cases.

But even with modern Win32 software, some applications are not designed to function optimally in a server environment. Microsoft Access applications are a good example. Because Terminal Services simulates a single-user environment to the user, it's tempting to think that single user applications are inherently appropriate. This is a sure path to disappointing performance.

Access and other file-based database systems are engineered to run on single-user PCs with full control of system resources. If you're running your applications in a server environment, you ought to use a database designed for a server environment, such as Oracle, Microsoft SQL Server, Sybase, and so on.

Monitoring Performance

Windows 2000 comes with a powerful set of performance monitoring tools that you can use to determine the source of performance problems on a server or network. If you've been a network administrator for a while you're probably already familiar with Perfmon, which can be found in the Administrative Tools program group, where it's named Performance.

The best way to use Perfmon is to use it first during your testing period. By running Perfmon during your tests and logging the results, you can establish a baseline for your applications, in terms of the CPU, memory, and other resources they consume. After you deploy the application, you can compare the real-world consumption and server performance to what you saw in your controlled test conditions. This can be invaluable in determining the sources of problems.

The Windows 2000 Server Resource Kit has a variety of performance measurement tools that I won't be going into in detail. Many of them are simple, single-purpose tools that illustrate data more fully explored in Perfmon and other tools.

Perfmon

Perfmon in Windows 2000 is an MMC program. If you prefer the old-fashioned Perfmon, the Windows 2000 Server Resource Kit comes with a non-MMC version. They work similarly and I saw all the same performance counters in each, but this discussion refers to the MMC version.

Perfmon works by monitoring performance-related activities, called performance counters, in the system and in applications. To be more specific, Windows 2000 has a wide variety of Performance objects and each has one or more performance counters. The most obvious, and often the most important, are items such as the amount of memory and CPU consumed by a particular program. Windows 2000 has a very large number of performance counters, and you may need to go fishing for the right one.

 NOTE: In the Add Counters dialog box, you can get an explanation for each performance counter. These make for useful reading.

Programs can create their own Performance objects and counters, and Terminal Services itself presents a variety of performance counters you can monitor to track its performance.

Add Counters to the Display

To add a counter to the display, select the + icon from the button bar. Unlike most programs, there are few menu equivalents for the most common operations and almost no keyboard shortcuts.

In the Add Counters dialog box, select performance objects and one or more counters for each object to add to the running graph of data. Perfmon also lets you connect to remote servers, assuming you have adequate permissions. You can monitor counters from different servers on the same graph, which can be useful if you have multiple servers running the same applications and you want to diagnose problems that are occurring on only some of them.

After you add your counters, they appear in a list below the graph that shows their data. As you select a counter, its last results are displayed between the counter list and the graph. Figure 7-1 shows the counter for Terminal Services Inactive Sessions.

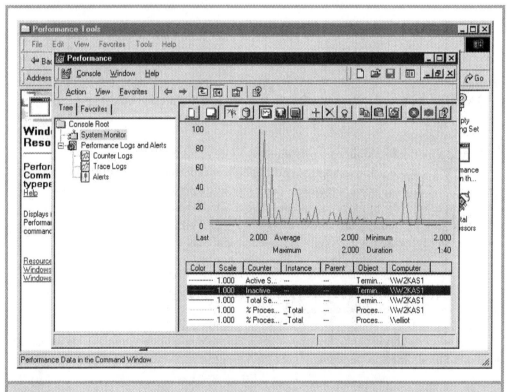

Figure 7-1.   Perfmon lets you track performance parameters on multiple systems

TAKE COMMAND

The **typeperf** command from the Windows 2000 Server Resource Kit outputs performance
data to a console session. It's not as useful a command-line tool as most; you can get the
same data by logging results in the regular Perfmon. But it's here if you want it.
The syntax for **typeperf** is:

 typeperf *nn counter [,counter…]*

where:

 nn is the number of seconds between samples of the performance counter.

 counter is the full path to a performance counter, such as *server_name*\Terminal
 Services\Total Sessions.

Setting Perfmon Properties

Right-clicking on any part of the Perfmon display and selecting Properties brings up a
property sheet that lets you customize characteristics of the program. I won't go into detail
on all aspects of the dialog box, as most of it will be obvious to any experienced Windows
user. However, there are some interesting features worth discussing.

On the Source tab, you can tell Perfmon to display data from current monitoring activity
or to read a previously recorded log file and display its data. As Figure 7-2 shows, you can
also specify the time range you want to display from the log file.

The list of counters on the Data tab is simply the list you created when you added
counters. But on the Data tab you can remove counters or change their graph color and style.

Logging Performance Data

The left pane of the Perfmon MMC has an entry for Performance Logs and Alerts that has
(by default) three entries: Counter Logs, Trace Logs, and Alerts. You should be concerned
mostly with counter logs and alerts.

Counter Logs Counter logs are simply log files of counter events. You can set these to
record specific counters to a specific log file, using the same Add Counter user interface.

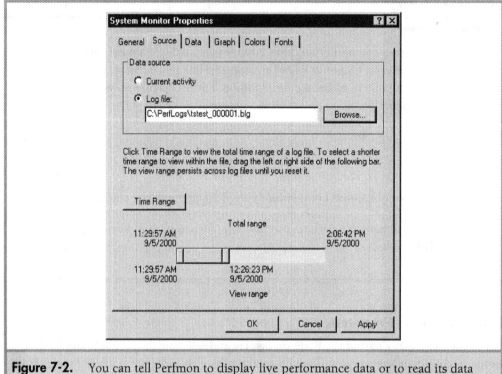

Figure 7-2. You can tell Perfmon to display live performance data or to read its data from a log file

You can schedule the log to be active at particular times. Log files can also be written in several different formats:

- ✦ A proprietary binary format
- ✦ A binary circular file format that lets you limit the size of the file
- ✦ Comma-separated text
- ✦ Tab-separated text

You can import these files into other programs, such as Excel, and perform analysis on them there. If you do serious logging, you will find yourself performing analysis in other programs, as Perfmon cannot even print its own data.

Alerts   Alerts are conditions you can test for on a counter, such as when CPU utilization reaches 100 percent. Create a new alert and add one or more counters, setting maximum or minimum values for them. When your conditions are met, the system issues an alert. You can define an alert as any of the following:

- An entry is written to the application event log (the default)
- A network message is sent to a particular computer
- A new performance log is started
- A program you specify executes

Key Perfmon Counters

With hundreds of counters available, you might want to know which are the most interesting from the point of view of Terminal Services performance. In this section, I'll define some counters that are particularly important, although depending on what your applications do, others could have relevance.

Generic Performance Counters   Generic performance counters are those that aren't specific to Terminal Services. The following are generic counters you should track:

- **% Processor Time**   The average of the percentage of time active on all processors in the system. (Active means the process is running a thread other than the idle process.) Under the Processor Performance object, choose % Processor Time from the counter list and choose _Total from the instance list on the right. If you have a multiprocessor system, you can also see the percentage of active time for each CPU, which is useful to ensure that all processors are servicing waiting threads. If some processors are servicing more than others, you are not necessarily seeing a problem; depending on the value of the Processor Queue Length counter, you may simply not have enough load on the system to use all your processors fully.

- **Processor Queue Length**   The length of the processor queue in terms of threads. Under the System Performance object, choose Processor Queue Length from the counter list. Since Windows 2000 uses symmetric multiprocessing, there is a single queue for all processors on the system. This is an instantaneous reading, not an average over time, so you should observe it over a period of time. According to Microsoft, a sustained reading on this value greater than two indicates processor congestion. This measure, in combination with others, can indicate whether your tested load could benefit from additional processors.

❖ **Data Transfer Over Network Interface**   Offers many counters, including Bytes Sent or Received over the network interface. In the Network Interface Performance object, select Bytes Received/sec, Bytes Sent/sec, or Bytes Total/sec counters, and then to the right select either all instances or a particular network interface. In a performance-stressed situation, one of the possibilities is that the network interface itself is maxed-out, and this measure can indicate whether your system would benefit from additional network segments.

❖ **Interrupts/sec**   The number of interrupts per second that the processor is receiving. If the computer has multiple processors, it's the total. There's no particular reason to suspect this metric in a Terminal Services environment, but it's always a good one to check, especially in a server that has many I/O devices in it. In addition to indicating a hardware problem, a high count could indicate that a device driver is consuming an inordinate amount of processor time.

❖ **Available Memory**   The amount of memory in a variety of memory pools which roughly sum up to available physical memory. In the Memory Performance object, select Available Bytes, Kbytes, or Mbytes. This is an instantaneous reading, not an average over time.

❖ **Page Inputs/sec**   Measures the number of pages read from disk to satisfy page faults, which are accesses to memory that has been paged out to disk. In the Memory Performance object, select Pages Input/sec. Microsoft considers this a primary indicator of system performance, as it shows how overcommitted the system is, and whether you might need additional physical RAM.

Terminal Services Perfmon Counters   There are two Terminal Services performance objects: Terminal Services and Terminal Services Session. The Terminal Services object has just three counters, Active Sessions, Inactive Sessions, and Total Sessions, the meaning of all of which is fairly obvious.

The Terminal Services Session object has, at my count, 75 performance counters, each of which you can measure for each Terminal Services session. These measures may be illustrative of a cause if you see a more general problem under Terminal Services that you didn't observe without it.

Another potential use would be to tune client-side settings for data compression and bitmap caching. You can turn these features on and off for a connection in Client Connection Manager. In the Terminal Services Client Registry Settings program in the Windows 2000 Server Resource Kit, you can fine-tune client use of some of these settings. See the "Tuning Client Performance" section later in this chapter for details.

Task Manager

Task Manager displays a lot of performance data on the system, although in a much more summarized form than Perfmon. For example, you can see all the processes in the system, their memory usage and CPU consumption. You can also see instantaneous and historical measures of overall CPU and memory utilization, as well as instantaneous measures of memory and other types of consumption.

Without dealing with all the details in Perfmon, you can quickly tell a lot from Task Manager, and sometimes it's convenient to be in a program where you can kill a process easily.

Netmon

You can use Network Monitor (Netmon) to detect and troubleshoot problems related to network traffic. Netmon is not installed by default on Windows 2000 Server. To install it, go to the Add/Remove Programs Control Panel applet, and select Add/Remove Windows Components to enter the Windows Components Wizard. Select Management And Monitoring Tools and click the Details button. In the Management And Monitoring Tools dialog box that appears, select Network Monitor Tools and then complete the Windows Components Wizard.

Netmon captures statistics on network traffic. The program's Capture window displays a graph representing current activity and offers statistics about network sessions. You can use the Frame Viewer window to display captured data. Use File | Open from either window to view a capture file (*.cap).

Netmon doesn't have a great reputation for being powerful or easy, and many network administrators prefer hardware-based network "sniffers" from companies like Network General, which are certainly easier to use.

The importance of using Netmon (or any network traffic monitor) is to see if problems you've been blaming on Terminal Services are really caused by a more basic issue such as a bad NIC or a problem with a router.

Using Windows Network Load Balancing Services

If your Terminal Services network is busy, you can use Windows Network Load Balancing Services to distribute client load across multiple Terminal servers. All of the servers will appear as one to the clients. Network Load Balancing requires Windows 2000 Advanced Server or Windows 2000 Datacenter Server.

Network Load Balancing Services was called Windows Load Balancing in Windows NT 4.0. It is not to be confused with Windows Clustering Services, which also requires Windows 2000 Advanced Server or Windows 2000 Datacenter Server, although Microsoft's documentation does a wonderful job of confusing the issue with liberal use of the term "cluster." Microsoft considers both server clustering and Network Load Balancing as Windows Clustering features. Falling right into line, and because there really isn't a better term, in this chapter I use the term "cluster" to describe a group of Windows 2000 servers joined together by Network Load Balancing Services.

When you use the Windows 2000 Cluster Service, multiple servers act as a single virtual system, providing failover capabilities. If you pair two servers as a cluster in this way, both run all the software; if one of them fails, the other can continue to provide uninterrupted service. In general, you can combine Cluster Service and Network Load Balancing to provide both the failover capabilities and high availability, but not with Terminal Services. Terminal Services is incompatible with Cluster Service, because of the way Cluster Service uses IP addresses.

How Network Load Balancing Works

The purpose of Network Load Balancing is to take a group of Windows 2000 servers and give them a single logical IP address. The Network Load Balancing software distributes the IP traffic to these servers based on rules that you set.

In the context of Terminal Services, you set up Network Load Balancing to increase the power of a Terminal server by distributing its work across two or more Terminal servers. Configure the servers in this cluster to be identical so that users encounter the same software environment no matter which server they connect to.

Network Load Balancing provides a simple form of failover, in that if one of the servers in a cluster fails, the others will continue to service requests, with priorities perhaps somewhat adjusted to account for absence of the first server. Unfortunately, this is likely of little solace to the Terminal Services users on that server, whose sessions and unsaved work are lost.

Client Affinity

An important concept in Network Load Balancing with Terminal Services is client affinity. Normally, with Network Load Balancing, if a client connects to the NLB cluster, the connection is made with whichever server in the cluster is most available.

Affinity establishes a relationship between specific clients and servers, so that if the client reconnects it will connect to the same server.

Network Load Balancing tracks clients for all these purposes by means of their IP addresses. In the aggregate, requests are still distributed across servers, because different clients are sent to different servers. But when affinity is assigned to clients and servers, once a session is established it sticks with the original server. To the extent that the workload of all sessions tends to be equal, the workload across servers tends to be equal (or distributed according to the specified percentages).

You don't need to set affinity for Terminal Services to work, but you do need it if you want to allow users to reconnect to disconnected sessions. In a related issue, if your clients are using DHCP to get their addresses, even affinity may not allow them to reconnect to disconnected sessions, unless they reconnect without logging off the network first. If they relog on to the network, they will likely have a new IP address and affinity won't be able to associate them with the same server. Depending on how your DHCP is configured, you might be able to work around this problem by using the Class C setting, covered next.

The Effects of Proxy Servers

The default affinity setting is Single, meaning that all requests from a particular IP address should be directed to a particular cluster host. Besides None, the other setting is Class C, meaning that all requests from clients whose IP addresses are in a particular class C subnet (addresses whose first three octets are the same) should be redirected to the same cluster host.

The idea behind this setting is that sometimes clients access servers from behind multiple proxy servers, in which case requests from one client system may arrive at the server with different IP addresses and appear to come from different client systems. By grouping all clients in the same subnet, requests from a client will end up at the right server, although at the expense of a good deal of distributive control over IP traffic.

Store User Profiles and Other Server States Centrally

Network Load Balancing is one of the few configurations that argue strongly for the use of Terminal Services profiles. The problem is that users should expect to have the same settings each time they connect to the same server or application. But when you are using Network Load Balancing, users may be logged on to any one of many different servers.

If you use local profiles for those accounts, settings changes are saved locally and are not necessarily available the next time the user logs on. If you use Terminal Services profiles, which follow the user no matter which server she logs on to, this problem is avoided.

In much the same way, any other server state, such as shared files, are best stored on some other central location, such as a file server outside the Network Load Balancing cluster. This allows you to refer to these locations using common names on all servers, and also makes it easier to keep the Terminal servers identical.

Configuring Network Load Balancing

If you didn't choose to install Network Load Balancing at Windows 2000 install time, you can do so in the properties dialog box for the Local Area Connection in the Network And Dial-up Connections window. If Network Load Balancing is not in the list of services, click Install | Service | Add | Network Load Balancing | OK. If Network Load Balancing is in the list but the checkbox is not checked, check it.

Before you begin configuring, there are a few rules of which you should take note. You will be creating a new IP address (variously called the virtual IP address or primary IP address) as the address for the NLB cluster. This address needs to be an IP address for all the servers in the NLB cluster. You will also be designating an address for the server as the dedicated address, which means the address used for non-NLB services.

Go to the properties dialog box for Internet Protocol (TCP/IP) and click Advanced to open the Advanced TCP/IP Settings dialog box. Add this address to the list of IP addresses in this server. The address you are listing as the virtual IP address in NLB must be after the dedicated address in the list of IP addresses in this dialog box.

NOTE: All server addresses need to be dedicated addresses, not DHCP addresses.

Select Network Load Balancing and then Properties to begin configuration.

Cluster Parameters

On the Cluster Parameters tab, the Primary IP address needs to be the virtual IP address for the cluster. This and all other settings on this tab need to be the same for all servers in the NLB cluster. Set the subnet mask as appropriate. See Figure 7-3 for reference.

◆ The Full Internet Name needs to be a unique DNS name to refer to the virtual IP address, and therefore the NLB cluster. Without this name you can still refer to the cluster by its IP address.

◆ The Multicast Support checkbox must be checked if your network hardware is configured to support multicast MAC addresses.

◆ The Remote Password and Remote Control checkbox fields are for allowing administrators to administer the cluster remotely using the WLBS program.

NOTE: If you enable remote control, it is essential that you block the remote control UDP control port, port 2504, at your firewall.

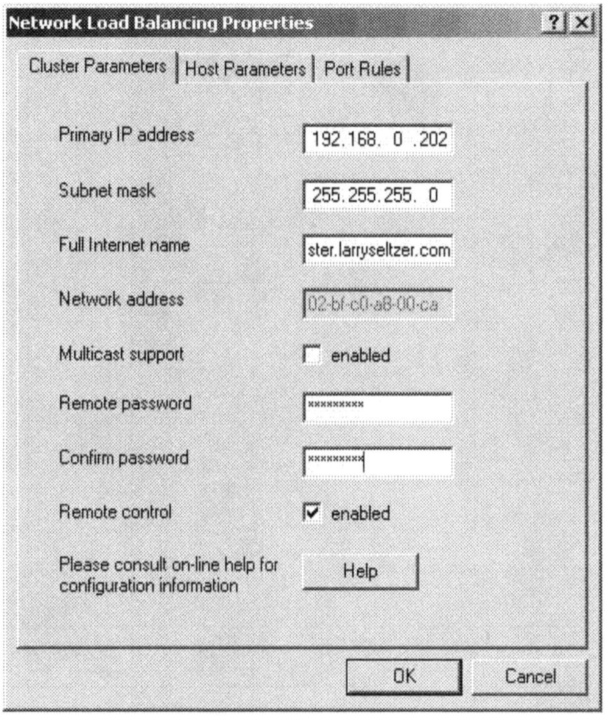

Figure 7-3. The Cluster Parameters describe network parameters for the entire NLB cluster

Host Parameters

The Host Parameters tab (see Figure 7-4) describes configuration information for the specific server in the NLB cluster.

✦ The Priority setting, which must be unique for each server in the NLB cluster, sets that server's priority for handling TCP and UDP services not described in the port rules (discussed next). This matters when a host goes offline and a decision must be made as to which server in the NLB cluster must handle the traffic. Lower numbers represent higher priority, with 1 being the highest priority and 32 the lowest.

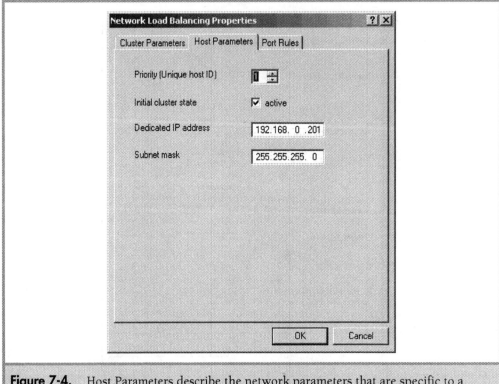

Figure 7-4. Host Parameters describe the network parameters that are specific to a particular server in the NLB cluster

The Initial Cluster State checkbox tells the server to join the NLB cluster immediately when Windows 2000 starts. If this box is not checked, you can add the server to the cluster later with the WLBS command-line tool.

◆ The Dedicated IP Address field is the unique address for that server.

◆ The Subnet Mask depends on your network configuration.

Port Rules

Exactly what goes into the Port Rules tab (see Figure 7-5) depends on all the services that you may be running on these servers, but let's assume that these are just running Terminal Services.

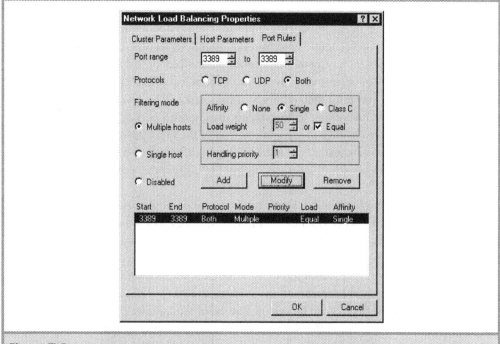

Figure 7-5. Port rules are the means by which different network services are shared among the servers in a Network Load Balancing cluster

By default, all TCP and UDP ports are enabled; the default Port Rule is set for TCP and UDP ranges 0 through 65535. For Terminal Services, it's common to configure the cluster so that it only services the RDP protocol. Change the range to 3389 through 3389 and set Protocols to TCP (RDP is a TCP protocol on port 3389).

Set the Filtering Mode to Multiple Hosts. This tells Network Load Balancing that this port rule should resolve to multiple hosts in the cluster. It's possible you might have port rules set to Single Host. It's not likely that this would be for Terminal Services, but rather for a light-load service running on a single server. You can, in fact, have multiple servers in the cluster set for Single Host Filtering for a port range, and the one with the lowest Handling Priority setting gets all the traffic; thus, this setting acts as a failover mechanism. Setting the Filtering Mode to Disabled blocks all traffic for that port range.

In the Affinity section, you should probably leave the default of Single selected. As described earlier in the chapter, affinity tells Network Load Balancing to tie specific clients with specific servers across requests.

By default, the Equal checkbox is also selected, meaning that requests are distributed evenly among the servers in the Network Load Balancing cluster. If you uncheck this option, you can assign a specific percentage (Load Weight) to this server, corresponding to the percentage of IP requests to the cluster that should be serviced on this host. If your servers are physically identical, or at least roughly so, you should leave this setting alone. If some of the servers are more powerful than others, you can increase the percentage of requests going to the more powerful servers. Unfortunately, in Terminal Services this does not guarantee that a larger percentage of the work will go to the more powerful servers. By sheer dumb luck of the draw, users who are performing more power-hungry tasks could end up assigned to the less-powerful servers. But in the big picture, work should tend to be distributed evenly.

Handling Priority is grayed-out; it's only available under Single Host Filtering mode.

If you are testing a Network Load Balancing configuration using the Terminal Services Capacity Planning tools, and are simulating multiple users from a single client, you may see the same problem as you would with a proxy server. Even if all your client systems have unique IP addresses, you have multiple Terminal Services sessions on some servers with the same IP address, which could present affinity problems to Network Load Balancing.

It's a limitation of Network Load Balancing, but these multiple sessions on the same client end up on the same server within the Network Load Balancing cluster. There's no easy way around the problem.

Using the wlbs Command

The **wlbs** command-line command is essential for efficient administration of live NLB clusters. You can use it to take individual hosts in and out of the cluster to perform administration on them. The rest of the cluster detects the absence but adjusts to it, and also adjusts automatically when you bring the host back into the cluster.

TAKE COMMAND

The **wlbs** command controls Network Load Balancing Services from the command line.

NOTE: "wlbs" stands for Windows Load Balancing Services, the name of the service under Windows NT 4.0. The program name was maintained for compatibility purposes.

The syntax for **wlbs** is:

> **wlbs** {**help** | **suspend** | **resume** | **start** | **stop** | **drainstop** | **enable** {*port* | **all**} | **disable** { *port* | **all**} | **drain** { *port* | **all**} | **query** | **reload** | **display** | **ip2mac**} [*cluster* [*:host*]]

where:

help opens the Windows help file for Network Load Balancing.

suspend suspends all cluster operations until a **resume** command is issued. All cluster commands except for **resume** and **query** are ignored until the cluster is resumed.

resume resumes a suspended cluster.

start starts the cluster service on the specified cluster and hosts. All ports that may have been disabled are enabled.

stop stops cluster operations on the specified hosts.

drainstop disables all new traffic on specified hosts that enter draining mode. When no more active cluster operations remain, cluster operations are stopped.

enable {*port* | **all**} enables traffic under the port rule which covers the specified port. Traffic on all ports under that rule are affected.

disable {*port* | **all**} immediately disables and ends traffic under the port rule which covers the specified port. All traffic is ended on all ports under that rule.

drain {*port* | **all**} disables any new traffic under the port rule which covers the specified port(s). All new traffic is blocked on all ports under that rule. New connections to the ports are not allowed, but active connections remain. (Use the **disable** command to disable active connections.)

query displays the current cluster state and host priorities for current cluster members. Cluster state can be any of the following:

- ✦ **Unknown**   The host is not responding.
- ✦ **Converging**   The cluster is attempting to come to a converged state. If the cluster persists in this state for a long time, it usually indicates an error in the cluster parameters. Check the event log.

✦ **Draining**   The cluster is attempting to drain active connections and eventually stop.

✦ **Converged as default**   The host is in a converged state and the current host is the default host for the cluster.

✦ **Converged**   The host is in a converged state and the current host is not the default host for the cluster.

reload reloads the Network Load Balancing driver parameters. The cluster service is stopped and restarted if necessary. This command may only be run locally on the specified host.

display displays extensive descriptive and historical information about the NLB cluster. This command may only be run locally on the specified host.

ip2mac displays the MAC address for the specified cluster or host. If multicast support is enabled, the multicast MAC address is displayed. You can use this command to create static ARP entries in your routing table.

cluster is the name or IP address of the cluster to which the command is being applied.

host is the name or IP address of the host to which the command is being applied. For example, host 2 in the cluster named bigcluster is referred to as bigcluster:2.

Tuning Client Performance

There are a number of performance parameters in the Terminal Services client that you can adjust. Some of these settings can help when clients are connected over low-speed connections, although some of the more advanced settings are not worth the trouble for most administrators.

Client Connection Manager

In the Connection properties of Client Connection Manager, you can check Enable Data Compression for the connection. Compressed data could improve performance in some low-bandwidth situations, such as dial-up clients using slow modems. The cost is mostly in terms of the compression that must occur at the server before data is sent to the client. Whether the benefits outweigh the costs is a judgment you must make, preferably in your testing.

You can also check Cache Bitmaps To Disk. The meaning of this setting is almost as obvious as the other one. Commonly used bitmaps are stored locally on the Terminal Services client system, cutting the need for some graphics to transfer from the server. Again, with low-speed connections this setting can improve performance and probably has no meaningful downside.

Terminal Services Client Registry Settings

The Windows 2000 Server Resource Kit has a program named Terminal Services Client Registry Settings that lets you fine-tune a number of settings in the Terminal Services client. In the vast majority of cases, none of these settings will have an appreciable effect on performance, but they might in some special cases. Of course, this program is only relevant to conventional Windows PC clients, as opposed to Windows-based terminals or non-Windows clients in a Citrix environment.

If you plan to use this tool, read the help file. It's not only that you ought to read the only documentation there is, but the help file lists which registry setting is affected by each setting in the program. Rather unusual on Microsoft's part.

You can change not only the sizes of the Bitmap and Glyph caches (a glyph is a rendered font character, as opposed to a bitmap or line graphic), but you can also adjust the way the caches are used. For example, you can specify what percentage of the bitmap cache is used for small bitmaps, medium bitmaps, and so on. Conceivably, if you know details about the sizes of bitmaps used in your applications, you can optimize the bitmap cache for them this way.

If you do want to dive into this issue, at least do it right. Use Perfmon to measure the bitmap and glyph cache hit data. In the Terminal Services Session Performance object, there are sets of three counters, Hit Ratio, Hits, and Reads, for four different kinds of items: Protocol Bitmap Cache, Protocol Brush Cache, Protocol Glyph Cache, and Protocol Save Screen Cache. (The Brush Cache and Save Screen Cache entries lead me to believe that there are registry entries for these that aren't manipulated by the Terminal Services Client Registry Settings program.) By monitoring the hit ratios on these caches, you can adjust the settings in the Terminal Services Client Registry Settings program to improve your performance.

Finally, you can save settings into a variety of profiles and load them as appropriate. But most users are best off with the default settings. Work with these at your own peril.

Chapter 8

Controlling Licensing

Terminal Services is unique among Microsoft products in the complexity and strictness of its licensing procedures. Some of you may view Terminal Services Licensing as an enhanced set of tools to ensure compliance, while others may see it as the end of the era of trust in software licensing. It's probably an omen of future Microsoft licensing practices.

Almost all of the discussion in this chapter has to do with Terminal Services' Application Server mode. If all of your Terminal servers run in Remote Administration mode, you can safely ignore this chapter.

The Rules of Terminal Services Licensing

Every client that connects to Terminal Services in Application Server mode must have a valid client access license (CAL), and Microsoft is going to make sure you have one.

If you have a Terminal server running in Application Server mode, you must have at least one server running the Terminal Services Licensing service. Windows 2000 clients come with a Terminal Services CAL built in. For all other clients you must purchase CALs and install them on the License server.

A single License server can service many Terminal servers, although you may want to have many License servers in your network both for performance reasons and for backup, in case one server is unavailable. For most applications, Microsoft recommends that each Terminal server have two available License servers.

How Many CALs Do You Need?

Remember that all clients connecting to Terminal Services also need a Windows 2000 CAL. Unfortunately, while Windows 2000 licensing permits per-server licensing, which allows you to buy as many licenses as the maximum number of clients that can connect to the server simultaneously, Terminal Services only has per-seat licensing. This means that you need a Terminal Services CAL for every client that may connect to the server, even if only one of them connects at a time.

High-Volume Licenses

Most Terminal Services client licenses are per client, but for special circumstances, there are two special client types: Internet clients and clients who work at home.

Internet Connector License

The Internet Connector License is a special license designed for software vendors who want to make Windows applications available across the Internet, either for demonstration purposes or for the actual services provided by the application. This license is best used in combination with the ActiveX control version of the Terminal Services Advanced client, in order to make Internet access even easier.

The Internet Connector License supports up to 200 concurrent users across the Internet. The administrator enables an Internet Connector License by installing the license on the License server, as with any other license, and then enabling the Internet Connector Licensing setting in the Terminal Services Configuration program. The Terminal Server must be in Application Server mode in order to enable the Internet Connector License.

All users who connect to the server under the Internet Connector License are automatically logged on using the TsInternetUser account, making the users effectively anonymous.

Once an Internet Connector License is enabled on a Terminal server, it becomes the only way to connect to that server. All other user attempts to connect to the server are rejected.

The Internet Connector License is not cheap. See http://www.Microsoft.com/ windows2000/guide/server/pricing/pricingwindows.asp for full pricing details for all Terminal Services licenses, but the last time I checked the license was $9,999. Also, none of the users who connect over the Internet Connector License may be employees of the company that owns the license; such users must use standard CALs, or the Work At Home license.

Work At Home License

The Work At Home license is a special license that allows a company to buy a second CAL for a worker to use at home. Work At Home is available to customers of Microsoft's Select program—in other words, people who spend a lot of money on Microsoft products.

The flip side of the Internet Connector License: all users of a Work At Home license must be employees of the company that owns the license.

Microsoft Clearinghouse

To activate a license, you must communicate in some way with the Microsoft Clearinghouse, a central repository, or database, of licensing information. The information you fill out in order to activate the license is stored in this database (see "Setting Up a License Server" later in this chapter).

As the diagram in Figure 8-1 shows, the Terminal Services Licensing server can be activated and have licenses installed on it over the Internet. Alternatively, the administrator can activate licenses after communicating with Microsoft via phone or FAX so that licenses can be registered with the Microsoft Clearinghouse, their central licensing database. Once licenses are installed in the Licensing server, they can be allocated to clients connecting over the LAN or Internet.

In case you are concerned, according to Microsoft, the information in this database is kept separate from any other information Microsoft maintains about you, and is used solely for the maintenance of licenses and determination of potential problems in licensing software.

If you lose licenses—for example, if a computer suffers an unrecoverable crash—you can call the Clearinghouse and Microsoft representatives will help you recover the licenses. The phone number is (888) 571-2048. For more details on the process, see "Reissuing Lost Licenses" later in this chapter.

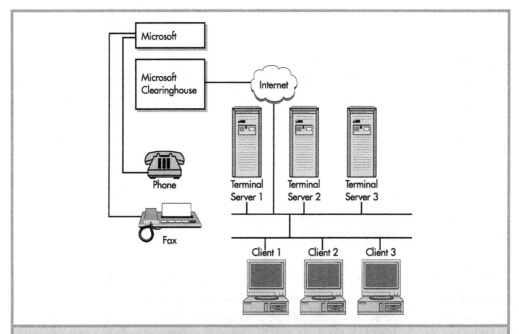

Figure 8-1. Microsoft has facilities for activating License servers and installing licenses securely over the Internet, or through phone or fax transmission

Microsoft Office Licensing Under Terminal Services

Microsoft Office is licensed strictly per seat, and you need an Office license for every computer on which it runs. Unfortunately, client systems of a Terminal server count as "computers" in this case. Here's an example that makes the point all too clear. Your employees access Office through Terminal Services at work, and you want to let them have access to the software from home as well. You set up your network so they can access the same Terminal server from home as from work. Even though the same number of users is using Office, you now need twice as many Office licenses. (You also need Terminal Services CALs for all the home computers, unless they are running Windows 2000.)

Third-Party Software Licensing Under Terminal Services

Without getting into legal blunders that third parties may have made, in general you should consider multiple users running an application as being in the same licensing situation as if they were running on multiple network clients. Certainly you have to check with each vendor for the terms when running under Terminal Services.

Citrix MetaFrame Users Require Terminal Services Licenses

If you are running Citrix MetaFrame on your Windows 2000 Terminal server, your ICA users need Terminal Services CALs in addition to Citrix licenses (and Windows 2000 Server CALs).

Setting Up a License Server

You can set up a License server during Windows 2000 installation, or later, using Add/Remove Programs. Select Add/Remove Windows Components and scroll down to select Terminal Services Licensing.

If Terminal Services is selected in the Windows Components list, you are led through the installation of that component again, and you have to decide between Remote Administration and Application Server modes, and permissions compatibility (if you choose Application Server mode). Depending on whether this server is a domain controller, you may have the option to make this server available to the entire enterprise or just the local domain or workgroup (more detail on these choices is available later in this section). You can also specify the location of the license server database, the default for which is the %SystemRoot%\

System32\LServer directory. The installation commences at that point, and you need the appropriate Windows 2000 Server CD-ROM or access over the network to the install files.

Selecting a License Server

The Terminal Services Licensing service makes very low demands on the server. Disk space consumed is less than 1MB for the code; the license database is only about 5MB (the service uses some additional space for temporary files). Memory consumption is less than 10MB, even when active. And even when the Licensing service is heavily used, the CPU and network needs are small.

Therefore, there's no reason to be concerned about the Licensing service slowing down a server that has other requirements. But the Licensing service itself must be available to avoid any delay in user logons, so running the service on a heavily-taxed server (such as a busy Terminal server) is not recommended. If a Terminal server has bandwidth to spare, however, the Licensing service runs fine on it.

Once a Terminal server discovers a License server, it continues to use that server for as long as it is available. The Terminal server pings the License server periodically to make sure that it is still available, and if it loses contact, it seeks out another License server. Microsoft documentation is unclear on exactly how frequent these pings are, but it appears to be either once or twice every hour. In any event, the pings will not pose a load problem on either the server or network.

Terminal servers have rules for the way in which they locate License servers. These rules differ depending on the network environment, and they're explained in this section.

Windows 2000 Domain

In a Windows 2000 domain, the License server must run on a domain controller. The load from a License server is light enough to avoid any worries that it might interfere with the other processes performed by the domain controller.

In a Windows 2000 domain, Terminal servers locate License servers by using a remote procedure call (RPC) to query all Windows 2000 domain controllers in that domain for the Licensing service. The Terminal server picks one of these License servers at random and then requests a license key pack from that server.

If the License server has no available licenses and there is an Enterprise License server in the installation (discussed later in this section), the License server passes the request on to the Enterprise License server.

If the Terminal server cannot find a License server in the domain, it searches Active Directory for the location of the Enterprise License server.

If the License server has no available licenses, and other License servers responded to the query, the Terminal server requests a license from one of the others.

Windows NT 4.0 Domain or Workgroup

In a Windows NT 4.0 domain or workgroup, the Licensing service must be running on a Windows 2000 member server. The Terminal server locates the License server by issuing a broadcast on a Win32 network facility called a mailslot. All License servers that receive the request respond, the Terminal server selects one at random and requests a license key pack from it. If the License server has no available licenses, and other License servers responded to the query, the Terminal server requests a license from one of the others.

Enterprise License Server

In a Windows 2000 network with multiple domains, you can choose to have a single server designated the Enterprise License server. Such a server can provide licenses to Terminal servers on many domains, but they all must be in the same physical site. As with all Windows 2000 domains, the Enterprise License server must reside on a domain controller.

Domain or Workgroup

If a License server is not an Enterprise License server, it only serves Terminal servers in the same domain or workgroup. If your network is not a Windows 2000 domain, this is the only choice available to you when you set up Terminal Services Licensing.

Forcing a Terminal Server to Default to a Specific License Server

You can make a Terminal server request licenses from a specific License server. This can be helpful for your own license tracking, and may speed up license acquisition if the License server is on a remote subnet.

On the Terminal server, open a registry editor and go to HKEY_LOCAL_MACHINE\ SYSTEM\ CurrentControlSet\Services\TermService\Parameters. Edit the REG_SZ value named DefaultLicenseServer so that its value is the NetBIOS name of the License server you want to be the default server. (If the data item doesn't exist in the subkey, you must add it.)

CAUTION: The Terminal server must be able to resolve the NetBIOS name of the License server, so if it cannot, you have to make it do so via WINS or the LMHOSTS file.

Activating Licensing

In order to perform any of its functions, the License server must be activated, which means you must contact Microsoft to begin the process of issuing licenses. This is a two-step procedure, beginning with activating the licensing process and ending with the installation of actual licenses (covered in the next section).

To begin, run the Terminal Services Licensing Wizard, which you access in the Terminal Services Licensing program (in Administrative Tools). If the server's Activation State is displayed as Not Activated, right-click the server name and select Activate Server, which launches a wizard.

After the obligatory "Welcome to this wizard" message, the wizard asks you to choose a method for connecting to Microsoft. In order to complete any of these choices, you need the product ID displayed on the welcome screen. The Internet activation method automatically picks up the product ID from the registry.

The connection method choices are as follows:

* **Internet**   A direct connection is made between the wizard and the Microsoft Clearinghouse. You are asked for information about your company and an e-mail address. A 35-character PIN is e-mailed to the address. You need to use this PIN to complete the process.

* **World Wide Web**   The wizard instructs you to go to https://activate.microsoft.com and fill out company information. Then, just as with the Internet method, a 35-character PIN is e-mailed to the address you provide.

* **Fax**   First, the wizard asks for your country, then for your company information, including your fax number. Then the wizard window offers a Print button so you can print the Activation Request form, which you are asked to fax to Microsoft at the number specified on the form. Microsoft responds via fax with the 35-character PIN.

* **Telephone**   The wizard asks for your country, and then instructs you to call Microsoft—the number is (888) 571-2048 in the United States. A representative on the phone will ask you for your company information and then read you the 35-character PIN.

With some of these methods, you have the option of closing the activation process temporarily while you await the code from Microsoft. (At this point, the Activation Status in the Terminal Services Licensing program is Pin Needed To Complete Activation.) To complete the process later, choose Activate Server again and tell the wizard to complete the activation process now that you have your PIN.

With all four methods, the end result is that you receive a 35-alphanumeric-character PIN, which you then enter into the appropriate field in the Activation dialog box (see Figure 8-2 for an example) to complete the activation process. In the final screen of the wizard, you have the option to move on to installing licenses after the wizard completes.

BUG ALERT: If you attempt to activate the License server while logged on with an account that uses a mandatory or roaming profile, and Terminal Services is configured to delete the local profile cache, you receive this error message at the activation:

```
The licensing wizard cannot connect to the selected License Server. Make
sure the licensing service is installed and running.
```

Also, the License server Activation Status is displayed as UNKNOWN. Microsoft claims to have a hotfix for this problem, although it is not fully tested. The hotfix is not available for direct download, so you have to call Microsoft Product Support to get it.

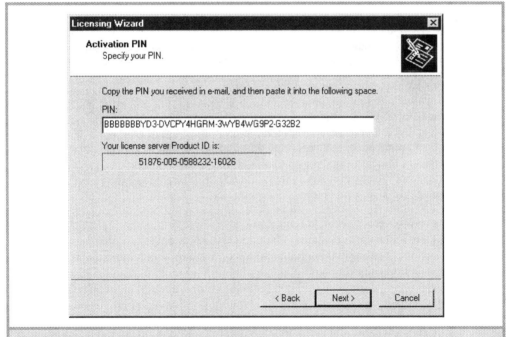

Figure 8-2. In this example, an activation code is entered to complete the Internet activation method for a License server

CODE BLUE

If you are attempting to activate a Terminal Services License server that came preinstalled on an OEM Windows 2000 Server or Advanced Server system, the activation may fail.

If you are using the Internet activation method, you might see the following error message:

```
The Licensing wizard cannot complete the license server activation process.
The PIN is not valid for this License Server. Click Back, and then compare
the Product ID with the Product ID in your e-mail. If the problem persists,
try using a different connection method.
```

If you are using the World Wide Web activation method, you might see this error message:

```
The Licensing wizard is unable to verify the license server ID. Check that
you have entered the correct ID for this server and retry this operation.
Message Number: 0x57.
```

The problem is that the activation routine in the OEM system does not verify the activation certificate obtained from the Microsoft Clearinghouse.

Windows 2000 Service Pack 1 fixes this problem. If you don't want to apply the full SP1, there is a specific hotfix entitled "Terminal Services OEM License Server Activation Failure" available at http://www.microsoft.com/Windows2000/downloads/recommended/q256854/default.asp.

Installing Licenses

Once a License server is activated, you need to install licenses on the server (although the server can immediately start issuing 90-day temporary licenses). To do this, select the License server in Terminal Services Licensing and choose Install Licenses. Welcome to the Obligatory Licensing Wizard!

After the opening window, you may be asked about how you purchase Microsoft software (the program refers to these as "licensing programs"). The choices are "Microsoft

Select or Microsoft Enterprise Agreement," "Microsoft Open License Program," and "Other." If you participate in either of the former programs, you need to have your agreement numbers for them. If not, choose Other.

> **NOTE:** You can change the information for your licensing programs as well as your connection method and company information later on by selecting Properties on the License server in Terminal Services Licensing.

You are then shown any license codes already entered and asked for another. License codes are just another alphanumeric string from Microsoft, in this case 25 characters. Enter the code and click Add to add it to the list of licenses. (Personally, I find the 8 and B characters in Microsoft's printed license codes to be easily mistaken, so watch out for that as you enter codes you received in CAL packs.)

CODE BLUE

If you upgrade a prerelease installation of Windows 2000 that had been running Terminal Services to the release level of Windows 2000, you may have licensing problems. Clients may be unable to connect, and if you attempt to install licenses, you may see an error message: "Invalid Serial #."

The problem is that licenses from the prerelease version of Windows 2000 were preserved in the upgrade. This license database is incompatible with Terminal Services in the release-level Windows 2000. You need to uninstall Terminal Services Licensing and reinstall it to generate a new database.

To do so, enter the Add/Remove Programs applet and start the Windows Components Wizard to uninstall Terminal Services Licensing. Re-enter the Windows Components Wizard to reinstall Terminal Services Licensing. Activate the License server as described earlier in this section.

You then have to obtain current licenses for your clients, unless they are Windows 2000 clients.

CODE BLUE

If you enter a proper license code into Terminal Services Licensing, but the program refuses to validate it, either the license code is not in fact valid or the license database is damaged.

First, you should call Microsoft at (888) 571-2048 and confirm the validity of the license code. (Don't hang up; you need more information after you check out the problem.)

If the license database is damaged and you don't have a backup (see "Backing Up a License Server" later in this chapter), you need to re-create the database by uninstalling and reinstalling Terminal Services Licensing.

To do so, enter the Add/Remove Programs applet and start the Windows Components Wizard to uninstall Terminal Services Licensing. Re-enter the Windows Components Wizard to reinstall Terminal Services Licensing. Next, activate the License server as described earlier.

If you had any license packs installed in the old, corrupt database, they are now gone. Get Microsoft back on the phone (unless you managed to keep them on hold) and request that they reissue the licenses.

Using the License

When a client attempts to connect to a Terminal server, the client may or may not present a CAL to the server. If it does present a license, the Terminal server validates the license with the Licensing service. If the client does not present a license, the Terminal server requests one from the Licensing service. If the Licensing service has any free licenses available, it allocates one to the client. If no licenses are available, it allocates a temporary license to the client.

Temporary licenses may only be issued or used when the License server is available. Clients with valid CALs can still connect to a Terminal server, but clients with no license or a temporary license are denied access if the License server is not available.

Temporary licenses are good for 90 days. The idea is that you have a grace period during which you can purchase a license. After 90 days, the License server rejects connections from the client until new licenses are added to the License server.

NOTE: The Windows 2000 Terminal Services Licensing service can only manage licenses for Windows 2000 Terminal Services. If you have Windows NT 4.0 Terminal Server Edition servers on your network, you must manage licensing for those servers separately.

MSDN, MSCP, and MSCTEC Licenses

Some companies with MSDN, MSCP, and MSCTEC licenses have, as part of those licenses, a 10-user Terminal Services license. If you have such a license, you can activate your licensing servers using the Internet, fax, or telephone methods, but you can only install licenses using the telephone method.

Activate your server as described earlier. You need to have your customer identification number (your MSDN subscription ID) when you call Microsoft to obtain a license key for your server.

Terminal Services and the 120-Day Evaluation Windows 2000

There is a 120-day evaluation version of Windows 2000 Server. If you want to use Terminal Services on the server, you should take advantage of the 10 temporary CALs that it includes.

You don't need to activate the server nor do you have to install the licenses in order to use them.

The temporary CALs operate just like regular temporary Terminal Services CALs. They begin life when you first use them and expire 90 days later. You may already have noticed that 90 days is 30 days less than 120 days. Yes, that is a hole in the "eval" concept. If you want to evaluate Terminal Services for 120 days, you should make sure to leave some of the licenses unallocated for at least 30 days into the evaluation.

Don't install real Terminal Services CALs on the evaluation version of Windows 2000. You won't be able to get them back.

Reporting and Managing License Information

The Terminal Services Licensing program is your main interface for license operations. In the main window of this program (see Figure 8-3) you can view information from multiple License servers, even those not in the current domain.

Each License server has one or more key packs, which are groups of Terminal Services licenses. Every Terminal Services License server has a key pack named Existing Windows 2000 License. This key pack is used for Windows 2000 clients that come, by default, with a valid Terminal Services CAL. Accordingly, the number of total and available licenses in that pack is unlimited.

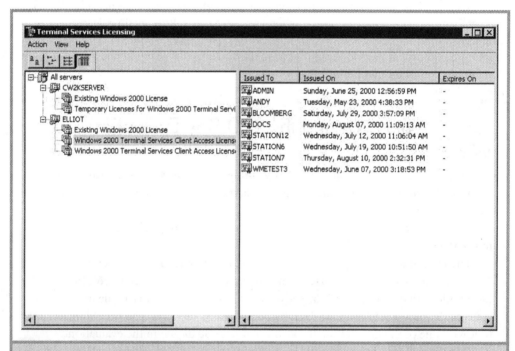

Figure 8-3. The Terminal Services Licensing program lets you administer multiple License servers

```
CODE BLUE
```

Microsoft warns that if you attempt to start the Terminal Services Licensing program within a Terminal Services session, you may receive the following error message:

```
The Licensing Wizard cannot connect to the selected License Server. Make
sure the licensing service is installed and running.
```

I personally have run Terminal Services Licensing within Terminal Services sessions a lot, and I have never seen this error, so I know it can't be all that common. The published workaround is to use Terminal Services Licensing from the console.

A possible alternative solution is to run Terminal Services Licensing across a network share. Run %SystemRoot%\System32\Licmgr.exe on the License server from any other Windows 2000 Professional or Windows 2000 Server system.

Depending on the license packs you install, you may have any number of key packs on your license server. Some of the common key packs are:

◆ **Temporary Licenses for Windows 2000 Terminal Services Client Access License**   This key pack exists to support temporary licenses.

◆ **Windows 2000 Terminal Services Client Access License**   This key pack results from the installation of a standard license pack.

◆ **Internet Connector License**   This is the key pack for the Internet licensing feature.

When you select a key pack (refer to Figure 8-3) you see an entry for each license issued by the License server. You only get the issue date and, if the license is temporary, the expiration date. See the information on the command-line program **lsreport** later in this section for more extensive reporting on licenses.

CODE BLUE

If you use cloning software such as Norton Ghost to make copies of systems, you need to be careful to give each computer a unique NetBIOS computer name. If more than one system with the same NetBIOS name connects to the same License server, the Terminal Services Licensing program (and the **lsreport** command-line program) shows multiple entries with the same computer name (see the following illustration).

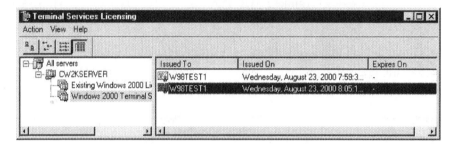

Of course, you have other, bigger problems if you have computer name conflicts on your network, but since it's possible for computers in different domains to share a License server, it's possible that the Terminal Services Licensing program is the first place you see symptoms of this problem.

Changing the computer name on one of the computers won't change the name entered in the Terminal Services Licensing program. To do that, you have to recover the license using the procedures described later in this chapter in "Reissuing Lost Licenses."

CODE BLUE

If you use some older Windows-based terminal (WBT) devices, buggy firmware in the devices may result in rapid depletion of your license pool.

You may see repeated entries in Terminal Services Licensing for the same devices. The bugs in the firmware cause the devices to request a new CAL each time they connect to the server.

To fix this problem, you must make two phone calls. First, call your WBT vendor, and insist that they provide an immediate and free fix for this problem. They will probably provide you with new firmware that you can flash into the devices.

Second, you must call Microsoft and have them reissue the licenses that were lost. If your entire license pool has been wasted by this problem, you may want to regenerate the license database by uninstalling and reinstalling Terminal Services Licensing and activating the server first.

TAKE COMMAND

The **lsreport** command from the Windows 2000 Server Resource Kit reports on licenses granted by a License server. The output of this command is a tab-delimited file that includes the server name, license ID, license key pack ID, client computer name, start date of the license, end date of the license (if any), issue type (active or temporary), and license type (the name of the key pack).

Most of the fields in this report are not available via the Terminal Services Licensing program. If you have many licenses and License servers to manage, running this report and importing the output into Excel, Access, or some similar tool provides the best reporting opportunities.

The syntax for **lsreport** is:

lsreport [/F *filename*] [/D *start* [*end*]] [/T] [/?] [*serverlist*]

where:

/F *filename* specifies that the output should go to a particular file. By default, output goes to lsreport.txt in the current directory. There's no explicit way to output to the console, but you can do so by using this parameter and specifying con: as the filename.

/D *start* [*end*] limits the report only to licenses that were in effect between the dates *start* and *end*. The end date is optional and defaults to today. Dates should be in the form mm/dd/yyyy.

/T limits the report to temporary licenses.

/? displays the command summary.

serverlist is a list of names of License servers. You can use either NetBIOS names or IP addresses.

TAKE COMMAND

The **lsview** command from the Windows 2000 Server Resource Kit brings up a grid display of Terminal Services Licensing servers (see the following illustration). According to the Resource Kit documentation, it's useful for monitoring and logging the status of License servers, but the program does almost nothing at all. It has no help files whatsoever.

Machine	Time	Type
ELLIOT	Wednesday, August 23, 2000 12:24 PM	Domain

The program polls for License servers every five minutes by default. It displays License servers it finds in the domain (and an Enterprise License server if one exists) and the date/time at which the server last polled successfully. It can write the same data to a log file on demand or automatically after each poll.

This program also creates a traffic light tray icon indicating the status of the servers.

Backing Up a License Server

Backing up the License server is both simple and important. If you're not going to back up the entire server, the minimum you should back up is the system state (an explicit option in the Windows 2000 Backup program) and the License server directory, which defaults to %SystemRoot%\System32\LServer.

According to Microsoft, the Licensing service must be running when you restore the system. If you restore the database and system state to a computer with the same system (SID), all the license and historical information, including unissued licenses, is restored.

If you restore it to a system with a different SID, only the historical license information is restored. Check the system log in this case. You see an event ID 25:

```
Database does not belong to this License Server; all available licenses in
registered license pack will be removed.
```

Following that is one event ID 26 for each key pack in the license database you restored:

```
All available n licenses for product Windows 2000 Terminal Services Client
Access License on server servername have been removed. Use Terminal Services
Licensing administrative tool to re-register licenses.
```

Servername is the name of the server to which you have restored the License database, and *n* is number of unissued licenses that have been lost. You can re-register these licenses, but you need to call Microsoft at (888) 571-2048 for assistance.

Troubleshooting Licensing

Sometimes things go wrong with clients or servers and the licensing system develops a problem as a result. For example, if a client hard disk crashes, or a system is physically destroyed (fire, flood, or whatever), you're out a license. The license existed on the client system and the License server has the license allocated to that client. There is no way in the Terminal Services Licensing user interface to make this change on your own. In such cases, you need to have Microsoft reissue the license. In addition, things can go wrong with the License server, specifically with the certificates in the server that identify it uniquely for licensing purposes.

Reissuing Lost Licenses

If a client license has to be reissued, you must go through a manual, but simple process. Call Microsoft at (888) 571-2048 and explain the situation to the representative on the phone. You need to have access to a system on which you can run Terminal Services Licensing when you make this call. The support person takes you through the Install Licenses Wizard so you can supply the 35-character License server ID. Support generates a new license code for you. After you enter that code into the licensing software, a new entry appears in Terminal Services Licensing with the number of available CALs that you asked to be reissued.

Figure 8-4 is instructive: I called Microsoft and explained that 8 of my 10 issued CALs had been for computers which no longer exist by the same computer name, or which had been upgraded to Windows 2000, and no longer need a CAL from the server. I read them my License server ID, they read me back the new license code, and I have a new license entry with 8 free CALs. The process took about five minutes.

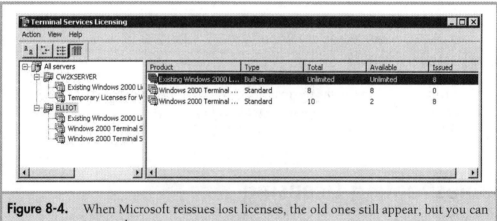

Figure 8-4. When Microsoft reissues lost licenses, the old ones still appear, but you can ignore them

If a client license certificate becomes corrupted, the client fails to log on and the License server has the following error in the Event Viewer:

```
Error 1003 - The terminal service client '%1' has provided an invalid license.
```

To correct this error, delete the HKEY_LOCAL_MACHINE\Software\Microsoft\ MSLicensing\HardwareID key from the client device's registry. Afterward, the Terminal server requests the license again from the License server and issues it to the client.

Reactivating the Server

There is a defined set of circumstances under which a License server cannot function and must be reactivated. The server is already activated, but the reactivation process fixes the problem. The circumstances are described in this section. In all such cases, select the server in Terminal Services Licensing, right-click, select Advanced, and then choose Reactivate Server.

Reactivating your server does not affect your issued licenses. All licenses issued from the server to clients remain valid, but unissued licenses must be reissued through Microsoft (see "Reissuing Lost Licenses" earlier in this chapter).

In the Reactivate Server Wizard, you have to supply, among other values, a "reason." There are four available reasons in the wizard, but there is no documentation and reasons themselves are somewhat ambiguous. The best I can do is list them for you. The options in the Reasons field are described in the following sections:

- ✦ The License Server Has Become Corrupted
- ✦ The License Server Is Being Redeployed
- ✦ The License Server Private Key Has Been Compromised
- ✦ The License Server Registration Has Expired

After you select a reason, the remainder of the process is similar to the activation process described earlier in this chapter, but you cannot use the Web or fax methods.

Reinstalling the Client OS

Sometimes, especially on Windows 9x clients, the most expeditious way to solve problems is to reinstall the client operating system. In such cases, if the client had been allocated a Terminal Services license, the license is erased, just as if you had reformatted the hard disk.

NOTE: Some Microsoft online documentation, specifically the Terminal Services Licensing FAQ at http://www.microsoft.com/WINDOWS2000/guide/server/pricing/tsfaq.asp#question23, incorrectly indicates that the client license is preserved when the operating system is reinstalled.

If the client is a Windows-based terminal, the license is preserved unless you flash the non-volatile memory of the device. If you perform one of the actions that destroys the license, you must have the license reissued through Microsoft.

Troubleshooting Terminal Services Event Log Entries

In this section, I'll cover some of the common event log errors you may find, along with their solutions, where available. There are also some non-error events described here for clarification purposes.

System Log Error 1000: Unable to acquire a license for user '%1', domain '%2'. A terminal server has requested a CAL for a client device, but an error occurred in acquiring the license from the License server.

System Log Error 1004: The terminal server cannot issue a client license. The Terminal server had a problem issuing a license to the client.

System Log Error 1007: Unable to log in the Internet user as TSInternetUser. If the problem is not corrected in 20 minutes, delete the account and run Setup again. The TSInternetUser account on the server is corrupted or has been modified in some deleterious way. This account is only used with an Internet Connector License. If you cannot fix the problem by undoing changes to the account, you must delete the account, then uninstall and reinstall Terminal Services Licensing using Add/Remove Programs.

System Log Error 1008: The terminal services licensing grace period has expired and the service has not registered with a license server. A terminal services license server is

required for continuous operation. A terminal server can operate without a license server for 90 days after initial start up. The Terminal server has failed to locate a License server within the 90-day period after it was started. This is the maximum lifetime for temporary licenses. You must activate a License server and install valid licenses in order to use the Terminal server again.

System Log Error 1009: The terminal services licensing grace period is about to expire on %1 and the service has not registered with a license server. A terminal services license server is required for continuous operation. A terminal server can operate without a license server for 90 days after initial start up. This error appears in advance of error 1008, and each day beginning 14 days prior to the end of the 90-day grace period.

System Log Error 1010: The terminal services could not locate a license server. Confirm that all license servers on the network are registered in WINS\DNS, accepting network requests, and the Terminal Services Licensing Service is running. The Terminal server could not locate a License server. Make sure that your License server is discoverable on the network. It must either be on the domain controller for the member domain or configured as an Enterprise Licensing server.

You may encounter this error when the Terminal server is a member server in a Windows NT 4.0 domain and the License server is located in a Windows 2000 domain that has a trust relationship with the Windows NT 4.0 domain. It may also occur in Windows NT 4.0-based workgroups. In either case, the problem is that the Terminal server cannot use Active Directory to locate a License server. The solution is to configure the Terminal server to look for a specific License server by default. See "Forcing a Terminal Server to Default to a Specific License Server" earlier in this chapter for instructions.

System Log Error 1011: The terminal services client %1 has been disconnected because its temporary license has expired. Client %1 has presented an expired temporary license to the Terminal server. You need to install additional valid CALs on the License server.

Security Log Success 627: Change Password Attempt: Target Account Name: TsInternetUser This event appears once a day in a system running a Terminal Services Internet Connector License. The TsInternetUser account is the account under which all users log on when an Internet Connector License is enabled on a Terminal server. The error is generated as the system changes the TsInternetUser password once a day for security purposes.

BUG ALERT: Microsoft reports that Security Log Success 627 can be logged when an Internet Connector License is not enabled on the server. I have not witnessed this in my own testing, but if it appears, know that it is a bug.

Chapter 9

Application
Compatibility
Scripts

You and your users fare best if you use modern, certified applications that have successfully been tested with Terminal Services. But the world rarely works that way, and many organizations have important applications that don't run properly under Terminal Services. The solution is in application compatibility scripts.These are scripts that you, the administrator, run after you install the problematic application. Many such scripts are included with Windows 2000 and many more can be downloaded from Microsoft at http://corporate.windowsupdate.microsoft.com/en/default.asp. Sometimes you have to edit these scripts to get them to work on your particular installation, and sometimes you may need to write your own script.

NOTE: The Corporate Windows Update site requires that you be running Windows 2000. If you access the site using another operating system, you will receive an error.

Writing a script requires some serious testing and research on the application. You may need to learn undocumented features of the program to get it to work, and you may learn in your research that no script can solve the problem. But I'll show you how to give it the old college try.

Application Compatibility Script Basics

Application compatibility scripts are run after installing an application and before any users access the application. The scripts modify the application settings, including the registry entries, so that the application will run correctly under Terminal Services.

NOTE: Before you begin researching and testing to create a script, call the vendor and give them a hard time for the problems you are having. Sometimes vendors just don't bother supporting products for different environments, such as Terminal Services, but they easily could.

If your application is internally developed, you may be able to correct the problems in it by fixing the program, instead of creating a script. (Programming guidelines for Terminal Services are at http://msdn.microsoft.com/library/psdk/termserv/ wtsstart_5in9.htm.)

How Application Compatibility Scripts Work

Application compatibility scripts do whatever they can, either to change an application's behavior so that it behaves in a way that is safe for Terminal Services or to trick the application into thinking that each user running it has a single-user computer.

The Significance of RootDrive and usrlogon.cmd

Almost all application compatibility scripts rely on RootDrive, a drive letter that is mapped to the user's home directory (by default this is %homedrive%%homepath%, such as "C:\Documents and Settings\lseltzer"). It is essential that you set this up properly, as the scripts need a single reference point to the currently logged-on user's home directory. If the same drive mapping points to the correct directory for all users, the scripts can work their magic for everyone.

In most cases, the first time you run a script, it checks the chkroot.cmd and rootdrv2.cmd batch files to see if the RootDrive environment variable has been set. If not, the script runs a batch file that opens Notepad with rootdrv2.cmd loaded in the window. rootdrv2.cmd contains a **SET ROOTDRIVE=** command, and you can complete the command to specify a drive (the batch file suggests **W:**). Save the file and rerun the script. Subsequently, when users log on, rootdrv2.cmd runs to set the ROOTDRIVE environment variable. When a user logs on to Terminal Services, the system runs %SystemRoot%\System32\usrlogon.cmd. This batch file performs a number of tasks, including the setting of the RootDrive drive letter to the user's Documents and Settings directory. Because of the importance of this batch file, I'll go over its contents:

```
@Echo Off
Call "%SystemRoot%\Application Compatibility Scripts\SetPaths.Cmd"
If "%_SETPATHS%" == "FAIL" Goto Done
```

The setpaths.cmd batch file uses the acregl.exe tool (discussed in the section "Command-Line Tools for Scripts" later in this chapter) to read certain paths for the current user from the registry; it creates a batch file to set those paths as environment variables that can be used by other batch files. Among these paths are the locations of the Start menu and Startup folder for the current user and for All Users, and the location of My Documents and Templates.

```
Rem
Rem This is for those scripts that don't need the RootDrive.
Rem
If Not Exist "%SystemRoot%\System32\Usrlogn1.cmd" Goto cont0
Cd /d "%SystemRoot%\Application Compatibility Scripts\Logon"
Call "%SystemRoot%\System32\Usrlogn1.cmd"
```

Some scripts (the Peachtree Complete Accounting v6.0 script, for example) create a %SystemRoot\System32\usrlogn1.cmd file that runs as each user logs on. In the Peachtree case, the file performs a search and replace on %SystemRoot%\btr.ini using the **acsr** tool (discussed in the section "Command-Line Tools for Scripts" later in this chapter). The search and replace action changes all references to the actual %SystemRoot% to the user's Windows directory in %homedrive%%homepath%.

```
:cont0
Rem
Rem Determine the user's home directory drive letter.  If this isn't
Rem set, exit.
Rem
Cd /d %SystemRoot%\"Application Compatibility Scripts"
Call RootDrv.Cmd
If "A%RootDrive%A" == "AA" End.Cmd
```

Here the script checks to see that RootDrive is properly set, and exits if it is not.

```
Rem
Rem Map the User's Home Directory to a Drive Letter
Rem
Net Use %RootDrive% /D >NUL: 2>&1
Subst %RootDrive% "%HomeDrive%%HomePath%"
if ERRORLEVEL 1 goto SubstErr
goto AfterSubst
:SubstErr
Subst %RootDrive% /d >NUL: 2>&1
Subst %RootDrive% "%HomeDrive%%HomePath%"
:AfterSubst
```

Here the script actually maps the RootDrive to the appropriate user directory. Notice the error handling code for the use of Subst. This probably handles some syntax difference in versions of Subst, but I'm not aware of the exact reason.

```
Rem
Rem Invoke each Application Script.  Application Scripts are automatically
Rem added to UsrLogn2.Cmd when the Installation script is run.
Rem
If Not Exist %SystemRoot%\System32\UsrLogn2.Cmd Goto Cont1
Cd Logon
Call %SystemRoot%\System32\UsrLogn2.Cmd
:Cont1
:Done
```

Here in the final section, the script runs %SystemRoot%\System32\usrlogn2.cmd, assuming the file exists. Some scripts (such as the Lotus SmartSuite 97 script) create this file. In the case of SmartSuite, the file checks to see whether a series of subdirectories (required by the software) exists in the user RootDrive, and creates them if they don't exist. It then sets the appropriate registry entries.

CAUTION: Never make changes to system-wide scripts such as usrlogon.cmd on a live server.

NOTE: If you want to change the drive letter used for RootDrive, edit the rootdrv2.cmd file to use the correct drive. You will also need to change the setting in HKEY_LOCAL_MACHINE\ Software\Microsoft\Windows NT\CurrentVersion\Terminal Server\RootDrive.

Remote Administration versus Application Server Mode

It's important at this point to reiterate that Remote Administration mode is not simply a two-user version of Terminal Services; it's a limited-function version. The tricks described here for application compatibility probably won't make an application work in Remote Administration mode, because that mode lacks certain software components necessary for supporting multiuser access to applications. Inside Microsoft, they say that Remote Administration mode doesn't do the "black magic" that Application Server mode does. The bottom line is that some applications don't work in Remote Administration mode, and scripts can't fix that.

Template Files

Sprinkled throughout the %SystemRoot%\Application Compatibility Scripts subtree are files that have elements in them surrounded by the pound (#) character. These files are template files, and the elements inside the # characters are replaced during script execution with the appropriate variables. For example, I will later analyze the Netscape Communicator script, which uses several templates with variables such as #NS4VER# that it resolves at runtime.

Microsoft includes special command-line tools for this job, including **acsr**, which does a search and replace on the contents of a file.

CAUTION: Don't pay much attention to the "templates" subdirectories in the %SystemRoot%\ Application Compatibility Scripts subtree. There are non-template files in those directories, and template files elsewhere. Somewhere along the line, the organizational aspect of this subtree was lost.

Finding Application Compatibility Scripts

You have two places to look for an application compatibility script for your applications:

♦ **The Terminal server** When you install Terminal Services, the installation program puts compatibility scripts in the %SystemRoot%\Application Compatibility Scripts subdirectory it places on your system.

♦ **At the Windows Update Corporate site** Travel to http://corporate.windowsupdate. microsoft.com/en/default.asp to find new application compatibility scripts. When you run the Windows Update process, a self-extracting .exe file is downloaded to a temp directory on your system. Open the file to install the scripts into the %SystemRoot%\Application Compatibility Scripts subdirectory.

Running Application Compatibility Scripts

After you install the application, either remain in or enter Install mode. Since you're probably in a console session to run the script, simply type **change user /install** to do this. Be sure that no users are logged on to the system. Change the directory to %SystemRoot%\ Application Compatibility Scripts\Install and run the script.

Some applications don't complete their installation procedures until they are run for the first time. If that's true of the application you are running, run the application while you're still in Install mode to complete the installation process. Then, after switching back to execute mode, test the application for Terminal Services problems. In some cases, you may determine that your application compatibility script can be more effective if you run the script before the second stage of installation (depending on the processes and configuration settings of the first stage). In other cases, your application compatibility script may work only after complete installation.

NOTE: If you upgrade or add components to an application installation, rerun the application compatibility script.

Other Compatibility Tricks

Windows 2000 and Terminal Services have some mechanisms—not strictly part of the application compatibility script system—that ensure compatibility with problematic applications. In this section, I'll discuss a couple of these tricks.

Compatibility Flags

Terminal Services maintains a group of registry subkeys in the HKEY_LOCAL_MACHINE\ Software\Microsoft\Windows NT\CurrentVersion\Terminal Server\Compatibility\ Applications key that contain data for each application that runs in Terminal Services. Each subkey name is the same as the .exe filename of its associated application. For example, the key for Excel is HKEY_LOCAL_MACHINE\Software\Microsoft\Windows NT\CurrentVersion\Terminal Server\Compatibility\Applications\EXCEL.

In the key for each application is a REG_DWORD data item named Flags that contains a bit mask describing certain compatibility options for that application when run under Terminal Services. Making changes in this value can solve some problems a program may be having.

The OS Bits

The least significant 8 bits of the Flags value are reserved for operating system coding, meaning the operating system for which the program was written. The values and their corresponding platforms are as follows:

DOS	0x00000001
OS/2	0x00000002
Win16	0x00000004
Win32	0x00000008
Win16 or Win32	0x0000000C

This OS setting is shorthand to Terminal Services and Windows 2000 for many types of behavior, and you should not change this data.

The Application Bits

The remaining bits are a series of flags that change the behavior of Windows and Terminal Services with respect to this application. Note that there are some gaps in the bit assignments (0x00000040 is not assigned, for example), so be careful with them.

0x00000010: Return username instead of computer name   Sometimes applications use the computer name as a unique identifier, but clearly this is a problem under Terminal Services. When this bit is set, applications see the username when they request the computer name.

0x00000020: Return Terminal server build number   When this bit is set and a program requests the Windows build number, the Terminal Services version number is returned instead. If this change is required, the application knows about it and sets it on installation, so don't change this setting.

0x00000100: Disable registry mapping for this application   When a user first runs an application, Terminal Services takes the registry changes that were captured in Install mode from the program's installation and copies them to HKEY_CURRENT_USER. There are programs (regedit, for example) for which this is inappropriate, and these programs should have this bit set.

0x00000200: Instruct application to create system global objects   Normally, when an application running under Terminal Services creates a system object (such as a semaphore), the session ID is attached to the name of the object to make the object name unique. This bit turns off that facility for the application, causing all objects to be system global. This is dangerous, as it can cause object conflicts.

0x00000400: Return systemroot, not user's Windows directory   This flag causes the GetWindowsDirectory() API call to return the actual Windows directory to Terminal Services clients, instead of the Windows subdirectory of their home directory. A number of applications require this setting.

0x00000800: Limit the reported physical memory (GlobalMemoryStatus)   Normally, applications are told that there are 32MB of memory available to them, and this can cause some to fail. Setting this flag causes the reported amount to be smaller, which solves problems for some applications, although this is not generally an issue in Terminal Services.

0x00001000: Log object creation to file   This bit tells Windows to log all object creation in the application to a file, the directory location of which is specified in the system environment variable named CITRIX_COMPAT_LOGPATH. This feature is not related to Terminal Services and, as far as I can tell, doesn't work.

0x20000000: Don't put application to sleep on unsuccessful keyboard polling (WIN16 only)   Some 16-bit DOS and Windows applications use keyboard polling to check for keyboard activity. Since this is a drain on CPU resources, Windows 2000 normally puts these applications to sleep, but this bit prevents that action.

The Windows Directory in the User Directory

Users and administrators are often confused by some of the mechanisms used by Terminal Services to create compatibility with a multiuser environment for single-user applications. One of the coolest is the fact that every user finds a Windows subdirectory under his or her Documents and Settings directory. Inside the Windows directory is a System subdirectory and a few files, including win.ini.

The Windows directory and its contents exist because some applications insist on looking for files in the Windows directory. If they determine the location of the Windows directory using certain "good" techniques, such as the GetWindowsDirectory API call, Terminal Services points them to the user-specific Windows directory. Any changes the applications make therefore remain user-specific.

This also means that if an application installs files that contain user-specific information in the Windows directory, you need to use a compatibility script to distribute those files to the individual user Windows directories. You must also send a copy to the Default User directory.

Creating Application Compatibility Scripts

If you need to create an application compatibility script, it's best to rip off an existing script wherever possible, rather than trying to write a new one from scratch. Unfortunately, that can be tough with these scripts, since the problems they solve are usually very application-specific. Nevertheless, you would do well to study other scripts and their approaches to problems so that you have some idea of how to address problems in the applications with which you are working.

Application Problems to Watch For

There's no way to create a complete list of problems an application might have with Terminal Services, but here are some of the most common behaviors to watch for. The best way to look for these in your testing is by using file and registry auditing when you install and run the application.

CODE BLUE

Many potential problems not discussed in this section occur if you install an application with Terminal Services in Execute mode. For example, if an installation program created Start menu icons in the currently logged-on user's menu, and the system were in Install mode, these icons would be copied to the All Users profile.

Sometimes the detective work you have to do to determine what the problems are, and how to solve them, can be difficult or even impossible. It may be worthwhile calling the application vendor and asking for some help with the problem. You might find someone in tech support who is knowledgeable and wants to help. Be friendly, not angry.

The Application Puts Per-User Data in HKLM

Even though it's always been a bad idea, many applications put per-user data in the HKEY_LOCAL_MACHINE sections of the registry. Consider a mail program that stores the location of the mailbox file in HKEY_LOCAL_MACHINE. Unmodified, this would result in all users using the same mailbox file.

If the problematic setting refers to a file, you can probably fix it by changing the file path to use the RootDrive letter. For example, if the setting were a REG_EXPAND_SZ and referred to %RootDrive%\mailbox.dat, every user would get her own mailbox because every user's RootDrive variable would point to a different directory.

Unfortunately, if the setting refers to raw data, such as color settings in the program, there is probably no way to change it.

The Application Uses Bad Pathnames for Per-User Configuration Files

Many older applications use central files, as opposed to registry settings, to store settings. If these settings should be user-specific in a Terminal Services installation, you have a real problem.

Bear in mind that some of these files may contain data that is not user-specific and can therefore be effectively shared, so don't assume that you need to treat this as a problem. This could be either global settings for the program, such as the location of the standard dictionary, as opposed to the user-customized dictionary, for a spell checker. Another good example is a set of template documents, which could be set as read-only and stored in a central location.

It can be difficult to determine whether there is a problem and exactly which files are at issue. This is another reason why you must test these programs before deploying them, and test them with multiple users logged on simultaneously. If there is a problem and it's not obvious from program errors where the problem is, you may need to use file auditing to pinpoint the problem.

The basic solution to this problem is to get the program to store user-specific information in the users' home directories. For this, you need to determine where the program stores its location for the file and change that location. Here are some handy tricks.

Use regedit or regedt32 to search the registry for the name of the file. The obvious candidate sections to search are HKEY_LOCAL_MACHINE and HKEY_CURRENT_USER, but probably HKEY_LOCAL_MACHINE (if the program was using HKEY_CURRENT_USER it would be less likely to have these problems). If you find the name of the file there and changing it solves the problem, then you can use regini.exe (discussed in the section

"Command-Line Tools for Scripts" later in this chapter) to fix this problem within an application compatibility script.

Scour the program settings menus and configuration files for possible references to the filename. If you turn file or registry auditing on when you make configuration changes, you can quickly see where the program is writing its configurations. If you can make a reference to the RootDrive in a central configuration file, you can still make the program multiuser-friendly.

In the end, it could be that the program hard-codes locations or other settings into the executable. While it might be possible to patch the .exe in some cases, especially if the variable is a null-terminated string and your value is shorter than the one in the file, this is a dangerous technique.

The Application Has Permissions Problems with Files

Under Terminal Services you want the user to have as few permissions to files on the server as possible. It's possible that an application will require a user to have some access to files in some location to which she doesn't normally have access.

Assuming you can't convince the application to move the program to some more desirable location, you can deal with this using the **cacls** utility (discussed in the section "Command-Line Tools for Scripts" later in this chapter) in the application compatibility script. You need to grant permissions to the appropriate group for users who use the application, but try to grant the most restrictive permissions you can get away with.

The Application Uses a Local Cache

Some applications use temporary files to store data that is user-specific. If the files cannot be moved to user-specific locations, and the program makes bad assumptions about the state of the data, the application might inadvertently delete data needed by another user.

Another potential problem to be aware of is that the program might expect, after one user ran it, that a temporary directory exists and continues to exist. What happens is that user A runs the program, so the program assumes that a temp directory exists. However, that temp directory exists in user A's RootDrive. Then user B runs the program. The program assumes that the directory still exists, but it doesn't, because now it's in a different RootDrive.

Check the logon script to see if the directory exists and create it if it doesn't. There's a handy batch file for this function at %SystemRoot%\Application Compatibility Scripts\Logon\ Tsmkudir.cmd.

The Application Can't Find Files in %SystemRoot%

Sometimes when a normal user runs an application, the program isn't able to find files in the %SystemRoot% tree. But when an administrator runs the program (also through Terminal Services), the application has no problems.

One explanation for this circumstance is that Terminal Services' mechanism for remapping the Windows directory to the user's RootDrive is interfering. The application may use the GetWindowsDirectory() API call to find the Windows directory and expect certain files there. This remapping doesn't happen for administrators, so the application will find the files it expects. This is basically a problem with shared files that must be in %SystemRoot%.

You may be able to fix this problem by setting one of the application compatibility flags (0x00000400: Return systemroot, not user's Windows directory) for that program (discussed earlier in this chapter). This is a tricky fix, since the change could easily cause other problems in the same program.

Analyzing a Script

I'm going to walk through the application compatibility script for Netscape Communicator 4.x. This is a program that is an obvious candidate for problems under Terminal Services. For example, it stores its own user-specific directory structures under the Program Files subtree and allows a default user logon.

```
@Echo Off
Rem #####################################################################
Rem
Rem Verify that the CMD Extensions are enabled
Rem
if "A%cmdextversion%A" == "AA" (
  call cmd /e:on /c netcom40.cmd
) else (
  goto ExtOK
)goto Done
```

The section above checks to see that command extensions are on for cmd.exe, the command interpreter. These extensions are new in Windows 2000 and enhance the behavior of many built-in commands (run **cmd /?** for more details).

If command extensions aren't running, the script runs a new, transient copy of the command interpreter to execute the script from the beginning.

```
:ExtOK
Rem #####################################################################
Rem
```

```
Rem Verify that %RootDrive% has been configured and set it for this script.
Rem
Call "%SystemRoot%\Application Compatibility Scripts\ChkRoot.Cmd"
If "%_CHKROOT%" == "FAIL" Goto Done
Call "%SystemRoot%\Application Compatibility Scripts\SetPaths.Cmd"
If "%_SETPATHS%" == "FAIL" Goto Done
```

The section above confirms that the RootDrive variable has been properly set on this system. chkroot.cmd tests to see if RootDrive is set and, if not, gives you the opportunity to set it (this process is explained earlier in "The Significance of RootDrive and usrlogon.cmd"). If this process fails, or if SetPaths.cmd, which reads certain user values out of the registry and writes them to environment variables, fails, the script ends.

```
Rem ###################################################################
Rem
Rem Get the version of NetScape (4.5x is done differently 4.0x)
Rem
..\ACRegL "%Temp%\NS4VER.Cmd" NS4VER "HKLM\Software\Netscape\Netscape
Navigator"
"CurrentVersion" "STRIPCHAR(1"
If Not ErrorLevel 1 Goto Cont0
Echo.
Echo Unable to retrieve Netscape Communicator 4 version from
Echo the registry.  Verify that Communicator has already been installed
Echo and run this script again.
Echo.
Pause
Goto Done
```

The section above uses aclreg.exe to create a batch file that sets the environment variable NS4VER to the Navigator version number (for example, 4.74). If it cannot find the value in the registry, it complains and exits. (acregl.exe is discussed in the section "Command-Line Tools for Scripts" later in this chapter.)

```
:Cont0
Call "%Temp%\NS4VER.Cmd"
Del "%Temp%\NS4VER.Cmd" >Nul: 2>&1
if /i "%NS4VER%" LSS "4.5 " goto NS40x
```

This section runs the batch file created in the previous section, deletes the batch file, and then tests the version number of Netscape. Notice that the test uses command extensions to the **if** command that developers of days gone by would have killed for. The script branches to two different sections based on whether the Netscape version number is greater or less than 4.5.

```
Rem ######################################################################
Rem Netscape 4.5x
Rem Get the installation location of Netscape Communicator 4.5 from the
Rem registry.  If not found, assume Communicator isn't installed and
Rem display an error message.
..\ACRegL "%Temp%\NS45.Cmd" NS40INST "HKCU\Software\Netscape\Netscape
Navigator\Main" "Install Directory" "Stripchar\1"
If Not ErrorLevel 1 Goto Cont1
Echo Unable to retrieve Netscape Communicator 4.5 installation location from
Echo the registry.  Verify that Communicator has already been installed
Echo and run this script again.
Echo.
Pause
Goto Done
```

In the above section, the script uses acregl.exe to read the Netscape installation directory from the registry and write a batch file named %Temp%\NS45.cmd that sets the environment variable NS40INST to that location. If it fails to find this value in the registry, the script exits.

```
:Cont1
Call "%Temp%\NS45.Cmd"
Del "%Temp%\NS45.Cmd" >Nul: 2>&1
```

Here the script runs the batch file it created in the previous section and deletes it.

```
Rem ######################################################################
Rem Update Com40Usr.Cmd to reflect the default NetScape Users directory and
Rem add it to the UsrLogn2.Cmd script
..\acsr "#NSUSERDIR#" "%ProgramFiles%\Netscape\Users"
..\Logon\Template\Com40Usr.Cmd ..\Logon\Com40Usr.tmp
..\acsr "#NS40INST#" "%NS40INST%" ..\Logon\Com40Usr.tmp ..\Logon\Com40Usr.tm2
..\acsr "#NS4VER#" "4.5x" ..\Logon\Com40Usr.tm2 ..\Logon\Com40Usr.Cmd
```

Here the script puts some of those previous sections to work. It uses **acsr** to search certain template files for codes and replaces them (in two of three cases) with values that it read earlier into environment variables. **acsr** overwrites files, so the script creates two temporary files to hold changes until it ultimately writes Com40Usr.cmd, which isn't run until near the end of the script. The temporary files are also deleted later on.

```
Rem ####################################################################
Rem Copy the "quick launch" icons to the netscape install directory so we can
Rem copy them to each user's profile directory
If Exist "%UserProfile%\%App_Data%\Microsoft\Internet Explorer\Quick
Launch\Netscape Composer.lnk" copy
"%UserProfile%\%App_Data%\Microsoft\Internet
Explorer\Quick Launch\Netscape Composer.lnk" "%NS40INST%"
If Exist "%UserProfile%\%App_Data%\Microsoft\Internet Explorer\Quick
Launch\Netscape Messenger.lnk" copy
"%UserProfile%\%App_Data%\Microsoft\Internet
Explorer\Quick Launch\Netscape Messenger.lnk" "%NS40INST%"
If Exist "%UserProfile%\%App_Data%\Microsoft\Internet Explorer\Quick
Launch\Netscape Navigator.lnk" copy
"%UserProfile%\%App_Data%\Microsoft\Internet
Explorer\Quick Launch\Netscape Navigator.lnk" "%NS40INST%"
goto DoUsrLogn
```

This section is fairly straightforward. The script wants to distribute the quick launch icons to all users' profiles, so it copies them temporarily to the Netscape program directory.

```
:NS40x
Rem ####################################################################
Rem Netscape 4.0x
Rem Get the installation location of Netscape Communicator 4 from the
Rem registry.  If not found, assume Communicator isn't installed and
Rem display an error message.
..\ACRegL "%Temp%\NS40.Cmd" NS40INST "HKCU\Software\Netscape\Netscape
Navigator\Main" "Install Directory" ""
If Not ErrorLevel 1 Goto Cont2
Echo.
Echo Unable to retrieve Netscape Communicator 4 installation location from
```

```
Echo the registry.  Verify that Communicator has already been installed
Echo and run this script again.
Echo.
Pause
Goto Done
```

This is the beginning of the Netscape 4.0 section, to which the script branched earlier if it determined that the Netscape version number was less than 4.50. Here, the script creates a batch file (%Temp%\NS40.Cmd) that sets the NS40INST environment variable to the Netscape install directory, which it obtains from the registry.

Notice that the format of the registry key is different in this entry than in the 4.5+ version above (there is no STRIPCHAR on this call to **acregl**). This is one of the reasons for the version branch.

```
:Cont2
Call "%Temp%\NS40.Cmd"
Del "%Temp%\NS40.Cmd" >Nul: 2>&1
```

Here the script calls and then deletes the batch file it created in the previous section.

```
Rem ###################################################################
Rem Copy the default profile from the administrator's home directory to
Rem a known location.  This profile will be copied to each user's directory
Rem during logon.  If the global default already exists, don't overwrite
Rem it.  Otherwise, an Admin could run this script much later and have all
Rem his personal information moved to the global default.
Rem
If Exist %RootDrive%\NS40 Goto Cont3
Echo.
Echo Default profile not found in %RootDrive%\NS40.  Please run the
Echo User Profile Manager and create a single profile named "Default".
Echo When prompted for the Profile Path, use the path shown above.  Leave
Echo all name and email name entries blank.  If any other profiles exist,
Echo delete them.  After you have completed these steps, run this script
Echo again.
Echo.
Pause
Goto Done
```

The script for this version (less than 4.5) of Netscape is odd. As the code and comments above indicate, it requires that you use the Netscape User Profile Manager to create a Default profile and put it in the RootDrive. From there it will copy the profile to the correct location. There are other ways it could have done this. If you have to ask the user to write the default profile somewhere, why not ask him to write it to the All Users profile? Perhaps he tried this and it didn't work.

```
 :Cont3
If Exist "%NS40INST%\DfltProf" Goto Cont4
Xcopy "%RootDrive%\NS40" "%NS40INST%\DfltProf" /E /I /K >NUL: 2>&1
 :Cont4
```

Here the script checks to see if a Default profile already exists. If it does not, the script uses Xcopy.exe to copy the one you created, as per its instructions, to where Netscape will find it.

```
Rem ########################################################################
Rem Remove Read permission for Users from the User Profile Manager start
Rem menu shortcut.  This prevents a normal user from adding a new user
Rem profile.  The administrator can still run User Profile Manager though.
If Not Exist "%COMMON_PROGRAMS%\Netscape Communicator\Utilities\User Profile
Manager.Lnk" Goto Cont5
Cacls "%COMMON_PROGRAMS%\Netscape Communicator\Utilities\User Profile Manager.Lnk"
/E /R "Authenticated Users" >Nul: 2>&1
Cacls "%COMMON_PROGRAMS%\Netscape Communicator\Utilities\User Profile Manager.Lnk"
/E /R "Users" >Nul: 2>&1
Cacls "%COMMON_PROGRAMS%\Netscape Communicator\Utilities\User Profile Manager.Lnk"
/E /R "Everyone" >Nul: 2>&1
 :Cont5
If Not Exist "%COMMON_PROGRAMS%\Netscape Communicator Professional
Edition\Utilities\User Profile Manager.Lnk" Goto Cont6
Cacls "%COMMON_PROGRAMS%\Netscape Communicator Professional Edition\Utilities\User
Profile Manager.Lnk" /E /R "Authenticated Users" >Nul: 2>&1
Cacls "%COMMON_PROGRAMS%\Netscape Communicator Professional Edition\Utilities\User
Profile Manager.Lnk" /E /R "Users" >Nul: 2>&1
Cacls "%COMMON_PROGRAMS%\Netscape Communicator Professional Edition\Utilities\User
Profile Manager.Lnk" /E /R "Everyone" >Nul: 2>&1
 :Cont6
```

This section uses the **cacls** utility to change permissions on certain files so that normal users can access their profile but not create new ones.

```
Rem ###################################################################
Rem Update Com40Usr.Cmd to reflect actual installation directory and
Rem add it to the UsrLogn2.Cmd script
..\acsr "#PROFDIR#" "%NS40INST%\DfltProf" ..\Logon\Template\Com40Usr.Cmd
..\Logon\Com40Usr.tmp
..\acsr "#NS4VER#" "4.0x" ..\Logon\Com40Usr.tmp ..\Logon\Com40Usr.Cmd
```

The two **acsr** calls above modify the profile and version tags in Com40Usr.Cmd for the appropriate values for Netscape less-than-4.5.

```
:DoUsrLogn
del ..\Logon\Com40Usr.tmp >Nul: 2>&1
del ..\Logon\Com40Usr.tm2 >Nul: 2>&1
FindStr /I Com40Usr %SystemRoot%\System32\UsrLogn2.Cmd >Nul: 2>&1
If Not ErrorLevel 1 Goto Skip1
Echo Call Com40Usr.Cmd >> %SystemRoot%\System32\UsrLogn2.Cmd
```

Here, first a couple of temporary files are deleted. Then **findstr** is used to see if Com40Usr is in the %SystemRoot%\System32\UsrLogn2.Cmd file. If it is not, Com40Usr.cmd is run and its output redirected to %SystemRoot%\System32\UsrLogn2.cmd to set the right variable when the user logs on.

```
:Skip1
Echo    To ensure proper operation of Netscape Communicator, users who are
Echo    currently logged on must log off and log on again before
Echo    running any application.
Echo.
Echo Netscape Communicator 4 Multi-user Application Tuning Complete
Pause
:done
```

That's all, folks.

Command-Line Tools for Scripts

Several tools are included with Terminal Services in the Application Compatibility Scripts directory. These tools (**acregl**, **acsr**, and **aciniupd**) weren't initially meant to be used outside of the scripts, so there is no documentation for them in Windows 2000. You need to understand them to understand the scripts, so I'll describe them here.

Additionally, a few advanced tools from Windows 2000 are used regularly in scripts, including **findstr**, **cacls**, and especially **regini**. Because these are not everyday tools for most administrators, I'll explain these as well.

Regini.exe

Regini.exe is a command-line tool that comes with Windows 2000 and the Windows 2000 Server Resource Kit (the version in the Resource Kit also comes with documentation!). **regini** runs scripts that make changes to the registry, and since application compatibility scripts make myriad changes to the registry, the scripts have a need for such a tool.

The **regini** command runs a specified script or scripts that makes modifications to the registry. The syntax of the script files is explained in the next section, "Formatting the Instructions for regini Scripts." The syntax of the **regini** command itself is:

regini *script_file_name* [, *script_file_name*, ...]

where:

script_file_name is the name of the file containing the script to execute. Script filenames can have any extension. Separate multiple filenames with a comma.

Formatting the Instructions for regini Scripts

regini scripts are not programming in any sense of the word, just instructions for modifying the registry. Each script file has a series of instructions in the following form:

\Registry*Key* [*ACL*] *ValueEntryName* = *DataType Value*

where:

Key is the name of the registry key that contains the data value you want to add or modify.

ValueEntryName is the name of the registry value in key *Key* that you want to modify.

DataType is the type of the entry (standard registry types, defined in the section "Standard Registry Types" later in this section).

Value is the value to assign.

ACL is an access control list, or set of permissions, you can choose to attach to the key.

Each statement may have multiple value assignments, and you may make changes in different parts of the same registry subtree in one statement. You can spread these statements out over multiple lines for readability. (See the examples later in this section.)

regini assume that any line that contains an equals sign (=) is a value assignment line. Any line that does not have an equals sign is assumed to be specifying the name of a registry key or subkey.

CODE BLUE

regini script files must have a carriage return at the end of each line. Some text editors don't insert these, at least not by default, so be sure you use an editor that performs this task. Unpredictable results may occur if you are missing them, and unpredictable results are not a good idea when you're working with the registry.

The following line is a valid **regini** script instruction:

```
\Registry\Machine\Software\Microsoft\Command Processor\CompletionChar = REG_DWORD
0x00000009
```

(The example enables filename completion in the cmd.exe command interpreter and sets the completion character to the TAB key.)

Registry Key Name Conventions

If you know your way around the registry, you'll notice that most of the example is self-evident, but the first parts of the key name are not quite right. **regini** has a shorthand system for the top levels of the registry names.

The top-level of the registry may be represented in **regini** scripts by aliases. These are optional, but you may see them in some scripts from third parties.

+ Use **\Registry\Machine** instead of HKEY_LOCAL_MACHINE.

+ Use **\Registry\User** instead of HKEY_USERS.

+ Use **\Registry\User**SID instead of HKEY_CURRENT_USER, where SID is the user's security ID. You can get the current user's SID with the **whoami /all** command. Or...

+ Use **USER:** instead of HKEY_CURRENT_USER.

You may also see the conventional HKEY_WHATEVER syntax, especially in scripts from Microsoft.

Personally, I recommend using the conventional HKEY syntax. You have to know it anyway, and adding a new syntax can't make the scripts any more readable.

Indent Your Key Names

If a line in a script does not contain an equals sign, and begins with one or more spaces, **regini** assumes the key defined in it is a subkey of the current definition. Consider the following example, stolen directly from a script used in the Lotus SmartSuite 97 compatibility script:

```
HKEY_LOCAL_MACHINE\Software\Microsoft
    Windows
        CurrentVersion
            SharedDLLs [1 5 17 13 30 28]
            Uninstall  [1 5 17 13 30 28]
            App Paths  [1 5 17 13 30 28]
                org32.exe [1 5 17 13 30 26]
            Explorer
                ShellExecuteHooks [1 5 8 13 17 30 28]
    Windows NT
        CurrentVersion
            Fonts      [1 5 8 13 17 30 28]
            Embedding [1 5 8 13 17 30 28]
```

Notice that both the Windows and Windows NT sections of the script are indented under the HKEY_LOCAL_MACHINE\Software\Microsoft section. **regini** takes this to mean that both are subkeys under HKEY_LOCAL_MACHINE\Software\Microsoft in the registry.

ACL Definitions

In the previous code listing, you saw key names followed by numbers in brackets, such as:

```
Fonts      [1 5 8 13 17 30 28]
```

The numbers represent ACLs or permission lists for the key. The numbers to use are represented in Table 9-1.

Code	User/Group	Rights
1	Administrator	Full
2	Administrator	R
3	Administrator	RW
4	Administrator	RWD
5	Creator	Full
6	Creator	RW
7	World	Full
8	World	R
9	World	RW
10	World	RWD
11	Power Users	Full
12	Power Users	RW
13	Power Users	RWD
14	System	OpFull
15	System	OpRW
16	System	OpRWD
17	System	Full
18	System	RW
19	System	R
20	Administrator	RWX
21	Interactive User	Full
22	Interactive User	RW
23	Interactive User	RWD

Table 9-1. ACL Codes for Regini Scripts

NOTE: When you set ACLs in this way, you are not adding them to the existing set of ACLs, you are overwriting the existing set with a new one. Be careful to include existing ACLs along with any you're adding.

Standard Registry Types

There are nine Windows 2000 registry types, although some are rarely used. The default data type for **regini** is REG_SZ.

REG_BINARY   This type defines raw binary data. You can express this as a stream of numeric data. The rules for formatting individual numbers are the same as with REG_DWORD (discussed next). Notice that you can break any data description among multiple lines by ending a line with a backslash (\).

```
\Registry\Machine\Software
    Microsoft
        NetDDE [17 1]
            DDE Shares
                CLPBK$
                    SecurityDescriptor = REG_BINARY 0x6C \
                        0x80040001 0x0000004C 0x0000005C 0x00000000 0x00000014 \
                        0x00380002 0x00000002 0x00180200 0x000F03FF 0x00000201 \
                        0x05000000 0x00000020 0x00000220 0x00180200 0x000002BD \
                        0x00000101 0x01000000 0x00000000 0x00000220 0x00000201 \
                        0x05000000 0x00000020 0x00000220 0x00000201 \0x05000000 \
                        0x00000020 0x00000220
```

REG_DWORD   This defines a 32-bit value, usually numeric or Boolean (0 or 1). You can express these numbers as decimal (base 10) by default hexadecimal by prefixing them with **0x** (see the script example for REG_BINARY) octal by preceding the number with **0o**, and binary by preceding it with **0b**. For example:

```
\Registry\Machine\Software
    Microsoft
        NetDDE [17 1]
            DDE Shares
                CLPBK$
                    Revision = REG_DWORD 0x1
```

REG_DWORD_LITTLE_ENDIAN   This is effectively the same as REG_DWORD. It specifies that the byte order should be most to least significant, left to right, which is the default for REG_DWORD.

REG_DWORD_BIG_ENDIAN   This specifies a REG_DWORD with reversed byte order. You won't see this very often.

REG_EXPAND_SZ   This defines a variable-length string that contains environment variables that are resolved when an application retrieves the data. For example:

```
\Registry\Machine\Software
    Classes
        AudioCD [10 1 17 5]
            DefaultIcon
                = REG_EXPAND_SZ %SystemRoot%\system32\shell32.dll,40
```

REG_LINK   This is a symbolic link between data in a program and a registry value.

REG_MULTI_SZ   This is an array of variable-length text strings. For example:

```
\Registry\Machine\Software
    Microsoft
        Rpc
            DCOM Protocols = REG_MULTI_SZ  "ncadg_ip_udp" \
                                           "ncadg_ipx"    \
                                           "ncacn_ip_tcp" \
                                           "ncacn_spx" \
                                           "ncacn_nb_nb" \
                                           "ncacn_nb_ipx"
```

REG_SZ   This is a fixed-length text string, although it isn't only used for text.

REG_FULL_RESOURCE_DESCRIPTOR   This is a series of nested arrays of binary data, usually describing a resource list for a hardware component or driver. You define in it the same way as you define binary data.

Special regini Registry Types

There are three special entries you can use in place of registry types with **regini**.

REG_BINARYFILE   This entry lets you include the contents of an external file as **regini** processes it. The point of this is to include large amounts of external binary data so as not to have it clutter up the rest of the **regini** script. For example:

```
\Registry\Machine\Software
Microsoft
        NetDDE [17 1]
            DDE Shares
                CLPBK$
                    SecurityDescriptor = REG_BINARYFILE "bin1.dat"
```

REG_MULTISZFILE   This tells **regini** to import the contents of an external file as the data for a REG_MULTI_SZ entry. This can be a convenient way to avoid cluttering up a script with large amounts of data. For example:

```
\Registry\Machine\Software
    Microsoft
        Rpc
            DCOM Protocols = REG_MULTISZFILE "strings1.dat"
```

DELETE   By using DELETE as a data type and supplying no data value, the registry entry is deleted. (**regini** offers no way to delete a key.) For example:

```
HKEY_CURRENT_USER\Software\Microsoft\Office\9.0\Access\Settings
    MRU1 = DELETE
    MRU2 = DELETE
    MRU3 = DELETE
    MRU4 = DELETE
    MRU5 = DELETE
    MRUFlags1 = DELETE
    MRUFlags2 = DELETE
    MRUFlags3 = DELETE
    MRUFlags4 = DELETE
    MRUFlags5 = DELETE
```

Creating regini Files with regdmp

The Windows 2000 Server Resource Kit comes with a tool called **regdmp** that dumps out the contents of the registry in **regini** format. It may be convenient to use **regdmp** on a test system to create a listing you can edit for your application compatibility scripts.

The **regdmp** command dumps registry contents in the same format read by **regini**. It writes to standard output, so you can redirect the results to a file if you want. The syntax is:

regdmp [-m *machine_name* | -h *hivefile hiveroot* | -w *win95_directory*] [-i *n*]

[-s] [-o *outputWidth*] *registryPath*

where:

-m *machine_name* is the name of the machine from which to read the registry (omitted for the local machine).

-h *hivefile hiveroot* is the name of the target hive root or file. A hive file is a section of the registry that is represented by a file (for example, HKEY_CURRENT_USER is %SystemDrive%\Documents and Settings\<*UserName*>\Ntuser.dat) and a hive root is a section of the registry (any key and its subkeys).

-w is the path to a Windows 95 machine's system.dat and user.dat files (the term "hive file" isn't used in Windows 9x).

-i *n* defines the number of spaces to use when indenting output. The default is 4.

-o *outputWidth* defines the width of the output. If output is redirected to a file, the default width is 240 or the width of the console if it is not redirected.

-s specifies summary output (only the first line of data is displayed).

RegistryPath is the point in the registry to read. This value may begin with HKEY_LOCAL_MACHINE, HKEY_USERS, HKEY_CURRENT_USER, or USER:, and may stand alone or be followed by a subkey path.

For example:

```
regdmp -i 2 HKEY_LOCAL_MACHINE\Software\Microsoft\Office\9.0\Outlook
```

The example above outputs the contents of the registry at and below HKEY_LOCAL_MACHINE\ Software\Microsoft\Office\9.0\Outlook with an indentation level of 2.

NOTE: **regdmp** will prefix any string entries that are missing their null-terminator with "(*** MISSING TRAILING NULL CHARACTER ***)". Failing to include the null terminator is a common programming error.

Acregl.exe

Acregl.exe is located in the %SystemRoot%\Application Compatibility Scripts directory, so it is not on the path.

The **acregl** command reads a value from the registry and writes it as a **SET** command to a file. This is not a generally useful command-line tool. Microsoft warns that this command was written to be used in the application compatibility scripts that Microsoft provides with Windows, and is not designed to be generally usable in other scripting conditions. It's easy to see why:

✦ **acregl** only supports reading string values from the registry. REG_SZ values should all work well.

✦ Only the first item in a REG_MULTI_SZ list is returned in a call to **acregl**. REG_EXPAND_SZ should work, but won't get expanded (for example, if the value is %SystemRoot%, it won't be translated to the actual location, such as C:\winnt).

✦ **acregl** returns an ERRORLEVEL of 1 for failure, 0 for success.

The syntax for **acregl** is:

acregl *filename env_var_name key value [options]*

where:

filename is the name of the file to write the **SET** command to.

env_var_name is the name of the environment variable to use in the **SET** command.

key is the name of the key from which to retrieve the value. The key must begin with HKLM or HKCU (for HKEY_LOCAL_MACHINE or HKEY_CURRENT_USER). If the key contains embedded spaces, surround it with quotes.

value is the name of the value to retrieve, and only string values may be used.

options can be either a blank string ("") or one of the following (enclosed in quote marks):

STRIPCHAR*xn*

STRIPPATH

where:

STRIPCHAR*xn* truncates the string from the *n*th instance of the character *x* from the right of the string. For example, if the value were "D:\WINNT\system32\LogFiles\W3SVC1" and the option "STRIPCHAR\2", the value to be written is "D:\WINNT\system32".

STRIPPATH removes the path portion of a filename. For example, the STRIPPATH applied to the string "D:\WINNT\repair\RegBack\NTUSER.DAT" would result in NTUSER.DAT.

For example:

```
acregl "%Temp%\foo.cmd" TEMPVAR  "HKCU\Software\MyCo\MyProd\Mydata" "some_var"
"STRIPCHARD1"
```

In this example, assume that the value of HKCU\Software\MyCo\MyProd\Mydata\some_var is ABCDEF. The command writes:

```
SET TEMPVAR=ABC
```

to the file %Temp%\foo.cmd.

ACSR.exe

Acsr.exe is located in the %SystemRoot%\Application Compatibility Scripts directory, so it is not on the path. This program performs a search and replace in a file, expanding environment variables in the replacement string if necessary.

Microsoft warns that this command was written to be used in the application compatibility scripts that Microsoft provides with Windows and is not designed to be generally usable in other scripting conditions. In fact, this tool is reasonably useful in many situations. Its purpose is similar to that of the much more powerful **sed** command, but **acsr** expands environment variables.

While **acsr** has generic value, for application compatibility scripts, use it to read the files in the templates subdirectories. **acsr** returns an ERRORLEVEL of 1 for failure, 0 for success.

The syntax is:

acsr *search replace input_file output_file*

where:

search is the string to search for in *input_file.*

replace is the replacement string.

input_file is the file to read.

output_file is the filename to write to.

For example:

acsr "#ROOTDRIVE#" "%RootDrive%" template\eudora4.key eudora4.key

This example reads the file template\eudora4.key and rewrites it to eudora4.key in the current directory, changing all instances in it of "#ROOTDRIVE#" to the value of the RootDrive environment variable.

Aciniupd.exe

Aciniupd.exe is located in the %SystemRoot%\Application Compatibility Scripts directory, so it is not on the path. This program changes the contents of INI files.

Microsoft warns that this command was written to be used in the application compatibility scripts that Microsoft provides with Windows, and is not designed to be generally usable in other scripting conditions. Given that .ini files are not used widely in modern software, it may be that these scripts are the only practical application of this program.

aciniupd returns an ERRORLEVEL of 1 for failure, 0 for success.

The syntax for **aciniupd** is:

aciniupd [/e | /k] [/u] [/v] *ini_file_name section key new_value*

where:

/e updates the key *key* in section *section* in file *ini_file_name* to *new_value*.

/k updates the name of key *key* in section *section* in file *ini_file_name* to *new_value*.

/u updates the INI file in the user's Windows directory instead of the system's Windows directory. The presumption is that application compatibility scripts are run while the system is in Install mode. Using the /u option temporarily switches to Execute mode, and then switches back to Install mode after the command.

/v tells the command to use verbose mode, in which error and status messages are supposed to be issued. In my tests, I never saw a single message.

ini_file_name is the name of the INI file to modify.

section is the name of the section in the INI file in which to find the key.

key is the name of the key to edit.

new_value is the name of the new value with which to replace the old one. If the value contains environment variables, they are expanded before being written.

For example:

```
aciniupd /e /u /v "win.ini" "Collage Capture" "Collage Capture Settings File"
"%RootDrive%\cshot.set"
```

This example changes the "Collage Capture Settings File" key in the "Collage Capture" section of win.ini in the user's Windows directory to "%RootDrive%\cshot.set". For example, if the RootDrive is Z:, the new value of the key would be "Z:\cshot.set". The command included the switch for verbose mode, although that doesn't actually show anything.

```
aciniupd /k "win.ini" "Mail" "CMC" "_CMC"
```

This example changes the name of the "CMC" key in the "Mail" section of win.ini in the system Windows directory to "_CMC". For example, the default line is probably "CMC=1" and this command would change it to "_CMC=1".

Findstr.exe

Findstr.exe is part of Windows 2000 and is in the %SystemRoot%\System32 directory. This command searches for strings in files and outputs the lines on which they are found. You can apply regular expressions (which are a complicated topic and are covered in the online help).

The syntax for **findstr** is:

findstr [/b] [/e] [/l] [/r] [/s] [/i] [/x] [/v] [/n] [/m] [/o] [/p] [/f:*filename*]
[/c:*search_string*] [/g:*search_string_file*] [/d:*dir_list*] [/a:*color_attributes*]
[*search_strings*] [*filename_to_search*]

where:

/b tells the command to match the pattern at the beginning of the line.

/e tells the command to match the pattern at the end of the line.

/l tells the command to use the search string literally.

/r tells the command to use search strings as regular expressions.

/s tells the command to search the current directory and entire subtree for matching files.

/i tells the command that the search is not to be case-sensitive.

/x prints only lines that match exactly.

/v prints only lines that do not match.

/n prints line numbers before matching lines.

/m prints only the filename if a file contains a match.

/o prints the character offset into the file before each matching line.

/p skips files with non-printable characters.

/a:*color_attributes* applies *color_attributes* as background and foreground color attributes to the output. See help for the color command for the format of this parameter (although why you'd be interested in it, I can't imagine).

/f:*filename* tells the command to search a list of files in the specified file.

/c:*search_string* uses the specified string as a literal search string.

/g:*search_string_file* tells the command to read the search strings from the specified file.

/d:*dir_list* tells the command to search the semicolon-separated list directories in the dir_list.

search_strings is the text to search for.

filename_to_search is the file or files to search.

For example:

```
findstr /c:"COMMON_STARTUP" setpaths.cmd
```

This example finds all lines in the file setpaths.cmd containing the string "COMMON_STARTUP".

Cacls.exe

Cacls.exe is part of Windows 2000 and is in the %SystemRoot%\System32 directory. This command displays or modifies permissions (access control lists) on files. The syntax is:

cacls *filename* [/t] [/e] [/c] [/g *usernamer:permission*] [/r username [...]] [/p *usernamer:permission* [...]] [/d *username* [...]]

where:

filename is the name of the file on which the operations are performed (wildcards are acceptable).

/t applies the operation to specified files in the current directory and the entire subtree.

/e changes ACLs instead of replacing them.

/c continues the operation even if an access denied error is encountered.

/g grants the permissions specified in *username:permission*.

username is the name of the user or users to whom permissions will apply.

permission is the permission code (any combination of N for none, R for read, W for write, C for change, or F for full control).

/r revokes the specified user's permissions for the file (requires **/e**).

/p replaces the permissions specified in *username:permission*.

/d denies the specified user access to the file.

Appendix A

Capacity Planning Tools

M icrosoft makes tools available for you to automate the testing of Terminal Services installations and recommends highly that you use them. Many problems in Terminal Services installations, especially large and complex ones, don't appear until all the different hardware and software products involved interact with each other. Only by creating a sufficiently complex and representative test network, and running the actual applications you will be running in production, can you test effectively.

Overview of Testing Tools

Unfortunately, these tools are internal Microsoft testing products that were released to the public without any of the usual thought that goes into their public products, even their development tools. When you read the documentation you see repeated references to tools, such as "the iostress and ntstress mix" that are acceptable vernacular in Redmond, Washington, but only vaguely meaningful to us outsiders. The clearest sign that no thought went into making the programs usable outside of Microsoft is that they have default server names that can only be the names of servers in the test lab at Microsoft.

 NOTE: You will see many references to "Hydra." This was the code name for Windows NT 4.0 Terminal Server Edition.

Even looked at in their best light, these tools are designed by Windows programmers for Windows programmers, and I don't mean VBScript. Effective use of these tools requires working at the level of Windows messages (mainly keystroke up and down events). You will need to use the Visual Studio Spy++ tool, or an equivalent, to capture events into a format that can be used in these scripts.

Microsoft was very helpful in clearing up some of the problems I encountered with software and documentation in this section—and not so helpful with others. It's only fair to point out that they expect those who use these tools to be the sort of pioneers who end up figuring things out for themselves anyway, but I hope this appendix makes things easier for all concerned.

How to Obtain the Tools

These tools are included in the Windows 2000 Resource Kit and are installed into the \Program Files\Resource Kit directory. You can also download current versions of the tools at ftp://ftp.microsoft.com/reskit/win2000/roboclient.zip.

CODE BLUE

Beware! The tools installed with the release version of the Windows 2000 Server Resource Kit do not work! It's not a common occurrence, but Microsoft just put the wrong files on the disk. Oops!

Resource Kit users should download and install the hotfix at http://www.microsoft.com/windows2000/library/resources/reskit/tools/hotfixes/ tscpt-o.asp. This launches a Windows Installer file that requires that you have Resource Kit already installed or at least that you have the Resource Kit CD.

If you don't have the Resource Kit, you can download the tools from ftp://ftp.microsoft.com/reskit/win2000/roboclient.zip, which are also current. (Of course, you should get the Resource Kit because it is so cool and useful that any Windows 2000 administrator should have it.)

Setting Up a Test Network

All Terminal Services Capacity and Planning test networks should have certain features in common. Only you can determine the best configuration of the test network, because only you know the applications to be run and the configuration of the production network that the test is simulating. Figure A-1 shows a typical, fairly simple example of such a network.

All test networks have a Terminal server. The Terminal server runs no special testing software, just the applications it would normally run in a production environment.

All test networks also have a Test Manager system. This can be a Win32 workstation that controls which tests are run on the network and when, and which also monitors the timing of the tests.

All test networks have test clients. The Capacity and Planning tools actually use Terminal Services clients to send RDP data to the Terminal server and run the applications. The test clients must be Win32 PCs, not Windows terminals.

The workstation domain controller in Figure A-1 is not strictly required as a separate system, but it's a really, really good idea. As in a production environment, domain controllers have important responsibilities for which they should have high availability. You should avoid sharing any tasks on a domain controller that have a non-trivial performance impact on it.

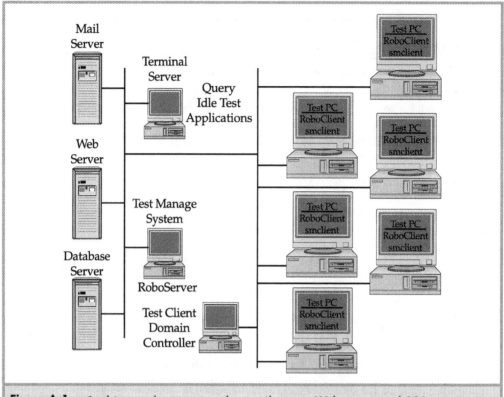

Figure A-1. In this sample test network, a mail server, Web server, and SQL server are included. These are not necessary for all test applications.

Figure A-1 also shows several other servers, and your test network should include other servers if the application calls for it. Your test network might also include multiple local segments and remote connections to other servers. You can either create these for real or use line simulators to emulate the performance impact they would have.

Overview of the Major Tools

There are four programs used in the Terminal Services Capacity and Planning tools.

RoboServer (robosrv.exe) runs on the Test Manager workstation and is at the heart of the testing process. It assigns scripts for clients to run and defines parameters such as the intervals between script invocations and how many sessions each client system should run.

RoboClient (robocli.exe) runs on each client workstation and communicates with RoboServer. It waits for commands from RoboServer to launch **smclient** to execute scripts.

Simulated Client (smclient.exe) is a scripting engine that runs on the client systems. It interprets scripts that you write and sends commands through the Terminal Services client to the server.

QueryIdle (qidle.exe) is a program that checks to see whether any of the client sessions have gotten stuck. In a complex test network, such errors are inevitable, but they usually happen when a test application is waiting for input and the script gets out of sync with where it is supposed to be. QueryIdle periodically checks client sessions to see if they have been idle for more than a specified period of time, and beeps if it finds such a client.

RoboClient

RoboClient is an extremely simple program, at least from the user interface standpoint. When you open it with no parameters, it looks for the Test Manager server named ts-dev. You can specify another server in the big, obvious field in the window or by using the -s parameter.

TAKE COMMAND

The **robocli** command launches the RoboClient program. Running it from the command line lets you specify the name of the Test Manager system. The syntax for **robocli** is:

robocli [-s *server_name*]

where:

server_name is the name of the Test Manager system controlling the tests.

After you start RoboClient and it connects to the server, there is usually no reason to bother with it again. The program sits around waiting for commands from RoboServer to run scripts.

RoboServer

RoboServer is not a very complicated application, thank goodness, since there is little documentation for it and no help system at all.

When a RoboClient logs on to the RoboServer, RoboServer tells the RoboClient how many connections to make to the Terminal server, based on the Number Of Connections Per Client graphical setting or the **-n** command-line parameter (the default value for this is 3).

Unless you're lucky enough that your Terminal server name is LABTS, you'll want to change the default name. You can also specify an IP address.

TAKE COMMAND

The **robosrv** command launches the RoboServer program. Running it from the command line lets you specify parameters that you would otherwise choose interactively in the graphical user interface. The syntax for **robosrv** is:

robosrv [**-s** *server_name*] [**-n** *number_of_clients*]

where:

server_name is the name of the Terminal server being tested. The default name is LABTS.

number_of_clients is the number of connections each client should generate. This must be a whole number from 1 to 5.

As the different client systems run RoboClient, they establish connections to RoboServer on the Test Manager system. As Figure A-2 shows, RoboServer shows these connections. Notice that each system establishes as many connections as is specified in the Number Of Connections Per Client control.

RoboServer runs a group of these clients, which is called a *set*. You can specify the number of clients per set, as well as how many minutes RoboClient waits between sets.

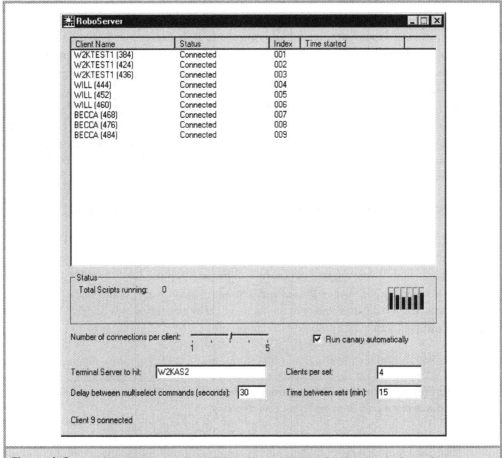

Figure A-2.   Before the tests start, all the client systems check in with the RoboServer

RoboServer Assumes Specific Usernames

Unfortunately, these tools assume certain specific usernames for the actual testing on the Terminal server. The usernames are smc001, smc002, and so on. This means that you have to have as many such users as you have test sessions. This number is the number of test client systems times the number of connections per client specified in RoboServer.

This is extremely bogus, but it's hard-coded into the program, so what are you gonna do?

The Create Program

The scripts you write to test applications are known to RoboServer and RoboClient as *template scripts*. That's because RoboClient actually creates the batch files that **smclient** runs at runtime, based on a number of parameters, including the name of the template script you want to run. The main goal of this is that all the sessions connected to the Terminal server under test log in under different usernames.

Microsoft's solution to this smells of a "cheap hack," although some would say "expedient solution." Unfortunately, the solution didn't work for me, and I had to handcraft a solution, as I'll explain later. RoboClient requires that you write a batch file named create.cmd. RoboClient executes this batch file with the following command line:

```
create.cmd 's/smc001/smcxxx/g' template_script_name tempy.scp
```

You can put whatever you want in create.cmd, but it's presumed that you will run **sed**, a UNIX command-line utility that applies regular expressions to input. The effect of the regular expression in this example is to change all instances of the literal smc001 to smcxxx, where xxx is the index number of the session. template_script_name is the name of the script you selected to run, and tempy is the name of the temporary script file that RoboClient will create and then run.

NOTE: You can download GNU **sed** from hundreds of public FTP servers around the world. Put **sed.exe** in the path or in the RoboClient directory.

The idea is that you make a create.cmd in the RoboClient directory and put this in it:

```
sed %1 %2 > %3
```

which means that the actual **sed** command line is:

```
sed 's/smc001/smcxxx/g' template_script_name > tempy.scp
```

I tried three different versions of **sed** that I downloaded from various places on the Net, and none of them accept the quotes around the regular expression. The result is that **sed** created no output and the script to run was an empty file. There's no way in batch language to strip the commas. Furthermore, RoboClient is hard-coded to run create.cmd.

What I did was to write a program in C (**createexe**) that I called from create.cmd instead of directly calling **sed**. **createexe** is very simple and naïve: it strips the first and last characters of the first parameter passed to it. Then it constructs a command line consisting of "sed," the modified first parameter, the second parameter passed to **createexe**, ">," and then the last parameter passed to **createexe**. It then executes this command line. If you put createexe.exe and create.cmd in RoboClient subdirectory, it should work fine.

Of course, you will have to run a non-standard create.cmd:

```
createexe %1 %2 %3
```

You can download **createexe**, its source code, and the create.cmd above from http://www.admin911.com. Select the link for "Book Downloads."

As I will discuss more fully later in this appendix, all user-specific references in the template scripts (usually just connect statements) should use smc001 instead of the actual username.

> **NOTE:** Since RoboClient changes only the usernames, all the smcxxx user accounts must have the same password. Since the password is specified in plain text in the script files, you may as well make it blank.

Acceptable Script Names

At the time Microsoft created this testing system, they used a Gartner Group study to define the actual workloads that would represent different profiles of workers.

Incredibly, and without any good reason, RoboServer is hard-coded to use only the script filenames that Microsoft used in their tests. Here are the active filenames:

- Knowledge Worker (knowwkr.scp)
- Fast Knowledge Worker (fastkw.scp)
- Data Entry Worker (taskwkr.scp)
- Structured Task Worker (stw.scp)
- Idle Session (blank.scp)
- Configuration Script (config.scp)

There are two other types of scripts that are grayed out in the RoboServer menus:

- Administrative Worker (adminwkr.scp)
- High Performance Worker (hpw.scp)

Microsoft obviously had special reasons for the Idle and Configuration scripts, which don't really represent a workload, but it doesn't really matter. You need to name your template scripts with one of the first six names and keep track of which name you are using, instead of any names you might prefer to use.

The Canary Script

The canary script is a separate program that can be run at the same time as the main tests are run. The execution time of the canary script is logged to the canary.csv file in the RoboServer directory.

The value of this is best explained by Microsoft's example in the white paper test described later in this appendix. In that test, Microsoft progressively added users to the test load until the time for the canary script dropped 10 percent from its time with no load on the server. This indicates that the other benchmark load is having a measurable effect on the server. The number of users on the server at that point was determined to be the capacity of the server.

The canary script is executed on the RoboServer machine, but must measure the performance of the Terminal server, which should be on a separate system. For this reason, the best way to implement it is for a batch file, canary.cmd, to call **smclient** to run another script on the server. Since you are running that script manually, and not through RoboClient, you can name the script anything you want. (Funny, but after a few days with RoboClient, this seems like a treat!) I suggest canary.scp.

NOTE: The canary script needs to run under its own user account. Be sure that you edit the script so that it uses a unique account (one not included in the accounts used by the test systems).

RoboServer runs the canary script if you check the Run Canary Automatically box on the RoboServer screen (refer to Figure A-2). The script may be any executable named canary in the RoboServer directory (canary.cmd, canary.exe, and so on).

The canary script should take some time to complete, but not too long. You'll need to experiment a bit to find the right length for the script. It should run long enough to be affected by the load on the server over a period of time, but not longer than a set of test clients takes to complete.

When you choose to use a canary script, it starts immediately when you tell RoboServer to begin testing. RoboServer pauses for the amount of time specified in the Time Between Sets (Min) setting before starting the first test. Afterwards, it starts the canary script before starting each set of test clients, the same number of minutes in advance. If you don't use a canary script, RoboServer starts tests immediately when you tell it to start testing.

The results in the canary.csv file are a simple table of the date/time that the test began, the number of test client sessions running then, and the time for the canary script to complete. As Microsoft did, you can make a simple graph of this data (the csv file reads straight into Excel) and watch any degradation in the performance of the canary script as the total number of users on the server increases.

Running Scripts

Once everything is in place, go to the RoboServer and select one or many client connections over which to run a script. Right-click on either a single client name or a selected group of them (see Figure A-3) and you can either reboot the client (I tried this and it didn't work for me) or run a specific script.

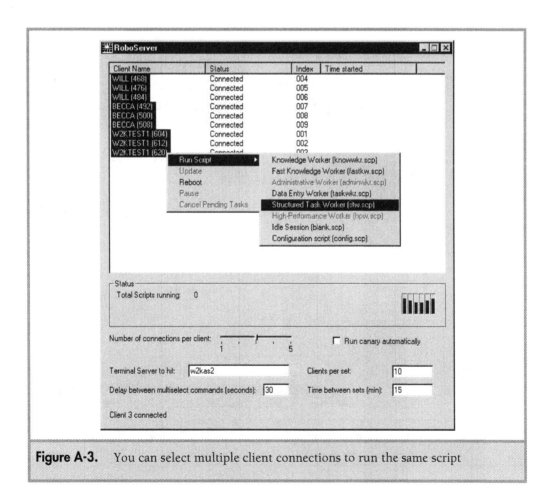

Figure A-3. You can select multiple client connections to run the same script

NOTE: if you select multiple clients, RoboServer will pause between starting each of them by the number of seconds specified in the Delay Between Multiselect Commands (Seconds) option in the program.

When you run a script, the status in RoboServer will change to "Script started successfully" (see Figure A-4). On RoboClient, the status in the Connection Status part of the window will change to "Now running *script_file_name* on *server_name*" where *script_file_name* is the name of the temporary script generated by **sed** and *server_name* is the name of the Terminal server being tested.

When the test is over, you'd expect the status on each side to change again, but it doesn't. This is apparently a bug.

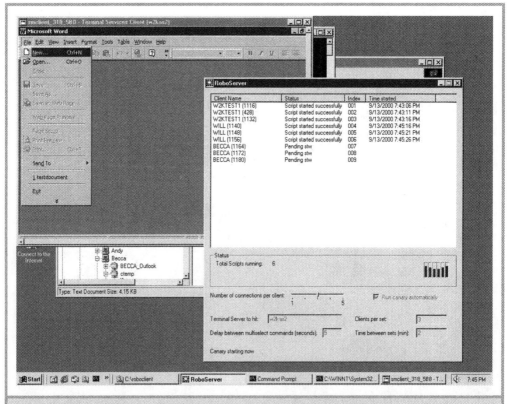

Figure A-4. Scripts start in batches in RoboServer. The Terminal Services session behind RoboServer is running the canary script.

CODE BLUE

Several error conditions can result in no execution when you run a script. If you run a script, either indirectly from RoboServer or using **smclient** from the command line, here are some things to check.

smclient, which actually parses and executes the script, calls the Terminal Services client to start the test session. If mstsc.exe, the Terminal Services client, is not in the same directory as **smclient**, it needs to be on the path.

Likewise, the applications that are run in the script need to be on the path or called with fully qualified names.

Any syntactical error in the script will cause **smclient** simply to exit while doing nothing. To check this, go to the command line and run:

```
smclient -f:script_name -c -v
```

This makes **smclient** test the syntax of the script and report on errors, albeit not in great detail.

QueryIdle

QueryIdle (qidle.exe) is a utility that monitors to see if any sessions have been idle for too long a period of time. Typically, you run it from a console session. Every 30 seconds, the program displays how many simulated clients and other types of users are connected to the server.

TAKE COMMAND

The **qidle** command launches the QueryIdle program. The syntax for **qidle** is:

qidle *server_name*

where:

server_name is the name of the Terminal server to monitor.

If a client is inactive for more than two minutes, QueryIdle beeps and displays the username and computer name for that session.

You can run QueryIdle on any Terminal Server. According to Microsoft, its load is so small that you can run it on the test server.

SmClient

Smclient is the program that actually reads scripts, invokes the Terminal Services client, and sends the events to the Terminal server. All RoboClient does is accept commands from RoboServer, create a temporary script from the template, and invoke **smclient** with appropriate parameters.

On occasion, it is useful to run **smclient** from the command line. As described earlier in the canary script section, you need to create a batch file to invoke **smclient** for that function. You also can run **smclient** from the command line to test the syntactical correctness of the script. Finally, you can, and probably should, run **smclient** from the command line on clients to confirm that they are configured properly, and that your scripts do what you expect of them, before running a fully automated test.

TAKE COMMAND

The **smclient** command interprets a script and uses it to run an automated test session on the Terminal server. The syntax for **smclient** is:

> **smclient** –f:*file_name* [-s:*server_name*] [-t:*num_threads*] [-l:*num_loops*]
>
> [-p:*protocol_name*] [-c] [-v] [-d] [-?]

where:

> *file_name* is the name of the script **smclient** will run.
>
> *server_name* is the name of the Terminal server on which the session will run.
>
> *num_threads* is the number of threads created by the application (default=1).
>
> *num_loops* is the number of times ("l" for "loops") the script is executed. If *num_loops*=0, the script runs forever. The default value is 1.

protocol_name is the name of the protocol the client uses to connect to the Terminal server. (This may have some meaning on Citrix products, but on Terminal Services there is only one protocol, so ignore this parameter.)

-c verifies the syntax of the script file instead of running it.

-v specifies verbose mode. **smclient** will emit a lot of information, mostly useless, about what it is doing.

-d runs **smclient** in debug mode. Extra information is sent to the debugger. If you don't work at Microsoft, pay no attention to this parameter.

-? displays the program syntax.

When you run a script from the command line, you must be aware of the username it uses when connected. By default, because of this **sed** nonsense, all scripts connect as smc001.

There is a smclient.ini file that specifies many settings, but most of them are undocumented, obsolete, or similarly useless. In the [servers] section, you can define your server names in this way:

```
[servers]
server1=\\MYSERVER1
server2=\\MYSERVER2
```

This tells **smclient** to search these servers if it is called without the **-s** parameter.

Don't mess with the [dlls] section. It defines the protocols for **smclient** to use when it connects to the Terminal server. The defaults work, and there's only one protocol that matters for Terminal Services.

The documentation refers to a [loaddlls] section and says that it lets you define DLLs to load so that a script may reference them easily. This section does not appear in the smclient.ini that comes with the software.

The smclient.ini that comes with the software does include a long [tclient] section, which I'm guessing changes settings for code in the tclient.dll file, which is a standard part of **smclient** and provides much of the core functionality in it.

The provided smclient.ini also has a short [clx] section, all of whose entries are commented out.

Have fun experimenting with smclient.ini.

Writing SmClient Scripts

The **smclient** scripting language is an extremely simple language, but it has some commands that can be a pain to write. In general, you connect, perform some work on the Terminal server, and log off. You can loop a series of statements a fixed number of times, but that's it for control structures.

The language has nothing like variables, I/O, or non-trivial control structures (if it had them there would be no need for the **sed** nonsense).

My Sample Microsoft Word Script

You can download a sample script, named stw.scp, from **http://www.admin911.com**. Use the link for "Book Downloads." I'll walk through the script and analyze its actions. I tested this script with Microsoft Word 2000, but the keystroke sequences are simple enough that it ought to work with Word 97 as well.

As with all **smclient** scripts, all the contents are inside a job {} structure. The first statement in the script is:

```
connect("smc001", "", "LARRYSELTZER", 640, 480);
```

Here, the script is connecting to the Terminal server specified on the smclient command line. It uses the username smc001, a blank password, the domain LARRYSELTZER, and opens the session in 640x480 resolution.

The next two statements instruct **smclient** to send a simulated carriage return to the Terminal server:

```
senddata("WM_KEYDOWN", 13, 1835009);
senddata("WM_KEYUP", 13, -1071906815);
```

Notice that both the press and release of the carriage return key are significant at this level of programming.

The purpose of the next statement is to check to see whether the Windows desktop has appeared. As a proxy for this, it checks for the string "MyComputer." As I discuss in the section on the check() call later, it is among the least documented facilities in the entire test toolset. Almost everything I know of it I picked out of existing scripts:

```
check("Wait4Str", "MyComputer");
```

After checking for the desktop, the script purposefully waits five seconds, mostly to make sure the system is ready for the next step of the script, and partly because real users do pause in their work now and then:

```
sleep(5000);
```

Now the real work begins. The script starts Microsoft Word. The next statement presumes that winword.exe is in the path, but it could also specify the full name of the file, including a UNC on another server:

```
start("winword");
```

The next statement waits to see that Word has been drawn on the screen. After that, it pauses another five seconds:

```
check("Wait4Str", "MicrosoftWord");
```

At this point, the script is in Microsoft Word, and it begins working there. First it presses CTRL-N to create a new Word document, then it sleeps some more. The next command can be very useful:

```
sendtext("Admin911 Test of Terminal Services",75);
```

This command sends a string of text to the server. Much more readable than **senddata()** commands, don't you think? The numeric parameter defines the number of milliseconds to pause between each character in the string.

After sleeping and typing some more, the script presses CTRL-S to save the document. Because it's a new document, the Save As dialog comes up. The script waits for it and then pauses some more. It types the name of the file and presses ENTER. Because no directory is specified, the document goes in the user's My Documents directory. At this point, it waits for the Replace dialog box to come up, which is to say that this script presumes that the document named "testdocument" already exists in the user's My Documents directory. After a few more seconds, it presses Y to replace the file. If you run this script once without the document there, it will fail, but succeed afterwards because the test document is there.

NOTE: If you run this script without the document present, it will wait endlessly for the Replace dialog box to come up. If you are running QueryIdle on the Terminal server, it should begin beeping after about two or three minutes because this session has been idle for too long.

Now that it has saved the document, it closes it by pressing ALT-F, waiting for the File menu to appear, and then pressing C to close the document. It then exits Word by pressing ALT-F, then X.

The **logoff()** command at the end of the script logs the user off of Terminal Services and thereby disconnects from the Terminal Services session.

Scripting Language Commands

Some of the scripting language commands are simpler than others. Many are thin wrappers over Windows API calls. Many are badly, incompletely, or inaccurately documented in the tscpt.doc file that comes with **smclient**.

I'm on my shakiest ground yet in some of the following descriptions, as the documents on which I am relying are not reliable, but I'll explain what I can and point out where the explanation for a command is uncertain.

In almost all cases, commands following a **logoff()** call are ignored. I will explicitly note all exceptions to this rule.

Call

The **call** statement is used to call a function in a DLL that is not specified in the standard DLLs listed in the smclient.ini file. The syntax is:

```
call(dll_library_name, function_name, function_parameters);
```

where:

dll_library_name is the filename of the DLL that contains the code.

function_name is the name of the function to call from the DLL.

function_parameters is a list of parameters to the function embedded entirely within the string. Since it is the function's responsibility to parse the string, the format of the parameters may vary from function to function.

Obviously, the called function must be exported from the DLL. You can check a DLL for its exports with the Visual Studio Dependency Walker tool (depends.exe) and many other tools. Unlike most commands in the script language, **call()** commands are executed even if there is no open connection.

Example:

```
Call("c:\program
files\MyApplication\MyApp.dll","SomeFunctionName","parameter1,
parameter2, parameter3");
```

Check

The **check** statement is used to validate that an operation in a script actually occurred. The **check** statement is under-documented, but you can pick many useful examples of it out of Microsoft's documentation and example scripts. The syntax is:

```
check("check_function_name","function_parameters");
```

where:

> *check_function_name* is the name of the check function. The full list of these is not given in Microsoft documentation, although there are example uses of "RegisterChat," "UnregisterChat," "Wait4Str," "SwitchToProcess," and "CheckRun."

> *function_parameters* is a single string containing parameters for the called check function.

Example:

```
check("Wait4Str","Command Prompt");
```

check is a generic way to call functions exported by the check DLL. According to the **smclient** documentation, this is supposed to be named check.dll, and also is supposed to be specified in the smclient.ini file. No check.dll file is supplied with **smclient**, and the relevant entry in smclient.ini is commented out by default. It does appear that the **check** call is exported by tclient.dll.

What is not at all clear is what the full list of **check** functions and their parameters are. From the documents and sample scripts I found these:

◆ **RegisterChat, UnregisterChat**   These are used in the sample Knowledge Worker document from Microsoft, but their meaning is unclear, and I couldn't get them to do anything in my own tests.

◆ **Wait4Str**   This causes the script to wait for the string specified in the parameter to be drawn.

◆ **SwitchToProcess**   This switches the current task to one with the name specified in the parameter. For example:

```
check("SwitchToProcess", "Excel");
```

◆ **CheckRun**   According to the documentation, this function checks to see that the application or applications specified in the parameter are running. Depending on what it finds, it creates an appropriate log file. The name of the file is not specified, and I couldn't find any candidates on my test systems.

Clipboard

clipboard is one of those unfortunate functions that is inadequately documented. You may be able to figure out more about it than I, so I'll relate what I know. The syntax is:

```
clipboard(operation, clipboard_file);
```

where:

operation is either copy or paste, unquoted (see the example below).

clipboard_file is the name of the file that contains the clipboard data.

Example:

```
clipboard(copy, "clipfile.dat");
```

Exactly what format the file is supposed to be in is unclear, as is exactly what is copied and what is pasted. I presumed that this was a script-based mechanism to copy a clipboard data file from the client and paste it to the server application, or paste data from a server application to a clipboard file on the client, utilizing the Terminal Services client's ability to share clipboard data.

Sadly, all my experiments on this call failed, and it is not used in any of the sample scripts available from Microsoft.

Comments

Comments in **smclient** scripts begin with //, just like C++. Everything from the // to the end of the line is ignored by the script processor. Example:

```
// This line is ignored by the script
```

Connect

The **connect** call establishes a connection to a Terminal server and logs the user on with the provided username and password. The Terminal server that the call connects to is taken from the value supplied in the **-s** command-line parameter to **smclient**. This value is passed automatically from RoboClient.

The syntax is:

```
connect("user_name","password","domain_name",xresolution,yresolution);
```

where:

user_name is the name of the user account to log on to the test session. Note: In a normal **smclient** script to be used with RoboClient, this value will always be "smc001," since RoboClient will use **sed** to change the username on the fly to an appropriate one.

password is the user's password. Note that since RoboClient will change only the username, the passwords of all the smcxxx accounts have to be the same.

domain_name is the name of the domain to log on to. If no domain is specified, the script logs on to the server locally.

xresolution is the horizontal resolution of the session, as in 640 in a 640x480 session.

yresolution is the vertical resolution of the session, as in 480 in a 640x480 session.

Example:

```
Connect("smc001","commonpassword","testdomain",800,600);
```

The example logs the user smc001 with password commonpassword on to the domain testdomain, using an 800x600 resolution session.

Disconnect

The **disconnect** call disconnects the user from the last opened connection. The user is not logged off. The syntax is:

```
disconnect();
```

If there is no open connection, calls to **disconnect** are ignored.

Job

A job is an artificial construct used by the scripting language to contain actual scripting statements that are executed in sequence. All scripts must have a job structure surrounding all their code. Since a job cannot be nested inside another job, this is the only place you will see it. The syntax is:

```
Job [
Statements
}
```

where:

> *Statements* is a sequence of scripting statements, such as **sendtext()** and **connect()**. Job itself is not technically a statement, and therefore cannot be included inside a job.

Logoff

The **logoff** call logs the user off of the Terminal server, and therefore implicitly disconnects the session. The syntax is:

```
logoff();
```

> If there is no open connection, **logoff** is ignored.

Loop

Loop lets you repeat a sequence of statements some fixed number of times.
The syntax is:

```
Statements
}
```

where:

> *counter* is an integral number specifying how many times the loop is to iterate. If *counter* is set to 0, the loop runs forever.

> *Statements* is a sequence of scripting statements, such as **sendtext()** and **connect()**.

> Loops may be nested. Consider this example:

```
Loop (2) {
    sendtext("This is the outer loop",75);
    sleep (2000);
    senddata("WM_KEYDOWN", 13, 1835009);
    senddata("WM_KEYUP", 13, -1071906815);
    loop (3) {
        sendtext("This is the inner loop",75);
        sleep (2000);
        senddata("WM_KEYDOWN", 13, 1835009);
        senddata("WM_KEYUP", 13, -1071906815);
        }
}
```

This example should write the following to the test document:

```
This is the outer loop
This is the inner loop
This is the inner loop
This is the inner loop
This is the outer loop
This is the inner loop
This is the inner loop
This is the inner loop
```

Senddata

The **senddata** call is the bread and butter call of **smclient** scripting. It is the main way to send special characters, such as CTRL and ALT key combinations, that are necessary for many operations in Windows. It can be used to send any kind of Windows message to the server, although many of those aren't appropriate for a scripting environment. The syntax is:

senddata(message_name, wparam, lparam);

Where:

> *message_name* is the name of the Windows message to send to the server.
>
> *wparam* is a parameter to the message, and depends on the specific syntax of the message.
>
> *lparam* is also message-specific.

Example:

```
senddata("WM_KEYDOWN", 32, 3735553);
```

The example sends a space bar press to the server.

In order to use this call, you either need to know Windows programming at the message level well or put yourself at the mercy of tools like Spy and hex2dec. You cannot use this effectively without some knowledge of the basics of how Windows messages work.

Sendoutput

The **sendoutput** call is undocumented to the point that it is not usable. It sends a file containing Windows message events to the server. Unfortunately, the format of this file is defined in a document (the "SpyHydra documentation") not released by Microsoft. The syntax is:

sendoutput(event_file, num_milliseconds);

where:

event_file is a file in the mysterious, missing format.

num_milliseconds is the number of milliseconds **smclient** should pause between sending each event.

Example:

Sendoutput("event_file_name.dat",200);

It seems clear to me that the file format is some variation of capture format created by Spy, the process for which is defined in the section "Using Spy to Capture Events" later in this appendix. But without a definition, there are too many possible formats to try.

Sendtext

The **sendtext** call sends a string of text to the Terminal server with a specified delay between characters. Only normal text characters, as opposed to, for example, CTRL and ALT combinations, may be sent with this statement. The syntax is:

sendtext(string, num_milliseconds);

where :

string is the text you want to send to the server.

num_milliseconds is the number of milliseconds **smclient** should pause after sending each character in the string. Microsoft commonly used 75 milliseconds in their test scripts, but you can adjust this value to simulate slower or faster typists.

Example:

sendtext("I am sending this text to the server",75);

If you used Spy to capture keystrokes and hex2dec to turn them into scripts, it's a good idea to edit the scripts to find large blocks of text being typed and turn them into a single **sendtext()** call. This will make the scripts much more readable.

Sleep

The **sleep** call pauses the script for the specified number of milliseconds. This can be useful either to help make sure that the script doesn't run ahead of the application on the server or to help simulate the pauses that real users have when running the applications you will simulate. The syntax is:

```
sleep(num_milliseconds);
```

where:

num_milliseconds is the number of milliseconds to pause.

Example:

```
sleep(2000);
```

The example pauses script processing for two seconds.

Start

The **start** command launches an application on the server. The syntax is:

```
start("command_line");
```

where:

command_line is a command line, just like one you might execute in a console session or at Start | Run.

Example:

```
start("\\appserver\apps\Microsoft Office\Office\excel.exe testdoc.xls");
```

or:

```
start("notepad");
```

Note that the command line can contain parameters.

Unicode Strings

Sometimes you want or need to use Unicode strings. The fact that the Capacity and Planning tools are not internationalized makes this a more complicated question. If you need to use these tools to test internationalized applications, you may need to send Unicode data to the applications.

smclient supports this, although in an inconvenient way. You can refer to any string in smclient as a Unicode string by their four-digit hexadecimal equivalents prefixed with \u. For example, the string ADMIN911 could be represented as \u410044004D0049004E0039003100.

You can get the Unicode numerical form for a character by hovering over a character in the **charmap** tool. This is not especially efficient, and the **smclient** documentation refers to a tool named **chgform** that performs this conversion and is supposed to be in the **smclient** directory. It isn't.

If you're interested in writing your own program to perform the conversions, the relevant Windows conversion routines are documented at http://msdn.microsoft.com/library/psdk/winbase/unicode_19mb.htm.

Using Spy to Capture Events

The most common scripting command is **senddata()**, which sends a Windows message from the client to the Terminal server. Unfortunately, these messages are tough to write in your head, as they involve a fair amount of data.

You can use the Microsoft Spy or Spy++ programs, included in various versions of Microsoft Visual C++, Visual Studio, and other tools, to monitor keystroke events as you manually run through a test and record the events to a file. Third-party development tools usually have an equivalent tool, although not all of them will write in the same format. Afterward, you can translate these events into a script for RoboClient to use.

Before you begin logging events, set up the system on which Spy is running with all the applications that will run on the Terminal server. You could even do this on the Terminal server itself. You might want to do a dry run through the sequence before actually capturing the events.

It's possible to capture and play back mouse events, but this is problematic. When you capture mouse events, you inevitably capture thousands of them. I recommend using only keystrokes in your test sequences. This will also make it easier to edit them later and recognize points where you may want to insert pauses.

Using Spy

In Spy, open the Message Options window with CTRL-M. You can set the program to capture events from all windows in the system or just a specific one (see Figure A-5), and there are further options. Unless you know what you're doing, it's simplest to capture all windows in the system and just be careful about what keys you press.

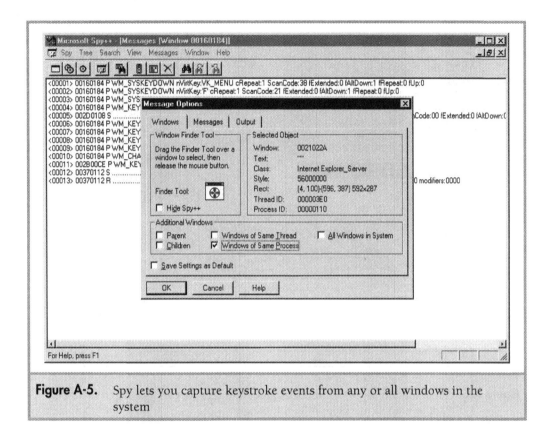

Figure A-5. Spy lets you capture keystroke events from any or all windows in the system

On the Messages tab (see Figure A-6) you can select which Windows messages to capture. By default, all messages in all message groups will be selected. If, as I have suggested, you want to restrict your captures to keyboard events, select Clear All and then Keyboard.

On the Output tab, you can restrict which data you want to go to the message log. For the purposes of making scripts for RoboClient and **smclient** to run, in the Show In Message Log section of this window, you want to select Raw Message Parameters and Raw Return Values, and deselect every other checkbox.

Below the Show In Message Log section, select the Also Log To File checkbox and specify a filename.

When you click OK, message logging will be enabled. You can press F8 or select the traffic light icon to pause it. At this point, begin performing your tests. At the end, go back to Spy and press F8 to stop logging.

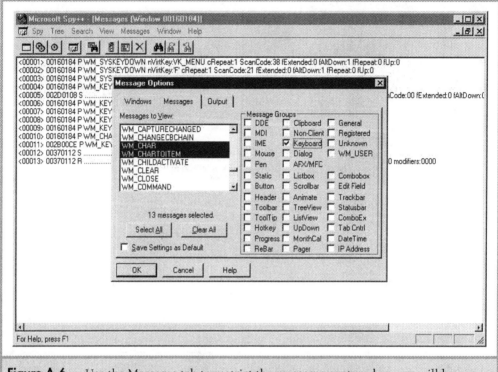

Figure A-6. Use the Messages tab to restrict the messages captured or you will have a lot of useless messages to sort through

Interpreting the Log File

The file will contain a list of keyboard messages. Here is a typical one, in this case the pressing of a SHIFT key:

```
000B01BC P WM_KEYDOWN wParam:00000010 lParam:002A0001
```

The fields in the file are:

◆ The window handle

◆ The message code:

> P means that the message was posted to the queue with the PostMessage function.

> S means that the message was sent with the SendMessage function.

s means that the message was sent, but its details are withheld for security purposes.

R is the return entry corresponding to every S line.

✦ The actual message, such as WM_CHAR.

✦ **wParam** This varies with different types of messages, but in a keystroke it is the virtual-key code.

✦ **lParam** This also varies with different types of messages, but in a keystroke it is the key data.

Translate the Logs into senddata() Calls

Now that you have the message log, turning it into a sequence of **senddata()** calls is mostly text editor work. But first, you have one problem: the parameter values are in hexadecimal, and **senddata()** wants them in decimal.

I wrote a program named **hex2dec** that you can download (including the source code in C) from http://www.admin911.com. Look for "Book Downloads." This program is a filter program that takes the message log in the format described earlier and outputs a stream of **senddata()** commands.

TAKE COMMAND

The **hex2dec** command converts message logs to a stream of **senddata()** commands that you can easily turn into a script. The syntax is:

hex2dec <*message_logfile_name* >*senddata_file_name*

where:

message_logfile_name is the name of the file with event messages created by the Spy program.

senddata_file_name is the name of the file that **hex2dec** should create containing **senddata()** calls.

Add Final Script Elements

The file created by **hex2dec** is missing some necessary elements for a script and some desirable ones. For example, you will need to add **job** { to the top of the script and a closing }.

But, as you can see from other scripts, such as the Word sample described earlier and the samples from the white paper test described in the next section, you have to connect and log on to the server, start an application, and you probably want to create pauses in the script at various points.

The Microsoft/NEC/Bull White Paper Test

The tools described in this appendix were first described publicly in a test performed by NEC and Groupe Bull engineers under the supervision of Microsoft's Terminal Services development team using the beta 3 version of Windows 2000 Server. The results of the testing were published in a white paper available from Microsoft at http://www.microsoft. com/WINDOWS2000/library/technologies/terminal/tscaling.asp.

I discussed this paper, its results, and how you could use them as guidelines for your own deployment in Chapter 2. But now I will reanalyze them as an example of how the Capacity and Planning tools described in this appendix can be used. The testing scripts used in the NEC/Groupe Bull tests are available from Microsoft at http://www.microsoft.com/ WINDOWS2000/library/operations/terminal/loadscripts.asp.

The idea of the tests was to classify certain types of users and create representative workloads in the form of scripts. The test engineers set conservative goals for the tests, determining a server to be at capacity when the performance of the canary script dropped by 10 percent. Different mixes of users were added to the test until this condition was reached. In this way, they were able to determine rough guidelines for how many of each type of user/workload could be supported on a particular configuration of server.

For example, at the high end, an 8-way Pentium III 500MHz server with 4GB RAM (NEC/Groupe Bull Model Express5800-HV8600) was able to support 105 Structured Task Workers and 160 Knowledge Workers. Based on these results, they were able to extrapolate guidelines for memory requirements per user, as shown in Table A-1.

The test setup for these tests was relatively elaborate. There were 64 test workstations, the obligatory domain controller and test manager systems, the Terminal server (the main variable in the test), plus an IIS Web server, Microsoft Exchange server, and Microsoft SQL Server. The test scripts, as you can see from the scripts, used these additional servers. Because Windows 2000 was in beta at the time, all systems except the Terminal server under test were running Windows NT 4.0 with Service Pack 5.

	Structured Task Workers	Knowledge Workers	Data Entry Workers
Memory per User (MB)	9.3	8.5	3.5
Base System Memory (MB)	128		

Table A-1. Memory Requirements for Terminal Services

As the NEC/Groupe Bull engineers did, you should probably run Perfmon during at least some of the tests, especially if you see problems, and have it log the critical metrics so you can analyze them for hints of how to tune your server. See Chapter 7 for details on how to use Perfmon with Terminal Services.

A good example of this sort of analysis is the white paper's graph of network utilization per user over time. As it shows, network utilization peaks early in the test as users log on and load profiles and their applications, and quickly settles down to a steady and low baseline. The paper also shows similar effects on server CPU utilization.

The tests used varying delays by means of **sleep** commands and delay parameters to **sendtext**, to simulate faster and slower typists. With Structured Task Workers, moving from 35 word per minute to 60 word per minute typing decreased the server capacity from 130 users to 90 users. On the other hand, changing the encryption level used by RDP from medium to high encryption had only a trivial effect on server capacity, even though high encryption does demand greater CPU utilization on the server's behalf.

These tools are the perfect opportunity for you to test other identifiable variables, such as AutoSave in Word, automatic spell checking and grammar checking, and new versions of applications.

For many people, this type of capacity testing is probably a secondary consideration. If you can set up a representative test network and just confirm that all your applications run correctly in the environment you will be using in production, and that the performance is at least acceptable, you will have accomplished a lot.

Appendix B

Terminal Services Command-Line Tools

A number of command-line programs and utilities are specific to Terminal Services administration. Some of them are covered within the chapters of this book. Because these commands are extremely useful, it seems appropriate to create one complete reference for all of the Terminal Services command-line tools. The commands are presented in alphabetic order to make it easier to find what you need.

Change Logon

The **change logon** command enables or disables logons from a Terminal server. You must have Administrator rights to use this command.

 CAUTION: If you disable logons while logged on to a remote session and then log off, you won't be able to get back in from a remote session. Instead, you must log on locally at the server console in order to re-enable logons.

The syntax for **change logon** is:

change logon [/enable | /disable | /query]

where:

/enable enables logons to the server.

/disable disables logons to the server.

/query displays the current logon status.

Change Port

Use the **change port** command to change COM port mappings for compatibility with MS-DOS applications. This command is most useful if you are using high port numbers (greater than COM4), which MS-DOS applications won't recognize. Remappings live only for the life of the session. They are deleted at logoff. The syntax for **change port** is:

change port [*portx=porty* | /d *portx* | /query]

where:

portx=porty maps port X to port Y.

/d *portx* deletes the mapping for COM port x.

/query displays current COM port mappings.

Change User

The **change user** command switches the system between Install and Execute modes. When you need to install an application for use in Terminal Services, you need to first switch the Terminal server to Install mode, which you may do either with this command or with the Add/Remove Programs applet in Control Panel. If you switch manually, using the **change user** command, it is critical to remember to switch back!

The syntax for **change user** is:

change user [/execute | /install | /query]

where:

/execute puts the system into Execute mode, the default and normal mode.

/install puts the system into Install mode, so that Terminal Services monitors changes in the system and makes the changes effective for all users.

/query displays the current mode for the system.

Cprofile

The **cprofile** command cleans user profiles in order to get rid of wasted space. You need Administrator rights to run it. Profiles that are in use are not affected, so you may want to schedule it to run at a time when the server is least busy. This program also removes user-specific file associations that are disabled. The syntax is:

cprofile [/i] [/l] [/v] *filelist*

where:

/I interactively prompts the user to confirm cleaning each profile.

/l cleans all local profiles. You can still add other files in the file list.

/v displays verbose information about the operation.

filelist specifies a list of files to clean.

Flattemp

The **flattemp** command enables or disables flat temp folders for users. You must have Administrator rights to execute this command.

By default, users' temporary folders are in a separate directory relative to their profile directory. Each session for Terminal Services creates a new subdirectory in this temporary directory with a name based on the session ID. This command lets you specify that the temp folder for Terminal Services should be the user's temp directory, not a temporary subdirectory of the temp directory.

This command is analogous to the Use Temporary Folders Per Session policy in Terminal Services Configuration. The syntax is:

flattemp {**/query** | **/enable** | **/disable**}

where:

/query displays the current setting.

/enable sets the system to use flat temporary folders.

/disable sets the system not to use flat temporary folders.

Logoff

The **logoff** command logs a user off from a session and deletes the session from the server. The syntax is:

logoff [*sessionid* | *sessionname*] [**/server**:*servername*] [**/v**]

where:

sessionID is the ID of the session from which you want to log off.

sessionname is the name of the session from which you want to log off.

/server:*servername* is the name of the server on which the session is running.

/v displays verbose information about the operations being performed.

Lsreport

The **lsreport** command from the Windows 2000 Server Resource Kit reports on licenses granted by a License server. The output of this command is a tab-delimited table that includes the server name, license ID, license key pack ID, client computer name, start date of the license, end date of the license (if any), issue type (active or temporary), and license type (the name of the key pack).

> **NOTE:** Most of the fields in this report are not available via the Terminal Services Licensing program. If you have many licenses and license servers to manage, running this report and importing the output into Excel, Access, or some similar tool provides the best reporting tools.

The syntax for **lsreport** is:

lsreport [/F *filename*] [/D *start* [*end*]] [/T] [/?] [*serverlist*]

where:

/F *filename* specifies that the output should go to a particular file. By default, output goes to lsreport.txt in the current directory. There's no explicit way to output to the console, but you can do so by using this parameter and specifying 'con:' as the filename.

/D *start* [*end*] limits the report only to licenses that were in effect between the dates *start* and *end*. The end date is optional, and defaults to today. Dates should be in the form mm/dd/yyyy.

/T limits the report to temporary licenses.

/? displays command help.

serverlist is a list of names of license servers. You can use either NetBIOS names or IP addresses.

Msg

The **msg** command sends a popup message to the specified session. This command has many advantages over the similar utility in Terminal Services Manager. For example, you can send messages to a list of many users and you can wait until they respond.

The syntax is:

msg {*username* | *sessionname* | *sessionid* | @*filename* | *} [/**server**:*servername*] [/**time**:*seconds*] [/v] [/w] [*message*]

where:

username is the username of the recipient.

sessionname is the name of the session to send to.

sessionid is the ID of the session to send to.

@filename is the name of a text file containing usernames, session names, and session IDs to send the message to.

* sends the message to all usernames on the system.

/server:servername* is the name of the server where the session resides. If no server name is specified, the server you are logged on is assumed.

/time:seconds* is the number of seconds the message should stay on screen before closing itself.

/v displays information about the message (where it's being sent, how long it will appear, and so on).

/w causes the **msg** program to pause until the user clicks OK on the message box.

message is the contents of the message to send.

Query Session

The **query session** command displays information about a session, although not the same information that Terminal Services Manager displays.

The result is a table of sessions and information about them, including the username, session ID, session state (see sidebar "Session States" in chapter 5), and type of session (console, RDP, and so on).

The syntax is:

query session [*sessionname* | *username* | *sessionid*] [**/server:**servername*] [**/mode**] [**/flow**] [**/connect**] [**/counter**]

where:

sessionname is the name of the session you are querying.

username is the name of the user whose sessions you want to query.

sessionid is the ID of the session you want to query.

/server:servername* is the name of the server where the session is running. If no server name is specified, the current server is used.

/**mode** displays current line settings.

/**flow** displays current flow control settings.

/**connect** displays current connect settings.

/**counter** displays counter information about sessions on the server.

Query User

The **query user** command returns session information, much like **query session**, but without some of the useless stuff, and with some additional useful information. Much like Terminal Services Manager, **query user** adds the time the user logged on to the session and the number of minutes a session has been idle. The syntax is:

query user [*username* | *sessionname* | *sessionID*] [/**server**:*servername*]

where:

username is the name of the user whose sessions you want to query.

sessionname is the name of the session you are querying.

sessionid is the ID of the session you want to query.

/**server**:*servername* is the name of the server where the session is running. If no server name is specified, the current server is used.

Query Process

The **query process** command lists information about processes running on a server or session with far greater flexibility than in Terminal Services Manager. For example, you can ask for processes associated with a particular executable or username. The syntax is:

query process [* | *processid* | *username* | *sessionname* | /**id**:*nn* | *programname*] [/**server**:*servername*] [/**system**]

where:

* list processes running in all sessions.

processid lists information on a specific process by ID.

username lists all processes running in *username*'s sessions.

sessionname lists all processes running in session *sessionname*.

/id:*nn* lists all processes running in the session with session ID *nn*.

programname lists all processes started by this executable.

/server:*servername* lists all processes running on this particular server.

/system lists information about system processes (such as ntvdm.exe, as opposed to applications like word.exe).

Query Termserver

The **query termserver** command lists Terminal Servers on the network in the current or some other specified domain. You can also get network address information on the servers. The command outputs a list of known Terminal servers. The syntax is:

query termserver [*servername*] [**/domain:***domain*] [**/address**] [**/continue**]

where:

servername is the name of a specific server on which you want information.

/domain:*domain* is a domain you want to search. The default is the domain to which you are logged on.

/address tells the command to output the network and node addresses of the servers.

/continue tells the command not to pause between screens if there is more than one screen of output.

Register

The **register** command changes the execution characteristics of a program so that it runs either in system global space or user global space.

By default, under Terminal Services, when a user runs a program it runs in an isolated memory space for that user's session. For example, copies of Excel running in session 2 and 3 are internally known to Windows as "Excel:2" and "Excel:3." A copy running in system global space is simply "Excel."

Some badly written programs may have problems running in user global space. You may be able to get them to work by running them in system global space, but only one user at a time can run them. Such applications are better thought of as incompatible with Terminal Services.

Changes in registration only take effect at installation, so you must run **register** before you install the program. If you want to change the status of an installed program, you must uninstall and reinstall the program.

You must have administrative privileges to run **register**.

The syntax is:

register *filename* [/**system** | /**user** | /**v**]

where:

filename is the file name of the program or DLL to change.

/**system** tells Terminal Services to run the program in system global space.

/**user** tells Terminal Services to run the program in user global space.

/**v** tells register to display verbose information about the command as it is executing.

Reset Session

The **reset session** command deletes a session immediately, without warning the user. It should be used only for malfunctioning sessions. The syntax is:

reset session {*sessionname* | *sessionid*} [/**server**:*servername*] [/**v**]

where:

sessionID is the ID of the session to which you want to reset.

sessionname is the name of the session to which you want to reset.

/**server**:*servername* is the name of the server on which the session is running.

/**v** displays verbose information about the operations being performed.

Shadow

The **shadow** command initiates a remote control session, which you specify by the session name or session ID. Unlike the remote control procedures in Terminal Services Manager, you cannot specify the keystroke to end a session. The syntax is:

shadow {*sessionname* | *sessionid*} [/**server**:*servername*] [/**v**]

where:

> *sessionname* is the name of the session to control.

> *sessionid* is the ID of the session to control.

> **/server:***servername* specifies the name of the server on which the session is running.

> **/v** causes the command to output extra descriptive text to the console.

Tscon

The **tscon** command connects you to a different session. The syntax is:

> **tscon** {*sessionID* | *sessionname*} [**/server:**servername] [**/dest:**sessionname]
> [**/password:**password] [**/v**]

where:

> *sessionID* is the ID of the session to which you want to connect.

> *sessionname* is the name of the session to which you want to connect.

> **/server:***servername* is the name of the server on which the session is running.

> **/dest:***sessionname* is the name of the current session to which the new session
> will be attached. If you have multiple sessions running, this parameter distinguishes
> between them.

> **/password:***password* is the password of the user who owns the session to which you are
> attaching.

> **/v** displays verbose information about the operations being performed.

Tsdiscon

Use the **tsdiscon** command to disconnect a session. The syntax is:

> **tsdiscon** {*sessionID* | *sessionname*} [**/server:**servername] [**/v**]

where:

> *sessionID* is the ID of the session you want to disconnect.

sessionname is the name of the session you want to disconnect.

/server:*servername* is the name of the server on which the session is running.

/v displays verbose information about the operations being performed.

Tskill

The **tskill** command allows you to end a process with precise control. Unlike the method available in Terminal Services Manager, you can choose to end all instances of a specific executable. The syntax is:

> **tskill** {*processid | processname*} [**/server:***servername*] [**/id:***sessionid* | **/a**] [**/v**]

where:

processid ends the process with the specified ID.

processname ends the process with the specified name.

/server:*servername* specifies the server on which the process is running. If none is specified, the current server is used.

/id:*sessionid* specifies a session ID in which the process is running.

/a ends all instances of the process.

/v displays verbose information about the operations being performed.

Tsprof

The **tsprof** command copies user profile information from one user account to another. It can also set the profile path for a user. You must have Administrator rights to use **tsprof**.
The syntax for **tsprof** is:

> **tsprof /update** [**/domain:***domainname*|**/local**] **/profile:***path username*

> **tsprof /copy** [**/domain:***domainname*|**/local**] [**/profile:***path*] *src_usr dest_usr*

> **tsprof /q** [**/domain:***domainname*|**/local**] *username*

where:

/update updates the profile path in domain *domainname* to *path*.

/**copy** copies the user profile from *src_usr* to *dest_usr* and updates profile path information for *dest_usr* to *path*.

/**q** displays the current profile path for *username*'s profile.

/**domain:***domainname* is the name of the domain in which the profiles exist.

/**local** applies only to local user accounts.

/**profile:***path* is the location of the profile.

src_usr is the name of the user whose profile you want to copy.

dest_usr is the name of the user whose profile you want to overwrite.

username is the name of the user whose profile you want to query or update.

Tsshutdn

The **tsshutdn** command shuts down a Terminal Services server in an orderly manner. The syntax is:

tsshutdn [*wait_time*] [/**server:***servername*] [/**reboot**] [/**powerdown**]
[/**delay:***logoffdelay*] [/**v**]

where:

wait_time specifies the number of seconds to wait after notifying users of the impending shutdown, before logging users off the sessions. The default value is 60 seconds. The administrator running the command has this amount of time to press ^C to abort the shutdown.

/**server:***servername* specifies the name of the server to shut down.

/**reboot** tells the command to reboot the server after the shutdown.

/**powerdown** tells the command to power the server off after the shutdown, assuming the hardware in the server supports software power-down.

/**delay:***logoffdelay* specifies the number of seconds to wait, after logging all users off from their sessions, before shutting server processes to finish the system shutdown. The default value is 30 seconds.

/**v** displays verbose information at the console about the operation. This command echoes to the console each shutdown message that it sends to each session.

Index

✦ S

www.ingramcontent.com/pod-product-compliance
Lightning Source LLC
Chambersburg PA
CBHW080151060326
40689CB00018B/3930